Scrum

3rd Edition

by Mark C. Layton, Steven J Ostermiller, & Dean J. Kynaston

for dummies®

A Wiley Brand

Scrum For Dummies®, 3rd Edition

Published by: **John Wiley & Sons, Inc.,** 111 River Street, Hoboken, NJ 07030-5774, www.wiley.com

Copyright © 2023 by John Wiley & Sons, Inc., Hoboken, New Jersey

Published simultaneously in Canada

For general information on our other products and services, please contact our Customer Care Department within the U.S. at 877-762-2974, outside the U.S. at 317-572-3993, or fax 317-572-4002. For technical support, please visit https://hub.wiley.com/community/support/dummies.

Wiley publishes in a variety of print and electronic formats and by print-on-demand. Some material included with standard print versions of this book may not be included in e-books or in print-on-demand. If this book refers to media such as a CD or DVD that is not included in the version you purchased, you may download this material at http://booksupport.wiley.com. For more information about Wiley products, visit www.wiley.com.

Library of Congress Control Number: 2022946398

ISBN 978-1-119-90466-3 (pbk); ISBN 978-1-119-90468-7 (ebk); ISBN 978-1-119-90467-0 (ebk)

SKY10036383_101322

Contents at a Glance

Table of Contents

Introduction

Welcome to *Scrum For Dummies*. Scrum is an agile product development framework with proven results in decreasing time to market by 30–40 percent, improving product quality, and heightening customer satisfaction — all while lowering costs by 30–70 percent. Scrum accomplishes these results through integrating business and development talent, improved communication models, increased performance visibility, regular customer and stakeholder feedback, and an empirically based inspect-and-adapt mentality. You can solve even the most complex problems more effectively by using scrum to increase your bottom line.

About This Book

The goal is to explicitly demonstrate how you can use scrum for any product or solution, not just software development. This book is intended to be a field manual for the application of scrum in real-world situations. Although it covers scrum fundamentals in detail, this book also delves into how to get out and experience the amazing benefits of scrum.

By design, scrum is easy to explain, but the application and mastery are often difficult. Old habits and organizational mindsets need to be shifted and new ways embraced. For this reason, we've included success stories so that you can see how scrum can fit into your situation.

The main thrust of understanding scrum lies in the three accountabilities, three artifacts, and five events that form its foundation — each of which is thoroughly covered in this book. We also include common practices that we and others in the field use so you can choose what works best for your product. Throughout the book, we use the word *product* to describe a channel for delivering value to a defined customer, whether a physical product, project, service, outcome, or even something more abstract.

Scrum isn't technical. In fact, its basic tenet is common sense. In many cases, we've wrapped this information within the technology world and used technical terms to help explain it. Where useful, we've defined these terms.

We also cover common practices from scrum experts throughout the world. You can learn so much from others who use this framework in a seemingly limitless spectrum.

Scrum falls under an umbrella of approaches to project management called *agile project management*. Neither *scrum* nor *agile* practices are proper nouns. *Scrum* is a framework for organizing your work, whereas *agile* is an adjective used to describe a variety of practices that align with the values of the Agile Manifesto and the 12 Agile principles. Scrum and agile are not identical or interchangeable, but you frequently see them used interchangeably in many written sources, especially online. In this book, you will see terminology from both scrum and agile because scrum is a frequently used subset of agile practices.

Foolish Assumptions

Several books about scrum are available, but this one differs in its practicality. Each of the authors has nearly two decades of experience with agile methods and scrum, and we bring this experience to you in a practical guide. We make no assumptions about what you already know: You don't need to be a rocket scientist or a whiz programmer; all you need are a problem to solve and a passion for getting it done in the best way possible. We give you examples ranging from building jet fighters to organizing a family vacation. We focus on the steps necessary to get scrum's magic working for you.

Our audience includes code programmers, sales professionals, human resource specialists, publishers, marketers, product manufacturers, executives, midtier managers, families, educators who are looking for a way to engage their students, and many others.

If you're in the technology industry, you've probably heard the terms *agile* and/or *scrum*. Maybe you've even worked in a scrum environment but want to improve your skills and vocabulary in this area and bring others in your firm along with you. If you're not in technology, you may have heard that scrum is a great way to run projects, which is true. Perhaps scrum is new to you, and you're searching for a way to make your project more accessible, or maybe you have a great idea burning inside and don't know how to bring it to fruition. Whoever you are, a simpler way exists to run your project, and that way is called *scrum*. Within these pages, we show you how to use it.

Conventions Used in This Book

If you do an online search, you may see the words *agile*, *scrum*, roles, meetings, documents, and various agile methodologies and frameworks (including scrum) capitalized. We shied away from this practice for a couple of reasons.

To start, none of these items are really proper nouns. *Agile* is an adjective that describes a number of product development items: agile projects, agile teams, agile processes, and so on. But it is not a proper noun, and except in chapter or section titles, you will not see us use it that way in this book.

For readability, we did not capitalize agile-related roles, meetings, and documents. Such terms include *agile project*, *product owner*, *scrum master*, *developers*, *user stories*, *product backlog*, and more. You may, however, see these terms capitalized in places other than this book.

Some exceptions exist. *The Agile Manifesto* and *The Agile Principles* are copyrighted material. The Agile Alliance, Scrum Alliance, and Project Management Institute are professional organizations. A Certified ScrumMaster and a PMI-Agile Certified Practitioner are professional titles.

Icons Used in This Book

The following icons in the margins indicate highlighted material that we think will be of interest to you.

TIP

Tips are ideas that we'd like you to take note of. These ideas are usually practical advice that you can apply to the given topic.

WARNING

This icon is less common than the others in this book. The intent is to save you time by bringing to your attention some pitfalls you're better off avoiding.

TECHNICAL STUFF

If you don't care much about the technical stuff, you can skip these paragraphs without missing much. If technical stuff is your thing, you may find these sections fascinating.

REMEMBER

This icon marks something we'd like you to take special note of, such as a concept, idea, or best practice that we think is noteworthy.

Beyond the Book

You can find an online Cheat Sheet for this book at www.dummies.com. The Cheat Sheet covers

>> *The Agile Manifesto*

>> The principles behind scrum

>> The roadmap to value we frequently reference throughout this book

>> A snapshot of various definitions for roles, artifacts, and activities related to scrum

>> A summary of scrum community resources

Go to www.dummies.com and type this book's title into the search field to find the Cheat Sheet.

Where to Go from Here

To start getting scrum working for you, you can begin applying it on smaller projects to get the feel of it. Soon, you'll be handling your most important projects similarly. This book applies to a diverse set of readers and is organized to allow you to find specific areas of interest relevant to you. Each chapter can be a reference whenever you have a technical question or want to see an example of scrum in real life.

>> If you're new to scrum, begin with Chapter 1 to understand introductory concepts and terminology; then work your way through Chapter 7 to find out about the entire framework. As you continue past Chapter 7, you see how to apply scrum in any situation.

>> If you're familiar with scrum and want to learn more about how it applies to many industries, check out Chapters 8 through 11, and read about scrum being practiced in various industries.

>> If you're a product owner, scrum master, or business leader and want to know more about scrum on a larger scale, start by reading Chapter 13 and all of Part 6 for valuable resources.

>> If you're familiar with scrum and want to know how it can help you address daily life, read Chapters 17 and 18 for inspiration and examples.

1

Getting Started with Scrum

IN THIS PART . . .

Connect scrum with the principles of agile product development.

Use constant feedback through transparency and adaptation to elevate the success rates of product goals.

Become tactically flexible to create strategic stability.

Chapter **1**

The Basics of Scrum

Scrum is an exposure framework based on empiricism, meaning people who employ the scrum framework gain knowledge from real-life experience and make decisions based on that experience. It's a way of organizing your work — releasing a new smartphone, coordinating your daughter's fifth-grade birthday party, or exposing whether your approach is generating intended results. If you need to get something done, scrum provides a structure for increased efficiency and more effective results.

Within scrum, common sense reigns. You focus on what can be done today with an eye toward breaking future work into manageable pieces. You can immediately see how well your effort is working, and when you find inefficiencies in your approach, scrum enables you to act on them by making adjustments with clarity and speed.

Although empirical process controls go back to the beginning of time in the arts, its modern-day usage stems from computer modeling. For example, in sculpting, you chisel away, check the results, make any adaptations necessary, and chisel away some more. The empirical exposure model means observing or experiencing actual results rather than simulating them based on research or a mathematical formula and then making decisions based on these experiences. In scrum, you break your work into actionable chunks, observing your results every step of the way. This approach allows you to immediately make the necessary changes to stay on track.

The Bird's-Eye Basics

Scrum isn't a methodology; it's a new way of thinking. It isn't a paint-by-numbers approach in which you end up with a product or outcome; it's a simple framework for clearly defining accountabilities and organizing your actionable work so that you're more effective in prioritizing and more efficient in completing the work selected. Frameworks are less prescriptive than methodologies and provide appropriate flexibility for the processes, structures, and tools that complement them. When this approach is used, you can clearly observe and adopt complementary methods and practices and quickly determine whether you're making real, tangible progress. You create usable results within weeks, days, or (in some cases) hours.

Like the process of building a house brick by brick, scrum is an iterative, incremental approach. It gives you early empirical evidence of performance and quality. Roles are distinct and self-ruling, and individuals and teams are given the required autonomy and tools to get the job done. Lengthy progress reports, redundant meetings, and bloated management layers are nonexistent. Scrum is the approach to use if you just want to get the job done.

TECHNICAL STUFF

Scrum is a term that comes from the rough-and-tumble game of rugby. Huddles, or scrums, are formed with the forwards from one side interlocking their arms with their heads down and pushing against the forwards from the opposing team, who are also interlocking arms with their heads down. The ball is then thrown into the midst of this tightly condensed group of athletes. Although each team member plays a unique position, all team members play both attacking and defending roles and work together to move the ball down the field of play. Like rugby, scrum relies on talented people with varying responsibilities and domains working closely together in teams toward a common goal.

We want to emphasize — and have written two-thirds of this book on — an overlooked concept of scrum: its amazing versatility. People who know about scrum commonly think that it's customized for software, information technology (IT), or tech use, but that's just the tip of the iceberg. Applications for using scrum can be found everywhere, including large, small, tech, artistic, social, and even personal use. In Chapters 8 through 18, we show you how. Be forewarned! Scrum is such an addictive framework that you'll be using it to coach your kid's soccer team, plan your neighborhood watch, and even ratchet up your exercise routine.

Roadmap to value

Throughout this book, we discuss techniques some expert scrum practitioners apply as common practice extensions to scrum. These techniques complement, not replace, the scrum framework. We point out the differences when they occur. All the common practices we include and recommend are tried and tested — always with a clear understanding these practices are outside the basic scrum framework and are suggested for consideration in your own situations.

We call this aggregation of scrum and vetted common practices the *"roadmap to value."* This roadmap consists of seven elements that walk you through the goal of your product to the task level and back again in a continual, iterative, and incremental process of inspection and adaptation. In other words, the roadmap to value helps you see what you want to achieve and progressively break that goal into pieces through an iterative cycle that leads to real results every day, week, and month.

You know that billion-dollar idea that's been lurking in the back of your head for years? Follow the roadmap to value. It will show you the feasibility or fallacy of your idea and where to make your improvements — step by step, piece by piece.

Figure 1-1 shows a holistic view of the roadmap to value. This figure shows that you begin with the product goal; work through planning; and then enter the cyclical world of sprints, reviews, and retrospectives.

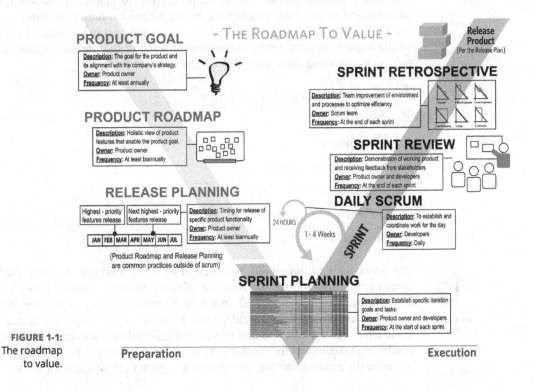

FIGURE 1-1: The roadmap to value.

Scrum overview

The scrum process is simple and circular, with constant and transparent elements of inspection and adaptation. First, a deliberately ordered to-do list — called a *product backlog* — is created and maintained. Then top-priority items are selected for a fixed, regular period — called a *sprint* — during which the scrum team strives for a predetermined and mutually agreed upon sprint goal.

Figure 1-2 shows a scrum overview.

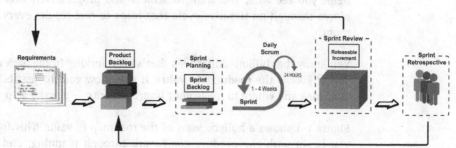

FIGURE 1-2:
A simplified overview of the events and cycles of scrum.

The scrum process allows you to adapt quickly to changing market forces, technological constraints, regulations, new innovations, family preferences, and almost anything else you can think of. The key is the ongoing process of working on the highest-priority items to completion. Each of the highest-priority items gets fully developed and tested through the following steps:

1. Requirement elaboration
2. Design
3. Development
4. Comprehensive testing
5. Integration
6. Documentation
7. Approval

REMEMBER

The seven steps to fully build the scope of each requirement are performed for every item. Every requirement taken on during a sprint, no matter how small or large, is fully built, tested, and approved or rejected. When a backlog item is approved and deemed "releasable," you know it works. Hope and guesswork are taken out of the equation and replaced by reality. You showcase these tangible results to stakeholders for feedback. This feedback generates new items that are placed in the product backlog and prioritized against existing known work.

What's more important: efficiency or effectiveness? Hands down, it's effectiveness — working on the right thing at the right time. Don't worry about efficiency until you figure out how to be effective. A very efficient team working on the wrong things is a waste of time. A super-effective team, however, can easily learn efficiency. Always work on the *right* things first. As economist and management author Peter F. Drucker said, "There is nothing so useless as doing efficiently that which should not be done at all."

The scrum cycle is run again and again. The constant flow of feedback and emphasis on developing only the highest-priority items helps you reflect what your customers are looking for, deliver it to them faster, and deliver it with higher quality.

Scrum teams

No matter what the scope of your product is, your scrum team will have similar characteristics. The sizes of teams vary somewhat, but the roles or accountabilities remain the same. We discuss the specific accountabilities in detail throughout this book. Figure 1-3 depicts a scrum team.

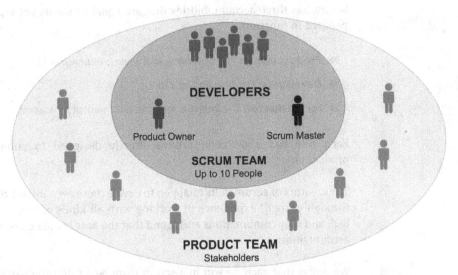

FIGURE 1-3:
A scrum team has the developers at its core.

The developers are the heart of a scrum team — the folks who work together to create the product, service, or solution itself. They work directly with a product owner and scrum master, who align business and development priorities for the organization and eliminate distractions so that the developers can focus on "developing" a quality result.

REMEMBER

Don't get hung up on the term "developer," thinking it refers to software development. Developers on a scrum team are simply the people with the skills needed to take an idea and "develop" it into something of value for the customer. Someone who writes software code is just one example of a scrum developer. There are many other skills a developer on a scrum team may possess, such as testing, writing, configuring, molding, waxing, teaching, designing, and so on. The word "developer" is used throughout this book to simplify, not exclude.

Stakeholders aren't scrum roles, but we include them in Figure 1-3 because they affect your product, service, or solution. Stakeholders can be internal or external. Marketing, legal, compliance team members, in-laws, and especially users and customers are examples of stakeholders.

The scrum team itself has ultimate accountability. Team members self-manage to figure out how to achieve their objectives within the environment in which they find themselves.

Governance

Scrum has three accountabilities that are equal in status yet separate and independent in function:

>> **Product owner:** The *why, what,* and *when* (not *how much*)

>> **Developers:** The *how* and *how much*

>> **Scrum master:** The *improvement* and *environment for success*

Each role has a defined purpose directly designed to enhance the team's productivity.

The creators of scrum didn't happen to devise these accountabilities by chance but through years of experience in working with all kinds of teams. They saw good, bad, and ugly combinations and found that the best results came from these three accountabilities.

TIP

We prefer that each person in a scrum team be a full-time participant dedicated solely to the scrum team's objectives. Don't thrash your team members across several priorities or use part-time players. How many professional football teams have part-time players or those who play for several teams? None.

REMEMBER

In scrum, no single person is above another. Everyone is a peer; no one is a boss or underling to anyone else on the team. *We* is the operative word rather than *I*. Scrum teams thrive on psychological safety, vulnerability, and trust — key attributes of peer-level team members.

Scrum framework

Scrum is a framework that provides clarity of responsibilities through roles, visibility through artifacts, and opportunities for inspection and adaptation through events. Within this structure, scrum is a container for other practices, processes, and tools that are appropriate for meeting the specific needs of a team, organization, product, or service.

REMEMBER

Scrum has:

>> Five values

>> Three accountabilities

>> Three artifacts

>> Five events

Each framework element fits within the scrum process, which is iterative and incremental. You incrementally create and improve your product, and you incrementally improve your process and environment with this simple framework, as follows:

>> **Values**

- Commitment

- Focus

- Openness

- Respect

- Courage

>> **Accountabilities**

- Product owner

- Developers

- Scrum master

>> **Artifacts**

- Product backlog

- Sprint backlog

- Increment

» **Events**

- Sprint
- Sprint planning
- Daily scrum
- Sprint review
- Sprint retrospective

TECHNICAL STUFF

In the scrum world, *artifacts* are lists of work to be done or work products that have been done and are deemed valuable and usable. Unlike archaeological artifacts, scrum artifacts aren't set in stone. Scrum teams continually inspect and assess artifacts to make sure that they're digging in the right direction.

Successful implementation of the scrum framework depends on people's ability to embrace the five scrum values in their culture and thinking. The new way of working needs to change the day-to-day habits of teams and individuals.

Each role, artifact, and event in scrum has a set purpose. You place your work in the scrum framework, moving through the roadmap to value (discussed earlier in this chapter), but the actual tools and techniques for accomplishing your goals are your own. Scrum doesn't tell you how to achieve your goal; it merely provides a framework within which you can clearly see what you're doing.

REMEMBER

Scrum is an empirical process control framework. It is actually process-agnostic; it does not tell you the processes to use to create your outcomes.

Scrum is simple, but it's not easy. Scrum is much like getting into shape physically. In concept, you need to exercise more and take in fewer calories; in practice, the process can be complex.

Following are some common practices that complement scrum and have produced incredible successes. (Extra elements are shown in italic.) Here, we've expanded the scrum framework with recommended practices:

» **Accountabilities**

- Product owner
- Developers
- Scrum master

- *Stakeholders*
- *Scrum mentor*

» **Artifacts**

- Product goal
- *Product roadmap*
- Product backlog
- *Release plan*
- Sprint backlog
- Product increment

» **Events**

- *Product planning*
- *Release planning*
- Sprint
- Sprint planning
- Daily scrum
- Sprint review
- Sprint retrospective

The framework is still simple but with additional roles, artifacts, and events designed to smooth the process. Throughout the book, we discuss these roles, artifacts, and events.

SCRUM'S ORIGINS

Although there have been almost 100 years of building toward the agile frameworks we use today, the first scrum team was created by Jeff Sutherland in 1993 after he applied the concepts outlined in a 1986 *Harvard Business Review* article titled, "The New New Product Development Game." With scrum co-creator Ken Schwaber, Jeff formalized the scrum framework at OOPSLA '95 (International Conference on Object-Oriented Programming, Systems, Languages, and Applications).

The Feedback Feast

One clear advantage of scrum over other frameworks is the feedback loop, which tells you early and continuously what's working, what's not working, what's missing, and what's extraordinary.

Feedback is generated regularly from scrum team members, stakeholders, and customers. The process goes something like this:

1. Developers receive daily feedback as they build their product or service.

2. Direct daily interaction occurs between the product owner and the developers for on-the-spot answers and feedback.

3. The product owner provides direct feedback as they accept or reject every completed backlog item.

4. At the end of each sprint, internal stakeholders provide feedback.

5. At the end of every release, feedback is provided by the external marketplace.

You get more from the scrum model than traditional project management models because scrum emphasizes results rather than artifact development, delivering tangible, validated products rather than tomes of reports on what's possible. You receive regular feedback along the way, enabling you to incrementally get your product or service to market as fast as possible.

In the end, you're not left wondering whether you produced what your customers want; you've been communicating with and receiving feedback from them all along the way. The inspection and adaptation process has been at work on your behalf, and you're delivering what your customers actually asked.

Agile Roots

To understand scrum, it helps to dip into the broader world of agile techniques because scrum is one of many approaches with common characteristics of agility.

Agile is a descriptor of approaches that align with the values of the Agile Manifesto and the 12 Agile Principles, which we outline in this section. Scrum is one agile approach.

TIP

For a thorough look at agile techniques, see *Agile Project Management For Dummies*, Third Edition, by Mark Layton, Steve Ostermiller, and Dean Kynaston (John Wiley & Sons, Inc.).

Three pillars of improvement

The empirical process control model sits securely on three pillars, which are common to agile techniques, including scrum:

>> Transparency

>> Inspection

>> Adaptation

Transparency

One distinguishing feature of agile techniques, in general, and scrum, in particular, is transparency. When channels of communication are clear and accessible, information is radiated broadly. Everyone involved knows what's been done, what's being worked on, what's left to work on, and any impediments blocking the way. Right from the start, you produce real results that are validated and approved or sent back for adjustments. Now, the lag time between the start date and usable results is days rather than months.

Transparency isn't just about seeing results quickly. Everyone needs to look through the same lens. A framework (such as scrum) is shared, along with an agreed-on definition of *done*. Both observers and participants can see what's being accomplished and interpret the results in a common language.

Inspection

As you discover in the following chapters, goals and outcomes are broken into the smallest actionable chunks possible (product backlog items commonly captured as user stories; see Chapter 3). Goals are set within fixed-length iterations called sprints. As each item is accomplished, it's inspected to make sure that it works and does what the customer wants.

These inspections are done by people closest to the job — those who do the work and those who represent the customer. This process eliminates the time lag required for an outside person to complete this task, and it also means that any adjustments can be made quickly because the required knowledge is at hand.

Adaptation

If the inspection shows inaccuracies and/or inefficiencies — that is, if the feature or desired outcomes don't work right — an adaptation needs to be made. The adaptation should be made as soon as possible and before moving to the next actionable item on the to-do list. In other words, when you move on, you know everything behind you is functioning properly.

Scrum allows inspections and adaptations to be accomplished immediately at the team and product or service levels through sprint reviews, sprint retrospectives, and the daily scrum (see Chapters 6 and 7).

One Agile Manifesto

Scrum is a framework, not a by-the-numbers methodology. You still need to think and make choices. Part of the scrum framework's benefit is that it is intentionally incomplete. It allows you to make the best decisions based on the reality in which you find yourself.

In 2001, 17 software and project experts agreed on the four values their experiments and approaches had in common. These values are known as the Manifesto for Agile Software Development (commonly referred to as the *Agile Manifesto*):

We are uncovering better ways of developing software by doing it and helping others do it. Through this work, we have come to value:

>> Individuals and interactions more than processes and tools

>> Working software more than comprehensive documentation

>> Customer collaboration more than contract negotiation

>> Responding to change more than following a plan

That is, while there is value in the items on the right, we value the items on the left more.

Agile Manifesto © 2001: Kent Beck, Mike Beedle, Arie van Bennekum, Alistair Cockburn, Ward Cunningham, Martin Fowler, James Grenning, Jim Highsmith, Andrew Hunt, Ron Jeffries, Jon Kern, Brian Marick, Robert C. Martin, Steve Mellor, Ken Schwaber, Jeff Sutherland, Dave Thomas

Even though the Agile Manifesto and principles were written by and for software experts, the values remain valid for whatever scrum project you embark upon. For example, the Global Positioning System (GPS) was designed by and for the military, but that doesn't mean that you can't benefit from it when you drive to a new part of town.

TIP

For more information on the Agile Manifesto and its authors, visit http://agilemanifesto.org.

Twelve Agile principles

The Agile Manifesto's authors also agreed on 12 Agile principles. You can use these principles to make sure your approach is true to agile values:

1. Our highest priority is to satisfy the customer through early and continuous delivery of valuable software.

2. Welcome changing requirements, even late in development. Agile processes harness change for the customer's competitive advantage.

3. Deliver working software frequently, from a couple of weeks to a couple of months, with a preference for a shorter timescale.

4. Business people and developers must work together daily throughout the project.

5. Build projects around motivated individuals. Give them the environment and support they need, and trust them to get the job done.

6. Face-to-face conversation is the most efficient and effective method of conveying information to and within a development team.

7. Working software is the primary measure of progress.

8. Agile processes promote sustainable development. The sponsors, developers, and users should be able to maintain a constant pace indefinitely.

9. Continuous attention to technical excellence and good design enhances agility.

10. Simplicity — the art of maximizing the amount of work not done — is essential.

11. The best architectures, requirements, and designs emerge from self-organizing teams.

12. At regular intervals, the team reflects on how to become more effective, and then tunes and adjusts its behavior accordingly.

REMEMBER

The principles don't change, but the tools and techniques to achieve them can. While some principles explicitly reference software development, their application is much broader. Try replacing the word "software" with other words relevant to your context, such as "product," "solution," "functionality," and so on.

Some of the principles are easier to implement than others. Consider principle 2. Maybe some parts of your company (or group or family) are open to change and new ideas. For them, scrum is natural, and they're ready to get started. But other parts may be more resistant to change.

Or consider principle 6. Working face-to-face may not be possible. With the Internet, the pandemic, and the globalization of workforces, you may have team members from Mumbai to Moscow to Miami. You could consider several video conferencing solutions, but none of these solutions meets the intention of principle 6, and none is as good as face-to-face communication. Regardless, you may actually find that only scrum allows you to maximize your results, even with a distributed team.

Your work is bound to have unique challenges. Don't let a hiccup or a less-than-perfect scenario stop you cold or cause your work to limp along. Part of the fun of using scrum is working through issues to get results. Stick with the 12 principles, and your team will get quality results quickly.

THE MARSHMALLOW CHALLENGE

In 2010, author and speaker Tom Wujec gave a remarkable TED talk called *The Marshmallow Challenge* that discussed a design exercise devised by designer Peter Skillman. In this exercise, small groups of participants are given 18 minutes to build a free-standing structure as tall as possible using strange, minimal tools: 20 sticks of spaghetti, one yard of tape, one yard of string, and one marshmallow. Wujec began giving this test and studying the results. Most groups struggled to create anything high or reliable. Group members discussed options, planned a final design, and assembled it, only to find that the structure wouldn't stand because they'd left out a crucial aspect.

The groups who performed the worst were recent graduates of business schools. The groups who performed the best were kindergarteners, who consistently produced higher and more creative structures.

Wujec said that when business students work on an idea, they believe that only one "correct" solution exists, so they spend much of their time contemplating and planning for that approach. The children, however, started by playing with the tools. They learned what didn't work and changed it; then, they figured out what did work and kept it. In other words, they built prototypes all along the way.

A takeaway in the context of scrum is that humans' natural state is inspection and adaptation. We want to do these things, but somewhere along the way, we get trained out of them. We're taught that planning and coming up with one solution is the correct way to do things. But kindergarteners remind us that this way of thinking may be wrong.

Three Platinum Principles

At Platinum Edge, our consulting and training firm, we've worked with agile organizations and scrum teams for more than two decades and consulted with dozens of companies, businesses, and not-for-profit organizations. We know how well the following "Platinum Principles" work because we've seen their value as we assisted in their implementation.

Here are three Platinum Principles that have consistently improved the performance of the teams we've helped:

>> Resist formality

>> Think and act as a team

>> Visualize rather than write

These principles can be applied to any work, not just software development. Part of the beauty of agile techniques is that you can use them for anything.

Resist formality

Have you ever seen a knockout presentation and wondered how much time someone spent putting it together? Don't even think about doing that with scrum. You can scribble it on a flip chart, stick it on a wall where people will look at it, and then get back to creating value. If discussion is required, walk over to the concerned parties (or at least spin up a quick video chat) and have the discussion. Each iteration of the design process takes very little time to visualize. Focus your valuable time and effort on accomplishing the goals instead of stylized presentations.

TECHNICAL STUFF

Pageantry is too often mistaken for professionalism and progress. With scrum, you're encouraged to communicate immediately, directly, and informally whenever you have a question and to work closely with your team members to increase efficiency and save time.

Avoid these unproductive traps:

>> Fancy, time-consuming presentations

>> Long and/or unfocused meetings

>> Tomes of documentation

>> Excessive effort justifying progress

Emphasize these productivity builders:

>> Be barely sufficient. In all things, the work should be barely sufficient to accomplish the goal. (Don't mistake sufficiency for mediocrity. Sufficient is sufficient; more is wasteful, and problems often arise in that bloat. See Agile Principle 10 earlier in this chapter.)

>> Communicate frequently with all parties to reduce the need for extensive updates.

>> Communicate simply and directly. If you can speak to someone face to face, do so.

Figure out the simplest way to get what you need, always with the goal of delivering the highest quality.

TIP

Before long, your concerted effort will evolve an agile culture. As people become educated in the process and see the improved results, their buy-in for being barely sufficient will increase. So, bear through any initial pushback with education, patience, and consistency.

Think and act as a team

The heart of scrum is working as a team, which can at first be challenging for traditional corporate cultures where individual contributions are valued most. In scrum, the results survive or die at the team level. Using each individual's talent on a team makes the work from average to hyperproductive. As Aristotle said, "The whole is greater than the sum of its parts."

How do you create this team culture? The scrum framework itself emphasizes teamwork. Physical space, common goals, and collective ownership all scream "team." Add the following practices to your scrum framework:

>> Eliminate work titles. No one owns areas of development; team members add value through their skills and collaboration. We want situational and informal leadership driven by expertise.

>> Pair team members to enhance cross-functionality and front-load quality assurance.

>> Always report team metrics, not individual or pairing metrics.

Visualize rather than write

On the whole, people are visual; they think pictorially and remember pictorially. Most kids like pictures — visual illustrations of text. Adults are no different. We're likely to start reading a long article by flipping or scrolling through its images and charts and then reading more about what piqued our interest.

Pictures, diagrams, and graphs relay information instantly. Written reports require reader buy-in, which drops as the reports grow.

TECHNICAL STUFF

Twitter was interested in studying the effectiveness of tweets with photos versus those that were text only. It conducted a study using SHIFT Media Manager and came up with some interesting results. Users engaged five times more frequently when tweets included photos as opposed to text-only tweets. And the rate of retweets and replies with photos was doubled. However, the cost per engagement of photo tweets was half that of text-only tweets (SHIFT Newsroom, January 17, 2014).

When possible, encourage your team to present information visually, even if that means sketching a diagram on a physical or virtual whiteboard. If someone doesn't understand the diagram, they can ask about it. The discussion coming from questions is usually valuable, as well. Changes can be made right there and then — simple graphs, charts, and models are at your fingertips.

The Five Scrum Values

Scrum is founded on five values that each member of the team uses to guide their decision-making:

>> Commitment

>> Focus

>> Openness

>> Respect

>> Courage

These values aren't rocket science. Instead, they fall into that familiar category of common sense. Yet, they're critical to the successful implementation of scrum, so they deserve discussion here.

In the following sections, we look at each of these values more closely to show how vital they are within scrum.

Commitment

Scrum team members must be committed to success and to each other. They must be willing to create realistic goals and stick to them. Everyone must participate. Scrum is an "all-in" situation in which everyone is part of a team and works together to meet the team's commitments. Fortunately, the scrum model ensures you have the authority and freedom to do just that.

At the core of scrum is a sprint event, which we cover in Chapter 5. A sprint requires clear goals set within fixed timeboxes. In this model, you break those goals into the smallest chunks of work possible, so you know what you're getting into. You know what's realistic, so you can set appropriate goals and meet your commitments.

Focus

Part of the magic of scrum is that it's built around the concept of focus. Focus on a few things at a time and do them well. You will have a clear role and clear goals within that role. Your job is to use your role to contribute to achieving the goal. Every day, team members know what to focus on for that day to be successful, which is liberating.

You made your goals and commitments earlier. Focus on those goals and nothing else.

Openness

Everything with your work, and everyone else's work, is transparent and available for inspection and improvement. The goals, challenges, and progress of anyone involved — you, your boss, your employees, your in-laws — are open and visible. Gone are the days of six-months-down-the-road surprises.

Fortunately, the basis of scrum is the agile pillars of empiricism: transparency, inspection, and adaptation. Information radiators (big, visible charts) and real-time intelligence allow unfettered action. Most people aren't used to this level of exposure. But after it catches on in your organization, they won't have things any other way.

Respect

Each team member is selected for their strengths. As a result, scrum teams are diverse — diverse personalities, backgrounds, skill sets, and perspectives. Each one is vital to success. Along with these strengths come weaknesses and opportunities to learn and grow. The golden rule within scrum is that each participant must respect everyone else. They respect each other to be capable, independent people and are respected as such by the people with whom they work.

Harmony is created by synchronizing roles and skills, which creates a development rhythm as the work progresses. If one person is out of tune for a bit, it's in your best interest to help that person because all team members are held accountable as a team.

People want to do good work; it's in our wiring. If you seek the positive, you'll find the positive. Likewise, if you seek the negative, you'll find the negative. Respect is the burning ember of positivity.

Courage

Scrum is about taking risks. It's about stepping into the unknown darkness. Every idea you have will get challenged in a scrum model. No procedure is justified because you've always done things a certain way. Say goodbye to procedures you've done by habit and say hello to a process that's built on what the team finds to be successful. Scrum team members have the courage to do the right thing, challenge the status quo, work on tough problems, and innovate ways to solve them. Philosopher Jacob Bronowski could have been speaking about the scrum model in his book *The Ascent of Man* when he said

It is important that students bring a certain ragamuffin, barefoot irreverence to their studies; they are not here to worship what is known but to question it.

Fiefdoms will be challenged. Rules will be tested. Routines will be broken. Improvements will happen. Change can be hard. Change takes courage. It takes courage to commit, focus, be open, and show and be worthy of respect — to embrace all the scrum values.

Scrum takes courage.

IN THIS CHAPTER

» **Quantifying the benefits of scrum**

» **Empowering product owner accountability**

» **Creating your product goal**

» **Enabling scrum master accountability**

» **Following common practices**

Chapter 2

The First Steps

Work expands so as to fill the time available for its completion.
— PARKINSON'S LAW

Scrum is simple in concept yet often difficult in application. Changing 70 years' worth of the project management paradigm is challenging. Still, achieving a 30 to 40 percent time-to-market increase and 30 to 70 percent cost savings are realistic. Jeff Sutherland, co-creator of scrum, has documented 1,000-percent performance improvements by using scrum. Given that potential, it's worthwhile to get out of your comfort zone and start dealing with the organizational dysfunctions that are holding you back.

Empirical process controls are best used when the outcomes are uncertain and the environment is dynamic, complex, and requires innovation. Applying scrum in such a context takes an open mind — something that's good for all of us. By the end of this chapter, you'll be up and running with your project and ready to take the next scrum steps.

Getting Your Scrum On

Two factors come into play as you convert to scrum:

>> **The technical nature of the work:** It's easy to find out whether the nature of the work fits scrum because scrum is for everyone. Any project for which you want early, empirical evidence of performance and quality can and should be done with a scrum framework.

>> **The social culture where the work resides:** Social culture is complex because people are complex. Changing processes can be easy; changing people isn't. Every person and every group of people has idiosyncrasies. As entertaining as these idiosyncrasies are at a barbecue, they can be a hurdle to overcome in teaching new agile techniques.

It's natural for people to resist change; people resist to different degrees and in different ways. However, the conversion is faster and easier when people understand how the changes will benefit them directly.

As you see in Parts 3 through 5 of this book, billion-dollar companies benefit from scrum, as do everyday folks. Steve used scrum to plan, day by day, a recent vacation to Hawaii. Because scrum allowed the right combination of structure with flexibility, he and his wife agreed it was the best vacation they'd ever had. (Chapter 17 provides additional examples of using scrum within a family.)

TECHNICAL STUFF

Empiricism, or the theory that all knowledge is derived from sense experience, is the essence of agility. Empirical process controls are all around us. We use them when we cook, play games, and even drive cars. While driving, we continually watch the road, check mirrors, react to other drivers, and monitor the gauges in the dashboard — each helping adjust steering and speed. As we drive, the transparency available to us enables inspection and adaptation — the three pillars of agility. Empirical process controls are best used to address dynamic, complex, and unpredictable situations mostly found in reality — like driving to grandma's.

Show me the money

Consider Net Present Value 101: A dollar today is more valuable than a dollar six months from now. The biggest problem in organizations isn't the efficiency of the tactical execution teams; it's poor portfolio management. Executives fail to show the leadership necessary to make the tough prioritization calls, which results in too many projects being pushed down to a lower level of management that lacks the power to fight back. (See Chapter 13 for more on this dynamic.)

This dysfunction is masked by stretching people across multiple projects so that each business unit gets something. Getting everything done takes considerably longer, but the managers of each project are placated by binders of documents telling them how great their products will be when they eventually get them. This thrashing between projects comes at a real cost.

Scrum is the opposite. You focus, you produce deliverable tangible results, and then you increment forward. The product backlog (described in detail in Chapter 3) forces you to be effective before worrying about efficiency.

Your organization may be a billion-dollar company or a mom-and-pop store struggling to get a great idea to market. Maybe you're one of a gazillion employees, and you've been given this one project to prove yourself. In each case, disciplined prioritization, increased effectiveness, and incrementally tested progress can help you survive.

Because of the prioritization within scrum, you're working exclusively on the highest-value features. You're not perfecting a third-tier widget instead of a high-value feature. You're going for the meat every time. As a result, what you produce during each sprint is what's most important, practical, and immediately desirable. In every release, you have something that the marketplace values. That's scrum. That's showing you the money.

REMEMBER

When your back is against the wall, everyone reverts to agile techniques, regardless of whether they realize it. If your company had 60 days' worth of cash left on hand, nobody would worry about whether a status report has the right cover sheet. Bureaucracy is the luxury of the financially bloated, and it's a luxury that can change overnight in today's economy.

DO SOMETHING BEFORE DOING EVERYTHING

Using the practice of doing something before doing everything, a client agreed to put a product out to market with only one way for the customer to purchase it. Instead of ensuring every credit card on Earth was tied in, PayPal was set up, and other payment options could be processed with speed, the client decided to take a chance on raising early funds with only one credit card payment option. The result? Between October and January, he brought in more than $1 million in sales through that one credit card option. Now the site can process multiple credit cards, PayPal, and several other payment options — each of which was rolled out one sprint at a time *after* the product was actively generating revenue.

In our seminars, we teach that it's better to do all of something than a little bit of everything. If you wait for everything to be ready, chances are nothing will get *done*. Instead, take those tangible steps of progress you achieve through scrum, get them out to market, get feedback, and let the value flow in.

Fortunately, scrum is built around delivering results early and often. You don't wait to see results. You see them after every sprint.

Try this approach for yourself. Ask yourself or your customer, "If we had only one month to deliver value to the marketplace, what would we build, and how?" See how taking this incremental approach brings value to the forefront?

Scrum may still be a fresh concept to many, but its usage is growing by leaps and bounds. We were thrilled to learn several years ago that more organizations were using agile techniques as opposed to waterfall techniques for software development. In 2016, Digital.ai reported that 8 percent of respondents said that all or most of their teams were agile. In 2018, it jumped to 25 percent and hit 52 percent in 2021. Jobs requiring experience and knowledge of scrum continue to climb, too. We have crossed the chasm, and this growth of agile product development has continued to increase.

I want it now

We live in a fast-paced world. It seems like our customers, bosses, and colleagues all demand "I want it now," or you may even hear that inner voice saying it. Scrum makes it more possible to see immediate results. Products developed using scrum get to market 30–40 percent faster. But how?

The answer is simple: Start your work early and thereby end early. You're creating usable products and solutions from the start. You don't wait for months or years for results that may have passed their sell-by date. You quickly plan, create, inspect, adapt, ship, and benefit. With this process, you churn out value early and continuously.

In science, as in business, the rule isn't survival of the fittest but survival of the fastest. Whoever could crawl into safety fastest missed being snatched up by the predator. In business, innovations are released to market at exponentially increasing speeds. Brands are created and killed overnight. You simply can't afford to be late.

That's not the only reason you want to experience increased speed to market. You order and prioritize items as you create your product backlog (the to-do list). When prioritizing, you consider two things:

>> Items with the highest value

>> Items with the highest risk and uncertainty

Both factors get to the top of the list.

I'm not sure what I want

Most people don't know what they want, at least not until they interact with it. Most people, companies, and organizations only realize what they want when interacting directly with the product or service. The gap is the difference between waterfall (seeing it in documents) and scrum (using it).

In your roadmap to value (see Chapter 1), you begin with a long-term objective of what you want your product to be. This product goal acts as a beacon for your team, the way any established destination acts as a beacon. The product roadmap allows a natural progression of decision-making — from large and fuzzy generalities down to small and specific operationalization of that goal. The goal provides the outer boundary of what can change. If the resulting product or service deviates from the intended goal, it's a different objective.

Scrum enables you to reach your goals, regardless of the outcomes. For example,

>> Developing a website where people can order organic, allergy-specific restaurant food for home delivery

>> Constructing an Alzheimer's patient residence with individual-specific, onsite monitoring; alerts; and security

>> Selling Grandma's doughnut recipe that you're convinced will lead to the next Krispy Kreme

How these ideas would pan out in reality is yet to be determined. The good news is that you develop the most effective path of progress through the scrum framework. The tangible creation, inspection, and adaptation process gives you the tools to create the needed product.

Is that defect a problem?

Each item the developers complete is tested and integrated to ensure that it works. The product owner is responsible for accepting or rejecting each item as it's completed. In other words, if something doesn't work, it doesn't make it out of the sprint.

Of course, issues can come up after a product makes it into the market. But the feedback cycle is so strong during creation that it can be corrected as soon as a defect or process inefficiency is spotted. The problem is fixed in that sprint or placed back in the product backlog to be prioritized against future work. Scrum is an exposure model.

Your company's culture

When people see the success and value of scrum, using it becomes easier. Employees discover that scrum improves communication and collaboration, creates *esprit de corps*, has a natural life cycle, develops an honest and transparent environment, and increases ownership and empowerment — all of which positively affect the company culture.

The level of resistance to change varies from company culture to company culture. The solution, as with so many things, is a tangible success. (You'll find no defense against demonstrated success!) Find what the key people need — increased profits, higher product quality, faster delivery, or improved talent retention — and show them how scrum delivers.

In any group of people, you'll find the influencers — the ones with clout who can get change rolling. Maybe you're an influencer, or maybe someone else is. Get that person on board (which may mean going to higher management), and your job will be easier.

The Power in the Product Owner

Involvement begets commitment. You want to build a team that can move the gears of change. The key to moving the gears of change is the product owner.

The product owner's primary job is to take care of the business side of the product or service. This person is responsible for maximizing the value of the product resulting from the scrum team's work. The product owner is one person, not a committee, and is dedicated full-time to owning the business-side duties, collaborating with the scrum team to maximize the value delivered to the customer, and representing the stakeholders and customers. Those wanting to change the backlog can do so by trying to convince the product owner.

The product owner is accountable for effective product backlog management, which includes:

- » Defining and explicitly communicating the product goal

- » Gathering and clearly communicating backlog items and the scope of the product

- » Making in-the-moment priority and trade-off decisions

- » Ensuring the product backlog is transparent, visible, and understood

- » Optimizing the work done by the scrum team

- » Setting product, release, and sprint goals

- » Determining with the scrum team which product backlog items go into the next sprint

- » Handling business aspects of the work, including ROI (return on investment) and business risk, and interfacing with business stakeholders and customers

- » Socializing the product goal and roadmap

- » Being available throughout the day to work directly with developers, thereby increasing efficiency through clear and immediate communication

- » Accepting or rejecting work results throughout the sprint, ideally the day they are completed

For product owners to succeed, the entire organization must respect their decisions. These decisions are visible in the content and ordering of the product backlog and through the inspectable increment at the sprint review (discussed in Chapter 6).

We're often shocked that organizations that plan to pour millions of dollars into a project say they don't have the people for a dedicated product owner to ensure that the business and technical priorities align and that the product created is the product needed. Yet, many of these organizations have a project manager to direct the project. Because the project manager role doesn't exist in scrum, the money for product owners can be taken from there. (Relevant duties are part of the three scrum accountabilities; see Chapter 1.)

Product owners clarify, prioritize, and set an environment for focus. They ensure that the scrum team is effective. The product owner determines which requirements are pursued and when work shifts to those requirements — that is, what and when but not how or how much. How and how much are the developers' responsibilities.

Imagine that your passion is building something. In scrum, you'd be a developer. For you, the product owner is a gift. This person excels in product management because they are empowered to make decisions, clarify, prioritize, and fight to ensure that team members focus on one goal at a time. Because of effective product owners, developers are freed from distractions and can focus more on getting their jobs done.

The product owner and the scrum master work to create the best environment possible for the scrum team to do the highest-quality work. The product owner handles and deflects business concerns and noise, and the scrum master ensures that other organizational interruptions don't affect the team.

The abstraction layer created by the product owner and scrum master doesn't mean less business noise. For the most part, developers don't have to deal with the noise.

On the other hand, developers can contact stakeholders or team/nonteam people directly when they need clarification on something they're working on. This model of filtering prioritization but not clarification is like a cell membrane, which is designed to let certain fluids travel in one direction but not the other.

The result is that the team is protected from outside interference but not hindered in their quest for knowledge. These boundaries are important and integral to the successful functioning of the team.

Why Product Owners Love Scrum

Product owners love scrum for the following reasons:

>> Development and stakeholders are aligned and held accountable as a single unit rather than being at odds as in historical methodologies.

>> Schedules and costs are empirically forecasted, and product owners have daily clarity on progress.

>> After every sprint, product owners know that they'll have the highest-priority items fully functioning and usable.

>> Customer feedback is early and continuous.

>> The earliest possible tangible measurement of the ROI is available — that is, after every sprint.

>> Systematic support is provided for changing business needs, giving the product owner continued flexibility to adapt to market realities.

>> Product and process waste are reduced by emphasizing prioritized product development, not process artifact development (usually, documents).

REMEMBER

The product owner's number-one characteristic should be *decisiveness*. This person makes tough, pragmatic, and uncomfortable decisions every hour of every day. They need to be able to create an environment of trust and pivot when changes are needed. The product owner must begin by doing what they think is right and then change based on empirical evidence. To be effective, a product owner must be empowered to make tactical decisions without escalating to a higher power.

A scrum product owner's role is much different from a traditional project manager's role. Imagine telling a golfer to hit the ball 400 yards and straight into the hole, and they'll need to run laps if they don't succeed. Traditional approaches work that way. With scrum, the golfer hits the ball, assesses the results, and adapts to achieve the goal in the best possible way, given where they are — not where they should be.

The Company Goal and Strategy: Part 1

Knowing what outcomes you want beforehand is key for successful agile delivery. These desired outcomes are often best described as a *product goal*.

TIP

When we coach clients, we always have them create a product goal statement, so their goal is right in front of them. We're looking for a crisp, concise, and clear elevator pitch that can be conveyed during the ground-to-fourth-floor ride. We ask them to have their product goal drafted before we first meet with them. Then we spend one hour with the people responsible for the goal, honing it into something with which we can work. It doesn't take long to create this invaluable artifact.

Product goals are so useful that we've added them to our roadmap to value (see Figure 2-1). Think of your product goal as a destination with a beacon. You may have 100 ways to get to the destination, and it doesn't matter which way you take; the point is to end there. With this beacon of a statement, you always know where you're headed because you have the goal in sight. From this stable, strategic destination, you have limitless tactical flexibility.

PRODUCT GOAL

Description: The goal for the product and its alignment with the company's strategy.
Owner: Product owner
Frequency: At least annually

FIGURE 2-1:
The product goal is on the roadmap to value.

A product goal is

>> Internally focused, with no marketing fluff

>> Fine-tuned to the goals of the marketplace and customer needs

>> Strategic in nature, showing why and what rather than how

>> Reviewed annually (when part of a broader vision that looks out further)

>> Owned by the product owner

REMEMBER

Your product goal must be communicated throughout the organization or group you work with. It is the scrum team's commitment to everything they do. The product backlog emerges from the product goal. Whether the team is designing a new sports car model or planning a wedding, everyone must clearly understand the goal, which sets expectations and the tone of the upcoming work.

Structuring your goal

In his excellent book *Crossing the Chasm* (Collins Business Essentials), Geoffrey Moore recommends an effective model for creating your product goal. We use this model often, with first-rate results.

The entire statement should be no longer than two or three sentences. Based on Moore's recommendations, the model we use follows this pattern:

>> For *<target customer>*

>> who *<statement of the need>*

>> the *<product name>*

>> is a *<product category>*

>> that *<product key benefit, compelling reason to buy>*

>> Unlike *<primary competitive alternative>*

>> our product *<final statement of product differentiation>*

We recommend adding this conclusion:

>> which supports our strategy to *<company strategy>*

Here are examples of what this format looks like in real life:

>> Tankless water heater

- *For* homeowners *who* desire continuous hot water flow and better energy conservation, *the* Acme Tankless Water Heater *is an* instantaneous water heater *that* efficiently heats water as you use it. *Unlike* tank-type water heaters, *our product* provides continuous flow at consistent temperatures with lower operating costs at 94 percent efficiency, *which supports our strategy to* provide for tomorrow's generation by reducing the waste of natural resources today.

>> Hawaiian vacation

- *For* my spouse and me, *who* are stressed out of our minds, *the* Hawaii or Bust 2022 vacation *is a* spontaneous, last-minute getaway *that* will remove us from our hectic lives long enough to provide new experiences. *Unlike* family vacations or structured itineraries, *our product* provides complete flexibility without expectations, *which supports our strategy to* make the most of each moment together.

TECHNICAL STUFF

Product and team goals should also be SMART goals. The SMART goal concept was developed by George Doran, Arthur Miller, and James Cunningham in their 1981 article, "There's a S.M.A.R.T. way to write management goals and objectives." SMART is an acronym for Specific, Measurable, Attainable, Realistic, and Timely (or time-bound).

REMEMBER

The product goal itself is functional, but the addition of business strategy is emotional. Bring purpose to your product in the form of a company strategy that makes people's lives better. It's never your company strategy to make money; it's to do something of such value that it can be monetized.

Finding the crosshair

The product goal is created and owned by the product owner and is integral to the business or endeavor. One mind, however, is just that: one mind. The product owner may own this statement, but they'll surely have better luck using collective intelligence to create and refine it. To this end, the product owner can choose to receive input from developers, the scrum master, external or internal stakeholders, and even customers themselves. Determining what to do with the input is the product owner's choice and the product owner's responsibility.

When product owners are open to input from others, the product owner may become aware of nuances, features, and market angles that one person alone wouldn't think of. The product owner may be wise to take feedback and then carefully filter it through their own understanding.

The Scrum Master

In *The New One Minute Manager* (William Morrow), Kenneth Blanchard and Spencer Johnson describe how some of the most effective managers they studied lacked their employees' technical skills. Oddly enough, they also had a lot of time on their hands. If they couldn't do the job themselves, what were these managers good at?

The managers could clear the path so that their employees could get the work done, which is the role of the scrum master. Whereas the product owner is a directing role, the scrum master is an enabling role. The scrum master is responsible for the environment for success.

Scrum master traits

After deep expertise, the scrum master's most important trait is influence. Diplomacy, communication skills, facilitation and coaching skills, and the ability to manage up are all good qualities, but the scrum master also needs to have the respect and clout to get difficult situations resolved. Where clout comes from — expertise, longevity, charisma, association — doesn't matter because it works in the scrum master role.

As a servant leader, the scrum master teaches, encourages, removes tactical impediments, and most importantly, removes strategic impediments, so the tactical ones don't reappear. As with the other scrum roles, the scrum master is most effective when dedicated full-time in the role, especially with teams, products, and organizations new to scrum.

TIP

If the product owner is the quarterback calling the plays and the developer is the running back gaining the yards, the scrum master is a blocker who clears the path. Yet, they're all peers with a common goal.

In our experience, developers who double as scrum masters and scrum masters thrashed across multiple teams throw off a team's ability to extrapolate past performance to future capability. This situation introduces availability variation and delivers inferior protection to developers. This rarely makes sense quantitatively because a minor improvement in a scrum team's velocity (see Chapter 4) often has a huge effect on the bottom line. If your team can schedule its organizational interruptions and is so mature that it can't improve further, contact us; we want to write a book about *you*.

Like every other role, the scrum master should be a full-time role, and the person who holds it should be solely dedicated to that job, especially for new teams, projects, and organizations.

REMEMBER

Scrum teams are typically ten or fewer people, so one scrum master improves the performance of up to nine people. Even a minor reduction in performance has a ninefold effect.

In addition to coaching the organization and scrum team on how to play scrum, the scrum master facilitates the events: sprint planning, daily scrum, sprint review, sprint retrospective meetings, and any team conversation and collaboration.

A scrum team is a bunch of intelligent, engaged people with a high degree of ownership in the work that they're doing. Put these folks in a meeting together, and the creative energy may cause them to explode — or at least go off on a lot of tangents. The scrum master's role is to focus this energy.

The scrum master's influence extends to everyone involved, including stakeholders and product owners. The scrum master is a coach to everyone because everyone needs ongoing education and smooth facilitation in scrum.

WARNING

If you're making decisions as a scrum master, you're not doing the right job. Developers will never become self-organizing if they're not making their own decisions. Scrum masters extract themselves from day-to-day decisions and create a conducive collaboration environment while shielding the team from interference.

As the scrum master shields the developers from external interference, the team's velocity increases dramatically. Think about how well you work when the door's shut, the phone's off, and everybody's away or asleep versus when you're fielding constant interruptions from colleagues, family members, and even the dog.

Even when outside interference is kept to a minimum, because social density is higher in scrum, it's not unusual for conflict to also be higher. The pressure to get valuable outcomes in short sprint windows can be wearing, so the scrum master's job entails managing conflict to the right level. Task conflict (being willing to fight for what you think is right) is healthy. Personal conflict (challenging someone personally) is not.

Scrum master as a true leader

The concept of *servant leader* dates to around 500 BCE and was developed by Lao Tzu, who is thought to be the author of the *Tao Te Ching*. Yet, this concept is mentioned in every major religion and is popular in modern-day corporate leadership models. That's staying power.

The servant leader puts others first so that they can do their jobs. The leader enables people rather than presenting the solution on a silver plate. If someone says, "I'm hungry," the servant leader doesn't hand him a fish. Rather, the leader asks, "How can I help you so that you're not hungry today, tomorrow, or next year?" The scrum master helps each person build skills and find the best solution for that person, whether the answer lies inside or outside the team.

As a servant leader, a scrum master teaches, encourages, removes tactical impediments, and removes strategic impediments so that tactical impediments don't reappear — characteristics of a true leader.

Why scrum masters love scrum

Scrum masters love scrum for many reasons, including these:

» They can focus on having quantifiable impact rather than administrative responsibilities. Rising velocity is directly tied to the additional value the scrum team can deliver.

» They coach people rather than serve as command-and-control managers.

» They get to enable people rather than direct them.

» They ask questions rather than give answers.

» They're involved with fewer meetings, and those meetings are shorter.

» They facilitate building empowered, motivated teams that think for themselves and act with authority.

» Performance accountability isn't outsourced to them (as in, "Hey, Joe, what's the status of the tasks Nancy is working on?"). Instead, accountability is sourced directly to the person doing the work.

TIP

A good scrum master's motto is "Never lunch alone." Always create and develop relationships. Influence is your currency, so make sure you create an environment in which you can easily video chat or walk to a person's desk and get results.

THE INTERFERENCE ISSUE

Studies have shown that it takes 15 minutes to get to the right concentration level for peak productivity — a state that's often called "being in the zone." Yet, it takes only a 2.3-second interruption to burst that bubble, so another 15 minutes is required to re-establish focus. A 4.4-second interruption *triples* the number of mistakes made in a sequencing task.

Three types of interference prevail in the workplace:

- **Personal interruptions:** Personal interruptions are email flashes, phone calls from Aunt Martha, and text messages with links to cat videos. Discipline is the solution. Silence your mobile devices to tune in to your task. Check out the nearby sidebar, "The Pomodoro Technique."

- **Team interruptions:** Team interruptions are those caused by workmates. The team needs to identify collaboration time versus concentration time and then balance these times based on team dynamics and project needs.

  - Collaboration time is the time when it's okay to interrupt, talk, and exchange ideas. This time is healthy and productive and should make up the bulk of each team member's day.

  - Concentration time can be indicated by physical indicators such as "Do Not Disturb" or "Busy" flags. This time helps team members get to a deep level of concentration and crank out the product. High-performing teams also set and honor online statuses set by their teammates.

- **External interruptions:** External interruptions are the scrum master's domain. These interruptions can happen anytime, all day, and every day. The scrum master's job is to shield team members from these interruptions.

Most interruptions are caused by higher-ups who pass tactical emergencies to the team responsible for creating quality products, which distracts team members from doing the work needed to reach the next goal. This is partly why the scrum master should be a full-time role, and the scrum master should have plenty of organizational clout. Sometimes, the scrum master needs to be able to run interference with the higher-ups to prevent current progress from being derailed.

THE POMODORO TECHNIQUE

The Pomodoro technique of time management, developed in the late 1980s by Francesco Cirillo, entails running personal work sprints of 25 minutes (though you can customize them) to get your own stuff done. The technique involves the following steps:

1. Create a to-do list and prioritize the highest-value items.

2. Work on the top-priority item for 25 minutes.

3. Take a five-minute break.

4. Go back to the same highest-priority item until it's completely done, and then move to the next highest-priority item.

5. After you've completed four Pomodoros (in this case, four 25-minute work periods), take a longer break of 15 to 30 minutes to reset your concentration ability.

Repeat these steps throughout the day to ensure you accomplish your most important tasks. Several apps and websites are available for using the Pomodoro technique.

Common Roles Outside Scrum

Product owner and scrum master are integral scrum roles created by the founders of scrum. Developer is another role (see Chapter 4). But like all good things, project management and product development are evolving and growing. Scrum remains a solid framework and foundation. Some common and proven practices can add value.

The following two roles aren't explicit scrum accountabilities of the scrum team, but we've found that acknowledging them adds enormous value and clarity. Consider clarifying these roles in your organization to optimize your scrum team's success.

Stakeholders

Stakeholders are people who affect or are affected by your work. Internal stakeholders are within your company or organization; they could be from the legal, sales, marketing, management, procurement, a neighbor, or even a friend. External stakeholders could be investors, users, or even your mother-in-law.

Although scrum prescribes only scrum team members, the stakeholder role explicitly interfaces with scrum teams, and we prefer to acknowledge this role so we can manage it. The product owner is the business interface for the scrum team, so stakeholders should work with the developers *through* the product owner. Stakeholders may communicate directly with the developers during sprint reviews or when a developer contacts them directly for clarification, but stakeholders generally work through the product owner.

Two roles deal with stakeholders:

>> The product owner is responsible if the stakeholders are on the business side (such as customers, sales teams, or marketing).

>> If the stakeholders are on the nonbusiness side (such as vendors or contractors), the scrum master is usually responsible.

The key to interacting successfully with stakeholders is recognizing and leveraging stakeholders' influence while shielding the developers from interference.

Scrum mentors

As we've said, scrum is a simple framework in concept, but it's not easy in practice. The same can be said of golf. Theoretically, you use a stick to whack a motionless white ball into a hole, using the fewest strokes possible. Yet, in practice, golf isn't easy. Like scrum, it's a game of nuance. Small factors make an enormous difference in performance.

The mentor, sometimes called a scrum or agile coach, will work alongside the team to help them develop maturity in practicing scrum. The benefit of using a mentor is that mentors are outside the normal politics and focus on getting the product out the door. They can step back and see objectively how the team works. Not only can they identify old habits, but they can also put the brakes on homemade modifications to scrum, which are simply ways to let an old dog do its old tricks.

You'll have the greatest ease and success with scrum if you stick to it in its truest form. A scrum mentor's job is to help team members keep good form. Like athletic coaches, they stand aside; see old, unproductive habits; and help you form new habits that make you successful.

SWINGING TO SUCCESS

Years ago, Mark took up golf for business and, in the process, caught the golf bug. He loved it, worked at it, and improved his game. But he always struggled with consistency. So, he hired a golf coach.

The coach teed up a ball in the first session, and Mark hit it. The coach watched that one swing and said, "I know what your problem is." Mark was incredulous. How could the coach possibly know what was wrong with Mark's swing by watching him just one time?

Then, the coach said, "You used to play baseball, didn't you?" Mark had played baseball for years. In fact, the coach could tell right away that Mark's golf swing was like his baseball swing. Mark had carried an old habit into the new sport.

When you convert to scrum, you, too, will carry habits (even ones that you don't realize you have) from a lifetime of managing your work differently.

2
Scrum Product Development

Chapter **3**

Planning Your Work

William of Ockham, a fourteenth-century logician and Franciscan friar, said, "Entities should not be multiplied unnecessarily." This statement is known as Occam's Razor in simpler, modern-day terms. (When you have two competing theories that make the same predictions, the simpler one is better.)

In other words, keep it simple. You can apply this mantra again and again when managing your work with scrum. If something doesn't feel right, it probably isn't.

In this chapter, you see that keeping things simple applies to a technique that we use to enhance scrum — called the *product roadmap* — and decompose your product's features into the smallest requirements possible.

Throughout this book, we point out common practices that scrum trainers and coaches use successfully. Although they're optional, we recommend that you give them a try. They will help you accomplish the outcomes you target.

The Product Roadmap

In the seven roadmap to value elements we outlined in Chapter 1, you begin with the end in mind by creating your product goal. The next step is creating a map to help you achieve that goal (see Figure 3-1).

A common agile practice outside of scrum

PRODUCT ROADMAP

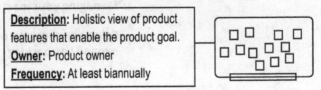

FIGURE 3-1:
The product roadmap in the roadmap to value.

Description: Holistic view of product features that enable the product goal.
Owner: Product owner
Frequency: At least biannually

Although the product roadmap is not a formal aspect of scrum, it is commonly used by scrum teams.

We should note that the word *product* will be used frequently throughout this book. According to the 2020 Scrum Guide, "A product is simply a vehicle to deliver value. It has a clear boundary, known stakeholders, well-defined users or customers. A product could be a service, a physical product, or something more abstract." The word *product* is meant to describe a much broader spectrum of value than simply software, hardware, or physical products. It's also broader than a project as it is long-term.

Creating a product roadmap is a common-sense way to set off on the journey and align an entire group. For example, if you were to go on a voyage with a crew and passengers, you'd want to know your destination and, most likely, route before you leave the safety of the harbor. The same holds true with almost any product. Following are the general steps in creating a roadmap:

1. Decide where you want to go (define the product goal).
2. Figure out how to get there (visualize the product roadmap).
3. Socialize the goal (communicate the plan).

The product roadmap can change, but it gives you something tangible to start with, thereby increasing effectiveness. By socializing the roadmap as an artifact of planning or replanning, you can make sure that influencers and stakeholders understand the direction and path. Adjustments to the plan are less costly, and a shared vision contributes to team unification.

Take the long view

The product roadmap is a holistic, high-level view of the features or capabilities necessary to achieve the product goal. Natural affinities are established ("If we do this, we should logically do that"), and gaps are made readily visible ("Hey, where is . . .?").

The product roadmap is the initial product backlog (your master to-do list). As the likelihood of product backlog items being developed increases, items are increasingly broken down (progressive elaboration). The product backlog expands to include items that are

>> Small (imminently realized; often referred to as *user stories*)

>> Midsize (midrange realized; often referred to as *epics*)

>> Conceptual (clear but lacking details; often referred to as *features*)

TIP

See the sidebar, "Roadmap and Backlog Terminology," later in this chapter for more information about features, epics, and user stories.

REMEMBER

The product roadmap isn't fixed in stone and fully paved; it's a living, dynamic artifact. We review and update these roadmaps at least twice a year, although this frequency varies depending on the work at hand.

Although the product owner fully owns the goal, the entire scrum team needs to be part of the roadmap-building process. Developers are the technical experts who will be doing the work and must provide constraints and effort estimates. If the developers haven't been chosen yet, include the functional managers after you create the initial product roadmap. These managers can help identify the skills that will be necessary and get the developers assembled as quickly as possible so that the scrum team can provide high-level effort estimates.

When we begin working with a client, we sit down with the business stakeholders, product owner, developers, and scrum master and create the product goal and product roadmap on day one. We finish these on day one so the actual development begins as soon as possible on day two.

Use simple tools

When creating your product roadmap, use the simplest tools possible. We prefer a whiteboard and sticky notes (either physical or virtual). Each product feature or capability fits onto a sticky note. Many digital whiteboards can also be used for this purpose especially if your team is distributed. This method is simplicity in its true working form.

Human brains weren't created in the digital age. Studies have proved that electronics have a dulling effect. In fact, it takes less brain-wave function to watch TV than it does to watch paint dry. Yet, using a simple system like sticky notes is physically and mentally engaging, and using it fosters an environment of change and creativity.

We have helped many clients create a product roadmap by simply placing sticky notes with major requirements on a wall or digital whiteboard and talking through ideas and issues. We put a roadmap together in less than three hours for one large product (worth almost half a billion dollars). We start with the highest priority items. As we talk through the product goal, stickies are simple to move as the roadmap begins to take shape.

Create your product roadmap

You can use seven easy, common-sense steps to build your product roadmap. Perform these steps on day one as part of your product planning; they should take no longer than a few hours. For smaller efforts, you'll get the job done over morning coffee. The product owner completes the steps with the rest of the product team (the entire scrum team and the stakeholders).

Using sticky notes, several colors of flags, and a whiteboard, follow these steps to build your product roadmap:

1. Write down one product requirement per sticky note.

Think of as many product requirements as you can.

TECHNICAL STUFF

You'll know you're on the right track for building a roadmap beneficial to your customers or target audience if you can read each sticky note as a completion of the sentence, "My customer can . . .<sticky note text>." For example, "My customer can now <Adjust the Temperature>" will make more sense to your stakeholders and customers than "My customer can now <Design the Temperature Touchscreen>." Product roadmaps lay out the requirement journey to value, not the tasks. Tasks come later in sprint planning (see Chapter 5).

2. If appropriate and synergistic, arrange some requirements in related categories or groups.

3. Prioritize the requirements on the roadmap.

At the macro level, the highest-priority items are on the left side, and the lowest-priority items are on the right side. At the micro level, the highest-priority requirements are at the top, and the lowest-priority items are at the bottom. The highest-priority items are top-left, and the lowest-priority items are bottom-right.

4. Identify business dependencies (noted by colored flags on the sticky note).

5. Have the developers identify technical dependencies (noted by flags of a different color).

6. Have the developers provide order-of-magnitude estimates for the sticky notes.

7. Adjust ordering based on dependencies, estimates, and feedback as appropriate.

TIP

Note the items that prompt the most discussion or concern from the team; these items may be the riskiest or require further breakdown. For estimation methods that your developers can use, check out Chapter 4.

Set your time frame

The nature of your product determines the quantity and timing of your releases. Focus on creating what is minimally valuable/usable that you can get into your customers' hands as quickly as possible. Smaller releases involve less complexity, smaller risk chunks, and faster end-customer feedback. Different customers and industries will have different thresholds of release frequency.

Ideally, you want to release working increments after every sprint or, even better, several times during a sprint (continuous delivery). However, sprints and releases do not necessarily need to be coupled.

Occasionally when working with clients, we create high-level product releases (for framing the requirements, not for timeline commitment) so we can see how those releases align with other product releases, budgetary cycles, holiday cycles, and so on. Chapter 14 provides more ideas on budgeting and incremental funding.

Figure 3-2 shows an example of quarterly product releases (common with publicly traded companies). The first release reflects initial release planning and has a level of commitment assigned to it. Everything after that shows how outside influences may affect the product.

If your time frame is shorter or isn't relevant, consider what your time frame is and break it into the initial logical groups, going no farther out than necessary (usually, no more than a year). Follow these steps:

1. Create the initial features or capabilities, starting with the highest-priority requirements and moving down.

2. At each release, assume you will deliver tested, verified, documented, and releasable results.

3. Above each release, write its conceptual theme.

4. Adjust as necessary.

TIP

The product roadmap and product backlog are excellent for scope control. In

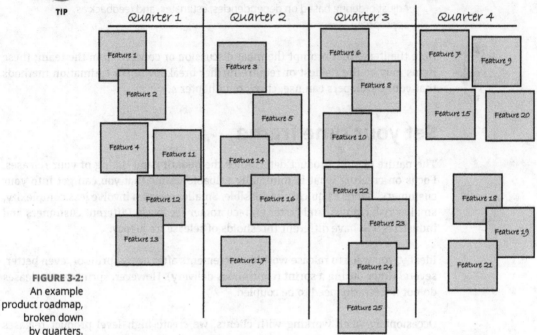

| Quarter 1 | Quarter 2 | Quarter 3 | Quarter 4 |

Feature 1
Feature 2
Feature 4
Feature 11
Feature 12
Feature 13

Feature 3
Feature 5
Feature 14
Feature 16
Feature 17

Feature 6
Feature 8
Feature 10
Feature 22
Feature 23
Feature 24
Feature 25

Feature 7
Feature 9
Feature 15
Feature 20
Feature 18
Feature 19
Feature 21

FIGURE 3-2:
An example
product roadmap,
broken down
by quarters.

traditional project management models, every new idea has to be justified. With scrum, if an idea brings you closer to the product goal, add it to the list. The idea's level of prioritization determines whether it gets completed. Sometimes, only the highest-priority items get done; at other times, every requirement gets done, depending on the budget and the organizational drag on the scrum team.

Breaking Down Requirements

It won't take long to notice that one product requirement can be broken into several pieces. Chances are those pieces can be broken down further, and those pieces, we're willing to bet, can be peeled apart too. In this section, we explain how to manage this decomposition process (also known as *progressive elaboration*, which was mentioned earlier).

Prioritization of requirements

With the product roadmap, you begin with the largest pieces. This roadmap truly provides an eagle's-eye view and is based on what makes sense according to business value and/or risk elimination. These pieces (requirements) are prioritized by the product owner, who decides what is most important to get to that customer first and which requirements logically belong together.

As requirements are prioritized, they become part of the product backlog. In scrum, you work on the smallest set of highest-priority items necessary to generate value, not just anything scoped for the product, which is why scrum teams achieve outcomes faster.

Take two things into consideration as you prioritize: business value and risk. Business value is easy. If a thing is high value, it has high priority. There are four reasons you also want to take on the highest-risk requirements first (assuming they are also high-value):

>> At the beginning, you have the simplest model to work with. You want to take on your highest-risk items within the simplest system.

>> You have the greatest amount of money at the beginning. If you're going to take on something that involves high risk, you should do so with the greatest resources at your disposal.

>> If you're going to take on a high-risk item, do so with the benefit of the longest runway possible.

>> If you're going to fail, fail early and cheaply. If a fundamental flaw exists, you want to know as early as possible. The highest-risk requirements are where the landmines are lurking.

TECHNICAL STUFF

Working the highest-priority requirements to completion isn't just convenient, it also saves money and is why products using scrum can come in at a 30–70 percent cost savings. If you run out of money 80 percent of the way through, you can say, without a doubt, that you have 80 percent of the highest-priority items completed, functioning, and accepted. What about the remaining 20 percent? If they were such a low priority, you can often live without them anyway. Efforts to develop products using agile techniques like scrum typically run out of value before they run out of time or budget. Chapter 5 talks more about maximizing value in a release.

The product roadmap creates your first cut of dependencies. Using our water heater example, you don't need to worry about having functionality to drain condensation until you have a controller to manage heat. Critical dependencies are revealed early and help the product owner prioritize the product backlog. Teams begin working on the highest-priority items on day 2, not day 120.

REMEMBER

A requirement must earn the right of your investment. Only the highest-priority items deserve your effort to break them into digestible requirements. Everything else can wait. This way, you're always working on only the most important things. Don't waste your time trying to boil the ocean. Learning and adapting are valuable even while building requirements.

Levels of decomposition

When decomposing your requirements into smaller pieces, you want to capture as little detail as possible. In fact, we want you to become an expert in doing the bare minimum, progressively elaborating requirements as the likelihood of bringing them into a sprint grows. Gone are the days of spending endless hours working on defining and refining requirements that never see the light of day. Figure 3-3 depicts the layers of requirement decomposition.

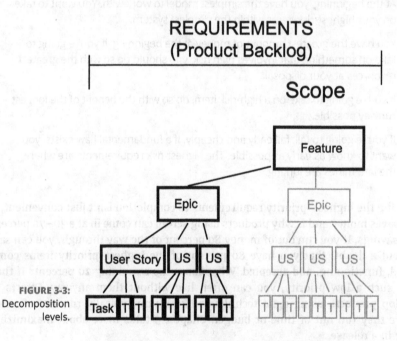

FIGURE 3-3: Decomposition levels.

Seven keys for product development

Seven types of work are involved in building valuable product increments. Using these approaches, you know the product works, can be integrated, and has been approved by the product owner. You're tangibly building products to showcase to stakeholders from whom you can garner feedback. This feedback is then used to refine and create new requirements that make the product better reflect stakeholder needs, and the cycle is run again. You incrementally improve the product based on reality.

The seven keys for building valuable products are

1. Requirement elaboration
2. Design
3. Development
4. Comprehensive testing
5. Integration
6. Documentation
7. Approval

TECHNICAL STUFF

Like *developer*, the term *development* simply means the act of creating a product or service. Development can include writing code in software development, but it can just as easily refer to any type of solution implementation or creating, configuring, sculpting, or even building. We've used the term *development* throughout this book to simplify.

ROADMAP AND BACKLOG TERMINOLOGY

Over the years, scrum teams have commonly used the following terms relating to product roadmaps and product backlogs. They aren't scrum, but they are part of a collection of common terminology that many of us use in the field:

- **Themes:** *Themes* are logical groups of features you create in your product roadmap. If a feature is a new capability that a customer will have, a theme is the logical grouping of these features. For example, the functionality enabling a customer to purchase items from a website is a theme. Your product roadmap usually identifies and/or groups features as part of a theme.

- **Features:** *Features* are capabilities that your customers will have that they didn't have before. The functionality that enables a customer to purchase items online via a mobile phone is a feature. Your product roadmap usually consists of feature-level requirements.

(continued)

(continued)

- **Epics:** *Epics* are a series of actions related to a feature and are the next stage in breaking features into actionable requirements. For example, the functionality allowing a customer to purchase an item via a mobile phone from a shopping cart using a credit card is an epic. An epic is smaller than a feature (purchasing an item online) but bigger than the credit card integrations that enable an item to be purchased.

TIP

We don't allow requirements larger than epics into a release plan because they aren't specific enough to plan.

- **User stories:** *User stories* are the smallest forms of requirements that can stand on their own. A user story consists of one action of value or one integration of value. Purchasing an item via a mobile phone from a shopping cart with a Visa card is a user story. Purchasing an item using a MasterCard is a different integration and a different user story. User stories are small enough to add to sprints and begin developing. We go into user stories in detail in the sections that follow.

TIP

This progressive breakdown (or elaboration) of feature, epic, and user story is one way to do it. Some people regard epics as being larger than features. It doesn't matter as long as you're consistent. The important thing to remember is your product roadmap will have larger-scope items, your release plan will have medium-scope items, and your sprints will have small-scope items.

- **Tasks:** *Tasks* are the steps needed to implement a user story. During sprint planning, a user story is broken into tasks.

REMEMBER

Requirements are things users do; *tasks* are what developers do to make a requirement work.

Your Product Backlog

The product backlog is a true scrum artifact and the to-do list for the entire product. All scrum products have a product backlog, which is owned and maintained by the product owner.

The requirements from the product roadmap initially create the product backlog, and the highest-priority ones are broken into user stories as early as day two of product planning. (We describe how in "Product backlog refinement," later in this chapter.) Figure 3-4 depicts a sample product backlog.

Order	ID	Item	Type	Status	Value	Risk	Estimate
1	121	As a homeowner, I want to adjust the thermostat so that I can control my water temperature.	Requirement	Not Started	High	High	5
2	403	Train team on latest standards for improving workplace efficiency	Improvement	Not Started	High	High	3
3	97	Adapt product to new tank standards	Maintenance	Not Started	Medium	High	8
4	68	As a homeowner, I want to remotely control my thermostat so that I can save money while on the road.	Requirement	Not Started	Medium	Medium	8
5	113	Update requirements traceability matrix	Overhead	Not Started	Low	Low	2

FIGURE 3-4: The product backlog is your product's ordered to-do list.

Each item in the product backlog has the following elements:

REMEMBER

» Specific order (priority slot in the product backlog).

   Although product backlog items may be similar in priority, they can't be worked on simultaneously.

» ID number (optional).

» Description.

» Type of item (optional), which could be a requirement, overhead, maintenance, or improvement. (See "The dynamic to-do list," later in this chapter.)

» Status (optional).

» Value to the business or product.

REMEMBER

   Highest-priority requirements get broken into the smallest actionable requirements possible in the product backlog. A small requirement, however, isn't automatically a high-priority item. Many small requirements have a low priority and never see fruition.

» Risk level associated with the item.

» Estimate of the effort required to complete.

REMEMBER

Anyone can write a product feature or requirement. A business stakeholder, developer, scrum master, product owner, and even the company barista can spark an idea or concern. Ideas are expected from everyone. Only the product owner has the power to accept or reject a requirement in the product backlog, based on whether it supports the goal for the product. The product owner is the full owner of this artifact. If accepted, the product owner will then number, refine, prioritize, and order the new requirement.

The dynamic to-do list

The product backlog never goes away while the work is active. If you have a product, you have a product backlog, which is always changing. As larger requirements are broken into smaller requirements, the backlog changes. As client feedback is received, the backlog changes. As your competitors bring new offerings to market, the backlog changes.

TIP

The product owner not only prioritizes items in the product backlog but also orders them in a logical sequence. This way, the next sprint can be quickly and efficiently organized from these ordered items.

The product owner makes all changes made in the product backlog. At any point, if anyone (product owner, developer, stakeholder) identifies a new requirement or design idea, it's given to the product owner to be prioritized along with everything else.

In traditional project management frameworks, change is viewed as a reflection of poor planning. If something had to be changed, it was because someone messed up. In scrum, we see change as a sign of growth and learning. As you discover your product more deeply, you will identify changes that need to be made. In scrum, if you're not changing, you're not learning, and that's a problem. It's a lack of change that is a sign of failure. Every day you need to learn something that causes change. With scrum, change is no longer something you crawl under your desk and hide from. Change is good. Change is life. Change is scrum.

Product backlog refinement

Product backlog refinement is how the scrum team advances its understanding of the items in the product backlog and prepares them for upcoming sprints. Product backlog refinement is a continuous process of breaking down and preparing feedback and responses to change for future development. This process is owned by the product owner and performed with the help of developers, who ask clarifying questions and provide estimates based on the best information available at that time. The scrum team, as a whole, may spend about 10 percent of its active sprint time in this process. The scrum master usually facilitates product backlog refinement activities to keep the group focused and on task.

The target outcomes of product backlog refinement are as shown below:

>> **Clarity:** All developers and the product owner reach a clear consensus on the scope of the product backlog items being discussed.

>> **Acceptance criteria:** All requirements (backlog items) include sufficient acceptance criteria.

>> **Risks identified and mitigated to the best extent possible:** Other known risks should be documented and accepted by the team as necessary.

>> **Sizing:** Requirements are estimated and broken down sufficiently to be accomplished within a sprint.

TECHNICAL STUFF

Acceptance criteria is a term frequently used in scrum practices that refers to a section on the back of the user story card or in the project software to communicate to everyone what success looks like for each story. It may include validation criteria and specific examples of the desired outcomes when the work is complete.

Backlog refinement should be a regular occurrence, but scrum doesn't prescribe how formal or frequent refinement discussions should be; neither does it prescribe an agenda. Here are suggestions that have worked well for our clients and us:

>> **Format:** The product owner presents one requirement to the team at a time. For each requirement, team members ask questions, challenge assumptions, explore implementation strategies, and use a whiteboard for drawing and clarification until they have a consensus on the details and scope of the requirement. Then the developers use estimation poker or affinity estimating (see Chapter 4) to assign a relative size estimate.

>> **Time:** On average, scrum teams spend about 10 percent of a sprint refining product backlog items and preparing for future sprints.

>> **Frequency:** Backlog refinement is a progressive activity. Requirements get refined gradually, just in time, and those closer to delivery are ready for sprints. Teams may prefer conducting backlog refinement on one of these schedules:

- Daily, at the end of each day

This schedule also acts as a demobilization exercise for scrum team members to transition into going home for the day.

- Daily, at some other agreed-on time

- Once per sprint during a regularly scheduled block of time

- Once per week during a regularly scheduled block of time

- Multiple times per week during a regularly scheduled block of time

- As needed, determined, and scheduled by the team in each sprint

>> **Activities:** Backlog refinement activities may consist of the following types of activities:

- Entire team discussions, including whiteboarding, review of upcoming priorities, modeling, question-and-answer sessions, and design discussions

- Research of items identified during team discussions
- Interviews of users, customers, subject-matter experts, or stakeholders to gain insights for determining the scope and suggested solutions to requirements
- Estimation poker or affinity estimation sessions

As the team discusses and refines the next-highest priority requirement candidates, use as many of the following questions and guidelines as needed to guide the team through the refinement process. Not all these items apply to every team and/or requirement.

>> Breaking down large requirements

- Does the user story satisfy the INVEST criteria (see the "INVEST" sidebar later in this chapter)?
- Can the requirement be completed within one sprint or part of one sprint?
- Is the user story a single action of value or a series of actions?
- Is the scope barely sufficient to deliver something of value?
- Has the product owner added technical tasks or other technical details that should be left to the developers to determine?
- Has the scrum team's definition of *done* (see Chapter 4) been considered before determining that the story is sufficiently broken down?
- Is more research required before the team can estimate?

>> Clarifying and refining where needed

- Do the developers understand the intent and/or value of the requirement?
- Have developers tried paraphrasing the requirement to make sure everyone is on the same page?
- Is the desired deliverable clear?
- Does an implementation approach make sense?
- Is the team considering all the work needed to complete and deliver the user story?
- Does the team know the tasks that will be required?
- Will the team be able to deliver a fully done increment of the product at the end of this sprint?

>> Ensuring adequate acceptance criteria

- If needed, have personas been identified (see "Product Backlog Common Practices," later in this chapter)?

- Are the acceptance criteria complete and adequate?

- Have validation-focused developers stated that the criteria are sufficient?

>> Addressing potential issues and risks

- Can the story stand alone, or are there dependencies?

- What conflicts may arise during implementation?

- What technical debt might this requirement introduce?

>> Assigning high-level estimates

- Have estimations revealed that any of the requirements are still too big?

If estimations bring up additional points needing clarification, use the guidelines above to refine them further before reestimating.

TIP

You need to watch a few factors in this process:

>> Only developers estimate requirements because they're the ones doing the work.

>> The product owner provides immediate clarifications to developers' questions by being actively involved in the refinement discussions.

>> The frequency and duration of refinement activities will vary from team to team, from product to product, and even from sprint to sprint.

Other possible backlog items

When we coach clients in building their product backlog, we encourage them to identify product backlog item types (refer to Figure 3-4 earlier in this chapter).

We use four types to clarify the nature of the item to be completed. All these items can be done (or not done) at the product owner's discretion:

>> **Requirement:** Basic business requirements make up the bulk of a product backlog. A requirement explains why a feature is being built (the value) and what needs to be done.

>> **Maintenance:** Periodic care to extend the health or life of your product. Maintenance items reduce the technical debt that is naturally incurred during past development.

>> **Improvements:** Based on results from the sprint retrospective, what can be done differently in the process? These are not product improvements (those are requirements). Instead, they are improvements to how we go about our work of creating the product.

>> **Overhead:** Companies often have overhead items that they like to see. They assume that it's free, but it costs time and money. We like to make that cost obvious.

TECHNICAL STUFF

Technical debt is a metaphor often used in software development to imply the cost of additional rework caused by previous technical decisions. If not addressed, the cost will accumulate and grow with time. Analogous to financial debt, as technical debt is not repaid, it accumulates "interest" that needs to be paid in the form of maintenance or refactoring infrastructure. The longer it goes unaddressed, the more difficult it becomes to implement new stuff. The same concept can be applied to nonsoftware products as well.

Product Backlog Common Practices

Thousands of companies and organizations practice agile techniques throughout the world. As a natural result, common agile practices abound. We incorporate some of these practices into our consulting business and discard others. We recommend that you do the same. No universal set of best practices exists.

User stories

User story is a common pattern for communicating and gathering requirements to achieve shared understanding across the entire scrum team. Developers create better value when they clearly understand the user's perspective.

User stories are an action of value that a user will achieve; for example, "As a homeowner, I want to adjust the thermostat so I can control my water temperature."

Multiple small user stories go into every sprint, and each is the highest priority at that time. On average, you may have six to ten user stories per sprint. Therefore, at the end of each sprint, if the developers concentrate on completing one user story at a time (a process called *swarming*, described in Chapter 6), you always have something valuable and usable to show for your work.

We use 3x5 index cards to write user stories. Even with these small cards, because we use a Card ⇨ Conversation ⇨ Confirmation model — the three Cs — we get rich requirement clarity. User stories aren't the only way to describe what needs to be done, but we've found them to be incredibly effective. Figure 3-5 shows example index-card user stories along with the three Cs.

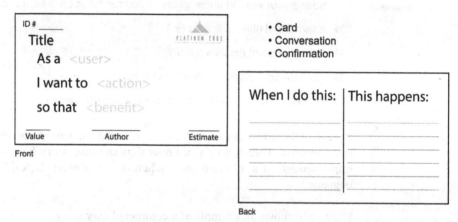

FIGURE 3-5:
A format for
writing user
stories.

TIP

TECHNICAL STUFF

Don't use technical jargon in your user stories. You're writing them with the user in mind. Keep them direct, customer-focused, and simple.

In the Card ⇨ Conversation ⇨ Confirmation model, the product owner uses the 3x5 card as a reminder of the requirement — a reminder that a conversation must take place to refine and clarify it. This model enables the immensely valuable activity of conversing with developers and answering their questions, supported by an explicit description of what success looks like on the back of the card. Previously, we created tomes of documents as we tried to answer all the questions we thought the team might have — an endeavor in which we invariably failed.

Personas

Sometimes, it's easiest to work with *personas*, which are fictional characters that are amalgams of your clients' target qualities. A persona for a dating product might be a professionally employed 35-year-old single male living in Portland, Oregon, looking for his future significant other. Use a persona to ensure that your product meets your target customer's needs.

A user story description is simple yet focused, clearly describing the user, the action, and the benefit. On each card, enter the following lines:

REMEMBER

>> An ID number that's the same as in the product backlog and assigned by the product owner when they accept an item into the product backlog

Keep your product ID numbers simple. You don't need to be able to track every item back to its more generic origin; you just need to give it a numerical name like 123, not like 10.8.A.14. You minimize the amount of work you do by ridding your work of timewasters so you can focus on the important things.

>> A shorthand title

>> A description of the user (who?)

>> What the user wants to accomplish (what?)

>> The reason the user wants to accomplish the task (why?)

Critical to the user story is what's written on the flip side of the card — the acceptance criteria. This is how you know that the user story has been successfully implemented. It's phrased as "When I do <insert task>, <insert result> happens."

Figure 3-6 shows an example of a completed user story.

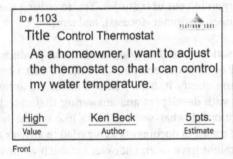

ID # 1103   PLATINUM EDGE
Title Control Thermostat
As a homeowner, I want to adjust the thermostat so that I can control my water temperature.

High   Ken Beck   5 pts.
Value   Author   Estimate
Front

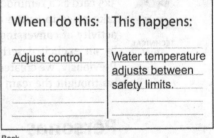

When I do this: | This happens:

Adjust control | Water temperature adjusts between safety limits.

Back

FIGURE 3-6:
A completed user story index card.

TECHNICAL STUFF

Each user story is written in the first-person point of view. ("When *I* do this, *I* get this.") First-person puts the author in the shoes of the user or customer.

The person who writes the user story gives it to the product owner to share with the scrum team. Often, the stakeholder also participates in the conversation, sitting down with the product owner and developers to go over every card. This act of direct communication is vital to a thorough understanding of the tasks necessary to achieve the desired result. As a result, communication is clearer, there are fewer mistakes, and product quality and delivery speed increase.

Further refinement

Developer effort determines whether a requirement needs to be broken down further to progress to the product roadmap, the release plan, or the sprint. (See Chapter 5 for details.) Especially at the beginning, as you discover how to apply user stories within your scrum framework, you may find that the ones you write are too big to fit into a sprint.

INVEST

Bill Wake, an early influencer in the eXtreme Programming (XP) movement, introduced the INVEST mnemonic for user stories. INVEST is an acronym for qualities that you want to look for in your user stories:

- **Independent:** To the best possible degree, the story doesn't need other stories to implement it or for the user to interact with it.

- **Negotiable:** The product owner and the developers must discuss and expand on the story's nuances and details. The value of a user story is in the conversation, not the card.

- **Valuable:** The story shows product value to the customer, not the technical steps (tasks) that the developer uses to enable the story.

- **Estimable:** The story is refined enough for developers to estimate the effort required to create the functionality.

- **Small:** Smaller stories are easier to estimate. A rule of thumb is to bring six to ten user stories into each sprint. Smaller individual user stories increase the likelihood of delivering value during a sprint.

- **Testable:** The story needs to be testable so that the developers know that the story has been done correctly. "It needs to be fast" or "It needs to be intuitive" isn't testable. "I need the controller to light the heater in less than a second" or "I need to complete the action in three turns or less" is testable.

Although most user stories have multiple steps, some are bigger than practical and can (and should) be broken into more granular requirements. This process is part of the discovery process and the benefit of using user stories.

You may find additional requirements that need to be placed in the product backlog during the user-story elaboration discussion. Excellent! These discoveries help you gain a deeper understanding of what the customer and/or user really needs.

Chapter **4**

The Talent and the Timing

Talent wins games. But teamwork and intelligence wins championships.
— MICHAEL JORDAN

Developers sit at the core of scrum. The primary focus of the product owner and the scrum master revolves around making sure that the environment is as ideal as possible for the developers to reach maximum productivity. This chapter reveals how developers self-organize and make their best contributions to the scrum team. To simplify this accountability, the word *developer* is used throughout this book. *Developer* refers to anyone with the technical skills and expertise to do the work. Consequently (and similarly), *development* is a developer's work to create a working product increment or outcome.

After you have your scrum team, product goal, and product roadmap in place, the next step is to estimate the amount of work for each requirement. The developers begin by estimating the effort involved in high-level requirements. Here, you create a starting point for future reference. You establish the numerator (product backlog total)/denominator (average velocity) relationship that gives you the estimated number of sprints necessary to complete all, or a target portion of, items in the product backlog. We show you how these high-level estimates can be achieved quickly and accurately.

The Developers

In Hollywood, actors and singers are referred to as *the talent*. They're the ones who get on stage and do the job. Everyone else facilitates this process because when the talent is successful, everyone is successful. Think of the developers as the talent. Retaining that talent is one of the byproducts of good scrum.

The developers are the talent responsible for creating and developing the actual product. They drive the how and the how much. In other words, they determine how they will develop the requirements and how many they can do in any one sprint. They are dedicated to one scrum team goal at a time, cross-functional, and self-organizing. The entire scrum team is self-managing with developers working alongside the product owner.

The number of developers on a scrum team is intentionally limited. Optimally, the team size is small enough to remain nimble and large enough to complete significant work within a sprint. Scrum teams are usually no more than ten people (a product owner, a scrum master, and up to eight developers). But we've found that five or six developers are optimal in most situations. This size allows for a self-sufficient and self-organizing group with diverse skills, yet it's not too big and unwieldy. Remember, for each new member, the lines of communication increase geometrically. You'll struggle to have a self-organizing team with more than eight developers. Under waterfall model, this issue is masked by a project manager responsible for coordinating all the communication. Scrum doesn't have the overhead cost of too many lines of communication or a project manager.

With scrum team size, the key factor is self-encapsulation. Can the developers elaborate the requirements, design them, develop them, test them, integrate them, document them, and have them approved? Have single points of failure been eliminated (that is, at least two people can do any one skill)? Is the total size of the scrum team no more than ten people? If all three answers are yes, you have a good-sized, cross-functional team. Whereas a product owner must be decisive and a scrum master must have clout, developers must be versatile, intellectually curious, and predisposed to sharing. Teamwork is expected. Developer team members' fires are lit with building and creating. Like all good teams, each team member is a peer and expected to bring their best performance every single day.

TECHNICAL STUFF

What's the difference between self-organizing and self-managing? Self-organizing means the team determines how to do the work and who will do it, typically discussed among developers. Self-managing means the team takes full responsibility for delivering a product through peer collaboration without a manager's guidance. The team is responsible for performance and quality, meaning the work gets done and done correctly. Developers self-organize throughout the day, and scrum teams self-manage (developers with product owner) through-out product development.

The uniqueness of scrum developers

In many ways, scrum teams are the opposite of traditional teams. In scrum, developers are going to develop cross-functional skills. They're part of the goal-setting process, and they have complete control of how they do their development. Additionally, credit is taken as a team.

Dedicated teams and cross-functionality

As mentioned previously, developers are dedicated to one product goal at a time. There's no making your developers switch back and forth between competing goals, known as *thrashing*. Instead, you want them to focus each day on the current sprint's goal. Whether functional management chooses the team members or someone else does, a diversity of skills is soughtafter, so the team has all the skills they need to succeed. (They're self-encapsulated.) This leads us to the next point: cross-functionality.

CREATING A MOTIVATING ENVIRONMENT

Daniel Pink writes about motivation in his excellent book *Drive: The Surprising Truth About What Motivates Us* (Riverhead Books). Here, Pink dispels the myth that the way to motivate people is through more and more money. Surprisingly, Pink found that the higher the monetary incentive, the worse the results. Money is a factor, but only enough to take the subject of money off the table.

As he continued to dig, Pink found three specific factors that produced the environment for the best-quality results, whether at home or work: autonomy, mastery, and purpose. Let your people determine how they will do their work, give them the space and time to master current and new skills, and communicate a sense of purpose in what they're doing.

The scrum framework can enable the environment that Pink discusses. The scrum team is designed to be self-managing and autonomous with regard to how it does the work. Cross-functionality and developing new skills are fundamental. Developers understand what they're working on (and why) through the product goal and direct communication with the product owner and stakeholders.

REMEMBER

People don't necessarily start out being cross-functional; they grow into this state. Start with a team of diverse talents and then organically build that team toward being individually cross-functional. Ideally, you want every developer to be able to do everything. This isn't always possible, but you at least want every developer to be able to do more than one thing and for every skill to have more than one person. Becoming cross-functional is a process, but it prevents bottlenecks in work delivery.

Figure 4-1 shows this progression of expanding their capabilities, so their skill sets are more T-, Pi-, or M-shaped.

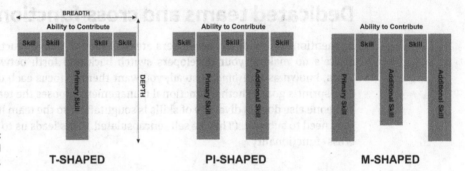

FIGURE 4-1:
Developer skill
progression.

Whatever your business or organization, the facts remain: People go on vacation; they get sick; they take on new roles and jobs. One day, they're there next to you, and the next day, they might be somewhere else. In traditional projects, when a key developer goes on vacation, product development goes on vacation. You're forced into delays as you wait for that person to return or (in the case of attrition) until you recruit and mobilize another person.

Strive for cross-functionality in your developers. In this way, you eliminate that single point of failure. If one team member comes down with the flu or is deeply involved in another task, someone else can take his place and get the job done. Cross-functionality also has these benefits:

>> It allows product owners to prioritize according to business value, not technical skills.

>> It allows for diverse input on the development of optimal solutions.

>> It enables pair development (described later in this section) to ensure higher quality.

>> It's one of the best ways to increase your primary skill. Learning an associative skill exposes you to other ways of thinking about your primary skill.

>> It allows people to work on various things and keeps the work interesting.

Several ways exist to create cross-functional individuals from cross-functional teams:

>> **Don't use titles.** Encourage an equal playing field. We've found that this stimulates junior developers to get up to speed faster, and senior-level skills increase because senior people don't want to be outdone by young, hungry talent. A lack of titles also emphasizes skills more than a fixed hierarchy, encouraging skill development. Informal status still exists, but now it's based on skills.

>> **Partner with a teammate.** Developers can use task pairing, mobbing, or working closely with a teammate to develop any type of product. Working together with a team member on a task leads to more innovation, creativity, and quality as they check each other's work. An example of this is pair programming.

>> **Two developers work together on the same task.** Developer A is tactically developing (at the keyboard, for example), while developer B is free to think strategically about the functionality (scalability, extensibility, risks, and so on). They switch these roles throughout the day. Because these developers work so tightly together, they can quickly catch errors. In our experience, developers stay more on task and make fewer errors as they pair, resulting in an overall shorter timeline.

>> **Do use shadowing.** Again, two developers are working together, but in this case, only one does the work while the other watches, ask questions, and learns.

>> **Shadowing also increases product quality.** Remember, visibility and performance are correlated: Increase visibility, and you generally increase performance. The working developer doesn't want to take a lazy shortcut in front of the learning one, and the learning one will ask those smart "dumb questions." Explaining something improves your own knowledge of it, and vocalizing something uses a different part of your brain and improves functioning. Finally, ownership is reinforced if you're teaching and explaining.

TECHNICAL
STUFF

The Hawthorne effect (or observer effect) is based on studies showing that a worker's productivity increases when someone is watching them. It's named after Hawthorne Works, an electrical company outside Chicago, where the first experiments took place.

TECHNICAL
STUFF

Rubber duck problem solving, rubber ducking, and *the rubber duckie test* are terms used to describe an interesting phenomenon. Developers are told to explain their technical problem *out loud and in detail to a rubber duck.* Most of the time, the answer comes to them before the explanation is complete. The same phenomenon occurs when a friend comes to you with a problem. Just the process of vocalizing the issue stimulates a different part of the brain, dislodging answers so they flow downstream.

TASK PAIRING

While task pairing may seem more expensive at first — employing two developers for the same job — you see that it reduces costs when you look at it holistically. The development cost may rise, but the quality assurance cost dramatically falls.

It's exponentially cheaper to prevent defects than to rip them out of a deployed system later, as described in these cases:

- If you catch the error on the spot, the cost to fix it is minimal.

- If the defect is found after committing the work, it costs 6.5 times more to remobilize, find, and fix it.

- If the defect escapes through testing, goes out to the production environment, and is finally identified several days or weeks later, the mobilization time is much longer, the discovery time is longer, and the cost is about 15 times greater.

- If this same defect makes it into the marketplace and must be corrected by a group that never developed the application — such as the production support group — the cost can be up to 100 times greater.

For every defect, the developers must find it, develop it correctly, and hope that the correction for that specific defect doesn't cause another defect. Remember, for every two defects fixed, another one is created in the process.

Ownership

The key word is *ownership*. Self-organizing and self-managing teams develop ownership in what they do. With scrum, whole team ownership is part of what creates such efficiency and success.

Clients sometimes ask us how we can assure them they'll get 100 percent from their developers. In response, we ask the clients how they can assure us that a professional sports team will give 100 percent. The answer is that the team gives 100 percent because they would lose if they didn't. The visibility and acknowledgment of their hard work increases drive.

TIP

Visibility and performance are directly correlated. Increase performance by increasing visibility.

To increase this visibility, sometimes, we'll work with two scrum teams to synchronize their sprints so the sprint reviews happen simultaneously on the same day. Then we invite an executive to come to both sprint reviews randomly for a few minutes and have them ask at least one question before leaving. Each team knows its performance will have executive visibility, and all teams want to look good. Historically, they may not have been given credit for their work. Now they can take pride in their product. They're on stage, getting all the credit. This is hugely motivating and increases drive and buy-in. Most world records are smashed during the Olympics. Why? The Olympics creates the largest stage in the world for athletes to compete.

Ownership and, therefore, accountability are increased in a scrum team in the following ways:

>> Developers are directly accountable for the deliverables that they create. This isn't always easy on them because visibility brings intrinsic pressure to perform, but this visibility also creates ownership.

>> Cross-functionality creates ownership because there isn't any *my job* versus *your job*. Everything is *our job*.

>> Individual performance is increased because the whole scrum team is held accountable. Everyone wins as a team, and everyone contributes to the success of every sprint.

>> Developers actively participate in creating the sprint goals and demonstrating the working functionality during the sprint review.

>> Developers are responsible for tactical status reporting every single day. In less than one minute of administration per day (see the burndown charts in Chapter 5), the organization gets a level of tactical status reporting that it's never had before.

WARNING

Developers perform best when they're stable. Feed them challenges to solve and give them what they need to do their best possible work. Every time you switch members on your team, it takes time to stabilize again. So, protect your developers to nurture good dynamics.

TECHNICAL STUFF

Cognitive consistency theory describes humans' tendency to seek out information, beliefs, and stimuli consistent with current beliefs and attitudes. In scrum, developers with a voice, buy-in, and control strive harder to achieve their work-related goals. They try to find consistency between the ownership that they created and their future output.

Team collaboration

Creating an environment for team success is essential. High performance results from many factors, but good communication and engaging collaboration are chief among them. Therefore, building an environment where team members can effectively collaborate and communicate is essential.

Here are a few recommendations for creating a healthy collaborative environment for team success:

Work as a team rather than a workgroup

A healthy scrum environment requires teamwork, not workgroups. Table 4-1 shows a summary of the key differences between teams and work groups:

TABLE 4-1   **Teams and workgroups**

Team	Workgroup
Shared leadership roles.	Strong, clearly focused leader.
Individual and mutual accountability.	Individual accountability.
Frequently come together for discussions, decision-making, problem-solving, and planning.	Come together to share information and perspectives.
Focus on team goals.	Focus on individual goals.
Produce collective work products.	Produce individual work products.
Define individual roles, responsibilities, and tasks to help the team do its work; often, they are shared and rotated.	Define individual roles, responsibilities, and tasks.
Concern with everyone's outcomes and the challenges the team faces.	Concern with one's own outcome and challenges.
The team leader and members shape the purpose, goals, and approach to work.	The manager shapes the purpose, goals, and approach to work.

Co-locating (or the nearest thing)

Face-to-face conversation is the most effective and efficient method of conveying information within a team. Although colocation is not always simple, like the work-from-home shift we saw in 2020, it does not change the data that continues to show people communicate complex issues best when face-to-face.

WARNING

Don't mistake *face-to-face* to mean video conferencing. Although video conferencing is pretty good and keeps getting better, it's not the same as face-to-face. In video conferences, you don't know what other participants are looking at or listening to while they're muted, even if it looks like they're looking at you through the camera. You don't know who is talking to them. Because of the low resolution, you may only see them from the nose up, hear every third word, and be unable to tell what nonverbal gestures or facial expressions they're giving. Face-to-face really does mean *face-to-face*.

REMEMBER

Scrum doesn't require co-locating. In fact, dislocated teams benefit from scrum as much (if not more) than anyone because of the clarity in accountabilities, short feedback loop for frequent course correction, and transparency of progress.

Here are a few benefits of a co-located team:

>> Increased speed and effectiveness of face-to-face communication, especially through kinetics, voice tonality, facial expressions, and so on.

The value of face-to-face communication shouldn't be underestimated. Albert Mehrabian, Ph.D., and professor emeritus of psychology at the University of California-Los Angeles, proved the following:

- 55 percent of meaning is conveyed through body language and facial expressions.

- 38 percent of meaning is *paralinguistic* (conveyed by how we speak).

- 7 percent of meaning is conveyed in the actual words spoken.

These statistics alone are a whopping case for co-locating your team.

>> Ease in immediate clarification of questions.

>> Understanding what other members are working on.

>> Ease in supporting other team members in their tasks.

>> Cost savings due to decreased lag times and fewer misunderstandings that lead to defects or wasted work.

>> Building relationships and trust.

Collaborative tools

Many tools exist for promoting a collaborative environment as well. Some we recommend are:

>> Whiteboards with 3x5 cards and sticky notes are the best tool for co-located teams. Distributed teams are finding varying levels of success in using virtual whiteboards.

>> Instant messaging platforms are also popular for team-written communication needs (sharing info, not resolving issues), especially for distributed teams. High-performing co-located teams prefer face-to-face communication more than digital communication.

>> Many digital agile project management platforms are available for managing both sprint and product backlogs. Some even enable product goals, roadmaps, and releases.

>> Collaboration tools for helping teams during retrospectives are also available. We'll discuss these more in Chapter 6.

REMEMBER

High-performing teams benefit from having developers with direct access to product owners and scrum masters all day, every day. All sorts of banality are exchanged, and it's tempting to think this might be wasteful. However, we've found during these exchanges is when the really good work gets done. Little things aren't actually little; they're differentiators and the things that matter. Quality needs input, and input needs access. When access is high, great things are possible.

TIP

Sometimes, outsourcing is the only viable solution for your company or organization. If this is the case, do it with both feet. Enable the entire scrum team to either co-locate or work as a near-proximity distributed team (meaning, at least, in the same time zone or geographic proximity). Your developers need an available product owner, so send one to the outsourcing location or develop a local product owner to work directly with the remote scrum team. The increase in quality and efficiency far outweighs the cost of the product owner.

WHY DEVELOPERS LOVE SCRUM

Developers love scrum for a variety of reasons, not least of which is that it's an empowering and motivating environment. When you allow people to contribute, they become part of the process and take ownership of the results. The effects snowball:

- Success is clearly defined with the sprint goal, the definition of *done,* and each requirement's listed acceptance criteria.

- Members participate in creating the sprint goal, thereby increasing ownership.

- It's a results-only work environment. Work any way you like; just show results.

- Direct communication with product owners is available.

- Team recognition is given in the sprint reviews.

- Structured process improvement is achieved through sprint retrospectives.

- Systematic knowledge is built through sprint retrospectives.

Getting the Edge on Backlog Estimation

In creating the product roadmap (see Chapter 3), the developers do a high-level estimate of the amount of work entailed in the product. The practical value of this estimation process doesn't come into play until the sprints start (see Chapter 5), but this initial estimation sets a mark from which future estimates may be calculated. The developers do the estimating because only the people who do the work should estimate the effort of the work.

REMEMBER

These backlog estimation techniques aren't requirements of scrum. They're common practices scrum practitioners have found useful in the field.

The product roadmap is the start of the product backlog. What's on your roadmap is what you will begin developing. So, how do you take all those items on your product backlog and estimate the work involved with any degree of accuracy? A few common practices are used depending on the situation. Before we look at these estimating techniques individually, it's important to understand what you're trying to achieve.

Your Definition of Done

If you ask the members of a scrum team what they expect to see when a requirement is done, you get as many answers as there are team members. So, before starting a product development effort, scrum teams define what it means for a requirement to be developed and tested to a releasable state with a definition of *done*. Until you have a consensus on this definition, estimations will be based on varying assumptions.

As described in Chapter 3, for each requirement within a sprint, you complete the following types of development work:

>> Requirement elaboration

>> Design

>> Development

>> Comprehensive testing

>> Integration

>> Documentation

>> Approval

This definition of *done* needs to be specific, refined, and focused on what it means to do these things to completion to achieve the level of quality you're striving for in your product. Consider the outcomes you're striving to accomplish.

Effective definitions of *done* encompass these four factors:

>> **Developed:** The product has been fully developed by the team.

>> **Tested:** The team fully tested the product to ensure it functions properly.

>> **Integrated:** The product has been fully integrated within the product as a whole and any related products.

>> **Documented:** The developers create whatever documentation is needed. Just remember that the goal is "barely sufficient."

TIP

When you've come up with your definition of *done*, write it out on a white poster board and tape it to the wall or make it your virtual background, and radiate it for the entire product team to see. You'll always have it right in front of the developers and product owner. We call it *in-your-face documentation*. No cover sheet, no table of contents — simply the lowest-fidelity way that communicates and makes the information the most visible.

In your definition of *done*, in addition to the development, consider the depth of testing and documentation you might need. You might consider the following types of testing:

>> Component

>> Functional

>> Integration

>> Security

>> Regression

>> User acceptance

Also, consider the documentation you need:

>> Technical

>> User

>> Maintenance

Each point may differ between the sprint and release levels, though we prefer the sprint-level definition of *done* to include everything necessary to release. You also may have organizationally specific items that you want to include. It's your choice. The point is to have a clear definition of *done* that's defined by the scrum team.

REMEMBER

A *release* occurs when a set of marketable features is released outside the scrum team. This could happen several times during a sprint, at the end of each sprint, or after a series of sprints. These requirements may be released into the market and to the users, or they may go to internal or external stakeholders for real-world use and feedback.

TIP

A regular sprint entails completing the development, testing, documentation, and approving items in the sprint backlog. However, before doing a product release, other activities may be needed that the developers wouldn't have access to in a regular sprint. Therefore, sometimes scrum teams have a release sprint just before the release itself to allow these additional steps to be addressed. The key is the requirements must work and be demonstrable at the end of every sprint. You can inspect and tune for scale in the release sprint, but the requirements must work every sprint.

Common Practices for Estimating

Estimating the effort involved in developing product backlog requirements is an ongoing process. (In Chapter 3, we discuss product backlog refinement.) For example, you could do estimations for 30 minutes at 5 p.m. every day before team members go home. This way, at the end of the week, you've covered lots of ground and will be ready for each sprint start. Some teams don't like to develop on Friday afternoons; instead, they do product backlog refinement on Fridays.

As part of breaking down the requirements for sprint-level execution, teams are likely to refine their estimates at three levels. Depending on your product, you may include more. Your estimate refinement usually goes in this order:

1. Product roadmap
2. Release planning
3. Sprint planning

REMEMBER

The developers are responsible for estimating the effort required to build the requirements fully. The scrum master can facilitate the process, and the product owner can provide clarification, but the decision is made by the developers doing the actual work.

TIP

We use relative estimating instead of precise (absolute) estimating because it's much more feasible in many situations. If you're asked to look out the window and say how tall the neighboring building is, how precise would your reply be? Very — it's 950 feet. How accurate would your reply be? Not very. Why? Because you honestly have no idea; you gave it a wild guess. But if we ask you to look at two nearby buildings and tell us which one is taller, barring some vision problem, we can guarantee you'll give us the right answer. Scrum teams value accuracy more than precision. Using *relative* sizing is an effective way to overcome humans' difficulty in making absolute estimates.

Fibonacci numbers and story points

The Fibonacci sequence is an excellent sizing technique for relative estimating.

With Fibonacci, if something is bigger, you get an idea of how much bigger it is. The last two numbers in the sequence are added to create the next number. Fibonacci numbers look like this:

> 1, 2, 3, 5, 8, 13, 21, 34, 55, 89, 144, and so on

As the numbering progresses, the distance between the numbers increases. We use this technique to acknowledge the lessened accuracy in predicting larger chunks of work.

REMEMBER

A *story point* is the Fibonacci number assigned to an individual requirement (that is, a user story).

TECHNICAL STUFF

Leonardo Pisano Bigollo, also known as Fibonacci, lived near Pisa, Italy, from about 1170 to about 1250. Widely recognized as a brilliant mathematician, he made the Fibonacci sequence famous and instigated the spread in Europe of the Hindu-Arabic numeral system — today, the most common symbolic representation of numbers worldwide.

Initial high-level requirements are estimated at the product roadmap level:

>> For the scrum teams we work with, the developers understand that requirements with Fibonacci number estimates from 1 through 8 can be brought into a sprint. This level of refinement usually results in a user story.

>> Requirements with estimates numbered 13 through 34 are those you would allow into a release but need to be broken down further before you would let them into a sprint. At this level of refinement, we call these *epics*.

>> Requirements from 55 through 144 are too big for a release but are estimable at the order-of-magnitude product roadmap level. These requirements typically reflect features.

>> Requirements larger than 144 need to be broken down before the developers can give any semblance of an accurate estimate, so we don't estimate beyond 144. These may represent broader themes.

TIP

Whatever the Fibonacci number, only the highest-priority backlog items get broken down into sprint-level sizes (which we recommend shouldn't be more than an 8). So, if you have assigned a 21 Fibonacci number to a high-priority requirement, it needs to be broken into smaller requirements before it can come into a sprint. This decomposition is the progressive elaboration we discussed in Chapter 3.

With the sizes established, we can apply a few techniques to estimate requirements:

>> When we have shorter lists of requirements, we begin with *estimation poker*.

>> When we have hundreds of requirements, we begin with *affinity estimation* (discussed later in this chapter).

In the estimation process with smaller work efforts, we have the developers begin as follows. We have the team sit down with their stack of requirements written on 3x5 cards (virtual whiteboards of sticky notes may also be used). Then we ask them to pick a requirement they agree has an effort level of 5, which creates a reference point.

We start with a 5 as an anchor because it's not trivial (1), it's not huge (55, 89, or 144), but it's somewhere on the lower mid-range of options. A 5 is small enough for a small group to agree on. They can imagine items that are smaller and also much bigger. It's a place to start — that's all.

REMEMBER

We then have them pick another card and, based on the first one being 5, ask them what number the next one would be. If it's greater than 5, is it 8, 13, or 21? If it's smaller than 5, is it 3, 2, or 1? Or is it similar to 5? This process continues until a few representational sizes have been established.

Estimation poker

A popular way to estimate requirements is to use a variation of poker. You need a deck of estimation poker cards like the one shown in Figure 4-2. (You can find them on our website at https://platinumedge.com/store/estimation-poker-cards). You can also download our poker estimation app for iPhone and/or Android by searching for *Platinum Edge Estimation Poker* in your device's app store, or you can make your own deck with index cards and a marker.

FIGURE 4-2:
Estimation poker cards for estimating the amount of effort required in each requirement.

Because only the developers decide how much it will take to develop a requirement, only the developers play estimation poker. The scrum master facilitates, and the product owner reads/tells the story and provides requirement details, but neither of those two gives estimates. It goes like this:

1. The product owner reads a targeted requirement to the developers, including acceptance criteria.

2. The developers ask any questions and get any clarifications they need.

3. Each developer picks a card from their deck (or from the app) with their estimate of the requirement's level of effort.

   The estimate is to accomplish the complete definition of *done* and acceptance criteria, not just a portion.

REMEMBER

4. Members don't show anyone else their cards because you don't want others to be influenced. (This is why we call it *poker*.)

5. After everyone has picked a number, the team members simultaneously show their cards.

   • If everyone has the same estimate, nothing is left to discuss. Assign that estimate to the requirement and move on to the next requirement.

   • If differences exist in estimates, the members with the highest and lowest estimates are asked to explain. Further clarification from the product owner is given as needed.

6. With increased knowledge, everyone picks a new number for that requirement by repeating Steps 3 and 4.

Normally, we do up to three rounds of estimation poker for each requirement to get the core assumptions on the table and clarified. Then, we usually have the estimates in a tighter cluster of numbers.

If all developers agree on a single number after three rounds, you're ready to move on to the next requirement. But not all developers will always agree on a single number after three rounds. At this point, we go on to a consensus-building technique called *fist of five.*

TECHNICAL STUFF

In true agile form, the conversation is the most important aspect of the relative estimation techniques. Take the time needed to help your team align on the approach and expected outcomes for their work by exploring the differences in their estimates. Individuals and interactions are more valuable than processes or tools.

Fist of five

Fist of five is a fast and efficient method of reaching consensus that can be used on its own or as a supplement to estimation poker. The purpose of fist of five is consensus — to quickly find an estimate that all team members can support (see Figure 4-3).

FIGURE 4-3: Fist of five is an efficient way of finding consensus in many situations.

5 = LOVE IT!
4 = Good idea.
3 = Yeah, I can support it.
2 = I have reservations, let's discuss further.
1 = Opposed. Do not move forward.

Perhaps when you tried estimation poker, after three rounds, some team members have given a requirement an 8, and others have given it a 13 — they're split.

For example, it begins with the scrum master holding up the requirement card in question and asking, "How comfortable would you be with this as an 8?" Each developer holds up the number of fingers associated with their comfort level. If everyone is holding up three, four, or five fingers, it's settled.

If some developers are holding up one or two fingers, as in estimation poker, the outliers would be asked to explain, and further information would be garnered if necessary. Fist of five would be performed again. You might even try asking for a fist of five vote on the 13 option to see if everyone can support it. Continue with this process until all team members can support a Fibonacci-sized amount with at least three fingers (which means, "All things considered, I can support it").

With the fist of five completed and requirements estimated, you're ready to move to release or sprint planning, which are covered in Chapter 5.

Affinity estimating

Estimation poker and fist of five are effective facilitation methods for establishing consensus with smaller backlogs. But what if you have several hundred requirements on the backlog? It could take days to complete. This is where affinity estimating is helpful.

Instead of beginning with Fibonacci numbers, you begin with a more familiar concept: T-shirt sizes (XS, S, M, L, and XL).

With affinity estimating, you first create several areas marked with each size (either physically or virtually) and then place each requirement in one of the size categories. It goes like this:

1. Identify small tables or set up a virtual whiteboard to sort the cards. Label one table or whiteboard section *Clarify*, and label other small tables or whiteboard sections for each size category (for a total of seven labeled tables or sections):

   - Extra-small

   - Small

   - Medium

   - Large

   - Extra-large

   - Epic (too large to fit into the sprint, given six to ten requirements are the target for each sprint; more on this in Chapter 5)

     - Clarify

2. For each size category, give your developers 60 seconds to pick a requirement from the overall stack of requirements and place it on the corresponding table. This establishes the *representational anchor* for each size.

3. Each developer grabs a stack of remaining requirements.

4. Each developer places the card they think reflects the size on the table. They use the representational anchors as a reference. Figure 4-4 shows the relationship between size piles and Fibonacci numbers.

TIP

Don't let team members linger too long on their stack of requirements. Establish a *timebox* for them to work within, such as 20 minutes for 20 cards.

Timebox is a term that refers to the allotted time for an event or activity. If your sprints last two weeks, the timebox is two weeks.

TIP

5. Have the developers play what we call *gallery* until all members agree on the requirements' sizes.

In the gallery, the team members flip through all the cards on all the tables or virtual sections and only provide feedback on the cards that don't appear to be in the right size pile.

For example, if one team member wants to move a story from small to medium, check to see whether the original person who placed it there disagrees. If the person disagrees, place that card on a separate *Clarify* pile. Don't get into extensive discussions just yet.

6. Invite the product owner to review for major disagreements:

   - If the product owner sees a requirement on the medium table they thought would be a small requirement, don't waste any time discussing it. The developers ultimately get to decide the requirement's size, and a difference of one-size isn't worth the time to discuss it.

   - If there is more than one size difference between where developers think a card should be placed and where the product owner thought it would be placed, put that card on the *Clarify* pile. Perhaps the developers didn't understand the product owner's requirement explanation.

7. For cards on the *Clarify* table, play estimation poker (discussed earlier in this chapter).

As you can see in Figure 4-4, these are like T-shirt sizes. Each "size" could eventually correspond to a Fibonacci number, as shown in Step 7.

Within a relatively short amount of time, you've been able to reliably estimate the effort on hundreds of separate requirements. Now, you're ready to plan your first release and/or your first sprint.

Velocity

After you have Fibonacci numbers assigned to your requirements, you have story points to work from.

SIZE	POINTS
XtraSmall (XS)	1 pt
Small (S)	2 pts
Medium (M)	3 pts
Large (L)	5 pts
XtraLarge (XL)	8 pts

FIGURE 4-4:
Affinity estimating uses T-shirt sizes for story sizes and gives each one a corresponding Fibonacci number.

Chapter 5 shows how to plan both releases and sprints. To plan your first sprint, among those requirements that are between 1 and 8 story points, a scrum team determines a modest number of combined story points to work on. Then, at the end of the sprint, a scrum team looks at the requirements that were done to completion and adds their story points. The result might be 15, 25, or 35 story points. This is the team's velocity for the first sprint and starting input for a team determining how much it can accomplish in the next sprint.

REMEMBER

Velocity is the combined number of story points your team completed in an individual sprint. It's a post-sprint fact used for extrapolation, not a pre-sprint goal.

TIP

To accurately determine velocity, you need more than one sprint to find an average. Velocity follows the law of large numbers; the more data points you have, the better. At a minimum, you need three data points to establish an optimistic, pessimistic, and most likely extrapolation of how many requirements will be met during the product development. After you have these, you can tell stakeholders optimistic, pessimistic, and most likely estimates for how many of the highest-priority requirements on the product backlog can be completed within a product development effort. Giving stakeholders this type of estimation range provides the level of detail they're looking for while allowing some flexibility for the developers as they're still getting into a development rhythm.

The team's velocity will usually vary greatly in the first few sprints. After that, it becomes more stable as the team gets into a development rhythm. Of course, team members or sprint duration changes will introduce variability into the team's velocity.

REMEMBER

Velocity isn't a goal; it's a fact used for extrapolation. Higher numbers are not automatically better than lower numbers.

When story points are used, you'll find that some teams are pessimistic with their estimates, so their numbers always come in high. Other teams are optimistic, so their story point total comes in low.

Consider that an optimistic team's velocity is 15, and the estimates for the release total 150 points. It would take them 10 sprints to complete the release.

If a pessimistic team's velocity were 30 and the estimates for the release total 300 points, it would also take 10 sprints.

TIP

Optimistic or pessimistic doesn't really matter. Teams will generally be consistent one way or the other and, therefore, balance out in the end. This is why you always value a team's velocity against itself, not against other teams. In fact, don't even share a team's velocity with anyone outside the scrum team. Consider it an extrapolation system, not a performance system.

STORY POINTS AND VELOCITY IN REAL TIME

A real-world example of the value of story points and velocity might appear like this.

Assume the following data:

- Remaining product backlog is 500 story points.
- Your sprint duration (timebox) is one week, Monday through Friday.
- The team velocity averages 20 story points per sprint.
- Today is Monday, January 10, 2022.
- Your annual team member cost is $100,000 per team member, and you have seven members — that is, $700,000 annually or $13,462 weekly.

Within minutes, you can make a solid estimate of the cost and delivery date of the product. Given this data, your product development effort will entail 25 sprints and, therefore, will take 25 weeks to complete. Your cost will be $336,550, and your completion date will be Friday, July 1, 2022.

What happens if your team increases its velocity to 25 story points per sprint? Just plug in the numbers. Now, you'll need only 20 sprints. Your cost will drop to $269,240 (saving you $67,310), and your final delivery date will be Friday, May 27, 2022. This is the benefit of having a dedicated scrum master who can remove impediments and organizational drag on the team to increase velocity.

When you have a clear method of estimating the effort required to complete each requirement and an average velocity established for the team, you can accurately predict the quantity of product that can be created within fixed cost and time constraints. This is because you're harnessing your variables.

Successful scrum teams need to share ownership of outcomes and value authentic transparency between the team and its stakeholders. Progress is visible to everyone.

Chapter **5**

Release and Sprint Planning

Scrum is simple. . .and is purposefully incomplete. . . . Various processes, techniques and methods can be employed within the framework. Scrum wraps around existing practices or renders them unnecessary.

— SCRUM GUIDE 2020

S o far, you have a product goal, a product roadmap, and a scrum team. Release and sprint planning is really where the rubber hits the road. As we've mentioned before, with scrum, you'll do just as much planning as in traditional models, but with scrum, it's more focused, continuous, results-oriented, and packaged such that you'll wonder how you ever managed your planning without it.

In this chapter, you find out how to plan the product's release in a logical and organized way. The purpose of release planning is to mobilize the wider product team around a specific set of functionality that the organization wants to release to the marketplace. This is when such departments or stakeholders as the marketing department, field support, and customer service get mobilized and prepared to support the functionality end customers will use in the real world.

We also walk you through the scrum event of sprints. Scrum at its core is the sprint cycle. We show you how to use this valuable process and get the best possible results.

REMEMBER

A *sprint* is a fixed timebox within which development is done to produce a working, potentially shippable product. A typical sprint might be one or two weeks in duration but could be as little as a day and as much as a month.

We discuss how prioritizing releases and sprints accelerates time to market and maximizes return on investment (ROI). We explain that by having feedback loops, you incrementally and iteratively create the product your clients want, with the features and capabilities they'll actually use.

But first, we can learn a lot about early, incremental, and iterative release approaches from the startup world.

Lean Startup

Forming your own startup company is no small endeavor. You have all the normal challenges associated with starting a business venture, including the use of personal funds to finance the endeavor and planning for success. Startups have certain portfolio advantages over larger established organizations and huge potential to bring value. Their small size increases their agility, and decisions can be made quickly without the weight of corporate bureaucracy. Still, making tough decisions early and getting minimum viable product out the door faster than everyone else is critical for entrepreneurial survival.

Lean Startup is scrum for startups.

Typically, in the waterfall method, many startups begin with an idea, spend time and money developing it into a formal multiyear business plan, and hope it's what the customer wants. Often, startups fail before they have a chance to show the client the product. Recent data shows that 80 percent of new businesses fail within the first 18 months.

REMEMBER

In one sense, an 80 percent failure rate is terrible. Those odds aren't betting odds. On the other hand, all those potential competitors are being swept away on the tide of ineffectiveness. With Lean Startup, new businesses can expand on their advantages and avoid unnecessary pitfalls.

In traditional project frameworks, the client is often left out of initial planning and prioritizing conversations, which misses the opportunity to collaborate and tailor the project. One size doesn't fit all, and the user could remain unsatisfied and unengaged.

With Lean Startup, the same inspect-and-adapt approach used with the scrum framework is applied from the beginning. The feedback loop is critical. Sprint planning, sprint reviews, and sprint retrospectives allow constant inspection and adaptation at the startup level.

REMEMBER

With Lean Startup, you don't have to wait months or years for valuable prototypes to be made. With the prioritization process of highest value and risk, you have products to place in stakeholders' and customers' hands within weeks. The feedback you gain, you can immediately use for future iterations.

You can also address critical yet often-overlooked questions such as these:

>> Should this product be created?

>> Does the product work at its most basic level?

>> Is the product economically viable?

Before you commit huge sums of money, basic questions and answers can be brought to light. "Fail early, fail cheap" is a form of success.

TECHNICAL
STUFF

Pivoting is part of the Lean Startup world. You pivot when you inspect and adapt and then adjust your course based on the information you gleaned from the feedback loop.

The prioritization process is driven by reality, not hope. As features are developed and feedback is gained, that data is immediately incorporated into new iterations (sprints) and requirements.

REMEMBER

The Lean Startup model follows the build, measure, and learn pattern, which is essentially the scrum model:

>> **Build:** The sprint cycle creates the product increment supporting the release goal (minimum viable product [MVP]).

>> **Measure:** The feedback is received in both the sprint review and the sprint retrospective.

>> **Learn:** New requirements are added to the product backlog as a result of customer feedback, intitiating the plan of action for the improvements learned from the retrospective.

DROPBOX

Dropbox, a file-storage and file-sharing application, was once a product that people didn't think they needed. The company used the MVP concept to get people to use its product early in its development. How do you sell something that people don't know they need? Henry Ford once said "If I had asked people what they wanted, they would have said faster horses." Lean Startup is a great agile tool for enabling entrepreneurial innovation.

Because developing Dropbox involved extensive integrations with computer platforms and operating systems, developing a full prototype wasn't feasible, given the complexity of the engineering necessary. Dropbox solved this dilemma by creating a video targeted to technologically savvy early adopters, showing why they needed the product and how easy it was to use. The company knew that it needed feedback as early as possible, and that feedback needed to come from the people who would give the developers the most knowledgeable feedback. Taking a Lean Startup approach allowed Dropbox to drive early traffic and grow its waiting list from 5,000 to 75,000. Literally overnight, the company had validation that its product was what the market wanted. The video was the first MVP and captivated the audience for the next MVP, which was the highest-valued file-storage and file-sharing features.

The Dropbox MVP was an opportunity to demonstrate to customers what they didn't know they needed and to quickly and inexpensively validate or nullify their hypothesis of the market demand.

Release Plan Basics

We began the roadmap to value in Chapter 1 with the bird's-eye basics: your product goal. This allows you to establish your destination and define the desired outcomes. The second part, the product roadmap, provides a holistic view of the features that support the accomplishment of the goal. As you narrow your focus and generate more detail, you come into release planning, which is the third element of your roadmap to value (see Figure 5-1). The release planning concept is not part of scrum. However, the release plan artifact is a common practice that many scrum aficionados use with success.

A *release plan* is a high-level timetable for releasing a set of product requirements. So, you're working down, segmentally, from the big-picture roadmap to the intermediate release plan. (Later in this chapter, we cover the immediate level of planning, which is the actual sprint.) The release plan provides a focal point around which the team or organization can mobilize.

RELEASE PLANNING

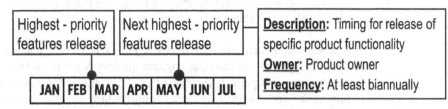

Highest - priority features release

Next highest - priority features release

Description: Timing for release of specific product functionality
Owner: Product owner
Frequency: At least biannually

| JAN | FEB | MAR | APR | MAY | JUN | JUL |

FIGURE 5-1:
Release planning on the roadmap to value.

REMEMBER

Do the minimum amount possible that still creates a working product. When planning a set of features or capabilities to release to the market, always ask yourself, "What is the minimum set of features that delivers value to my customer?" This is what is commonly referred to as the *minimum viable product* (MVP).

You should release to the market as often as you have something of value to offer your customers — the minimum viable product. Your product releases could also come on a regular schedule (for example, four times a year, at the end of each quarter). But with the need to be quick to market, releases now may be monthly, weekly, or even multiple times a day in some cases.

AC + OC > V

Applying a simple formula to your product development effort helps you know when you've achieved the best possible results. In other words, you know to terminate the current work as soon as the actual cost (AC) of working on the remaining product backlog added to the opportunity cost (OC) of not working on other products is greater than the value (V) you're expecting to get from the remaining product backlog.

As a formula, it looks like this:

$$AC + OC > V$$

This formula helps you determine when it is time to end development. You'll see how you can achieve the 30–40 percent time savings and 30–70 percent cost saving we've realized so many times by

- Having stable, dedicated teams

- Prioritizing to avoid building features that customers won't use

- Iterating through consistent feedback loops with your customers

TIP

Consider the pen-and-pencil rule. You can use a pen to commit to the plan for the first release, but anything beyond this plan is written in pencil. It's just-in-time planning for each release.

A product may have multiple releases. For each release, you start with the goal, which is supported by the next-highest-priority features and requirements. You'll see that this is a pattern you follow at each stage of the roadmap to value. Each release has a release goal, and you commit to only one release at a time. Figure 5-2 depicts a typical release plan with an optional release sprint.

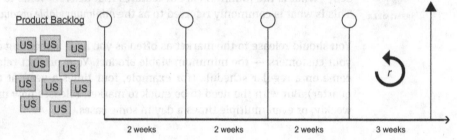

Release Goal: Enable customers to purchase tankless water heater base model 7.
Release Date: March 31, 2023

FIGURE 5-2:
A typical release plan with the release goal, date, and an optional release sprint.

US = User Story
r = optional "release" sprint

TECHNICAL
STUFF

The number of sprints within each release can vary depending on the release goal and what's required to complete the requirements to achieve that goal. An option is to use release trains, in which each release has a set time schedule. Releases are set so that everyone knows when to expect them.

At each scheduled release, the product owner decides which of the completed functionalities will be released on that date. This way, organizations and customers know to expect new features on a set schedule. Scrum teams can predictably organize their release plans to cadence.

Scrum is an empirical approach. Each step of the way, you inspect your results and adapt immediately to the changing needs of your customers. These fundamentals enable you to achieve significant cost and time savings while delivering what the client wants. You may have a bird's-eye view of four releases for your product, but you plan in detail only one release at a time. What you learn in the first release may change what you do in the second release.

WARNING

Your organization may be afraid to release incrementally. You may find it difficult to release completed work before the entire backlog is complete. Sometimes that hesitancy derives from a sense that once the product is released you can't improve it or add to it. Overcome these antipatterns to support more effective and frequent releases.

Prioritize, prioritize, prioritize

You've heard this before when we've talked about scrum, and you'll hear it throughout this book. Identifying the highest-priority requirements, according to business value and risk, and working with only those requirements are key common practices within the agile community.

Think of each release as the next incremental MVP of your product. When planning each release, ask these questions to identify the highest-priority features:

>> What makes a requirement important for this release?

>> What "barely sufficient" set of features provide enough business value to the customer we need to bring to market next?

>> Which requirements present the greatest risk and should be addressed sooner than later?

TECHNICAL
STUFF

A famous Standish Group study updated in 2015 by Jim Johnson showed on more than 1,000 representational software development projects that only 20 percent of the features were used always or often by the customers. Thirty percent were infrequently used, and half were hardly ever used. This means that 80 percent of features were never or rarely used. With scrum's emphasis on prioritization, only those most important and useful features are developed first. What if your development effort runs out of funding, and you're only 80 percent done? Based on the Standish study, you might not have needed the remaining 80 percent anyway. AC + OC > V means end the effort. Redeploy that capital to a higher and better use.

Following are the four key reasons you want as small a set of features per release as possible:

>> First-mover advantage of speed to market and increased market share.

>> Accelerated customer feedback cycle.

>> Maximized ROI. (A dollar today is literally worth more than a dollar will be worth six months from now.)

>> Reduced internal risk from such factors as organizational change and budget poaching.

The product owner fully owns the release plan, prioritizes the requirements in the product backlog, and sets the release goal (as shown in the following section). While the product owner decides the priorities and when to release completed shippable functionality, they consult with stakeholders and the scrum team to make their decisions. Figure 5-3 applies the 80/20 rule to the value versus effort idea. It isn't a magic formula, but it's a helpful way to understand and explain the value.

The Pareto Principle (80/20 rule) and the Law of Diminishing Returns

	Imagine a current unstarted project and let's apply the 80/20 rule a few times.	Delivered Business Value	Expended Effort	Value Leverage
Low hanging fruit	80 percent of business value delivered with 20 percent of the effort (a good value by delivering the highest value and best defined stories first)	80%	20%	4:1
Hard or risky but needed	Now taking 80% of the remaining part (20) of business value leaves us with 16% and taking 20% of the remaining effort (80)	16%	16%	1:1
Whoops we feel stuck	We've delivered 96% of the business value so far with only 36% of the effort! Let's do it one more time. 80% of 4% = 3.2 value and 20% of remaining 64% effort = yields 12.8 effort.	3.2%	12.8%	1:4
	We still have over 50% of the estimated effort remaining to gain hardly business delivered value.	99.2%	48.8%	

This illustration isn't intended to be an exact project estimation but rather to demonstrate something scrum professionals experience across projects. If the roadmap to value is followed you will do the most valued stories first.
- More than half of software features don't get used (see the Standish study).
- **Law of diminishing returns** refers to a point at which the level of benefits gained is less than the amount of effort (time, money) expended.

FIGURE 5-3:
Applying the Pareto Principle (80/20 rule) to scrum.

Release goals

Each release plan has an overall business goal called a *release goal*. This goal is created by the product owner and ties directly to the product goal. The release goal establishes the midterm boundary around specific functionality that will be released to customers to use in the real world.

Having an explicit release goal expedites the prioritization process: If a requirement doesn't align with the goal, you don't have to worry about that requirement in this release. Any given requirement should earn the right of your investment. Leave it tucked away in the product backlog until it can support a priority goal. Figure 5-4 shows a matrix to help you determine the priority stories.

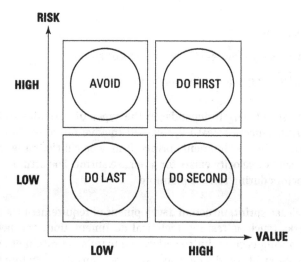

FIGURE 5-4:
Backlog
priority matrix.

TIP

Think of the three layers of goal setting as a prioritization filter system. The product goal is the highest boundary. If a feature doesn't fit the overall goal, it doesn't belong in this product development effort. Don't even put that requirement on the product backlog. The requester needs to get funding for that idea separately. Don't allow features to be stowaways on your product backlog.

Next comes the release goal. This is the midterm boundary. If a requirement doesn't fit this goal, it stays in the product backlog but stays at a high level. Finally, the shortest-term boundary is the sprint goal that focuses on "What do we need to achieve now?"

REMEMBER

Goals drive the product backlog and the release plan, not the other way around. Every feature and requirement must be thought of in terms of whether it fits the goal. This is *purpose-driven development (or goal- or outcome-driven development).* Goals drive what makes the product backlog. Goals drive what gets included in a release. And goals drive what gets included in each sprint.

Release sprints

Sometimes, releasing product features into the marketplace requires completing certain jobs that can't be done within a normal developmental sprint because of organizational dysfunctions or constraints, such as siloed departmental structures or outdated policies. Ideally, all activities required to release a product to the market are done within a normal sprint. But if the way an organization is set up doesn't allow it, a release sprint may be used to accomplish such purposes as

- » Verifying scaling

- » Broader testing activities (for example, focus groups)

- » Internal training required to support the release

The release sprint length depends on the types of activities to be done in the release sprint. Since a release sprint will involve different types of work than what's done in the development sprints, it may be a different length. This is also why no concept of velocity exists for a release sprint. The scrum team determines all these factors during release planning.

REMEMBER

During a release sprint, no actual development of requirements is done. All development tasks (such as testing, technical documentation, and peer reviews) are completed during each sprint to satisfy the team's definition of *done*, ensuring a potentially shippable product at the end of each sprint. But before the product can go out to the market, other things may need to be done.

WARNING

The release sprint is a form of antipattern in organizations that can't do organizational support tasks within the sprint. If you don't need it, don't do it.

Including examples already given, uses for release sprints may include the following:

- » Conducting focus groups (keep in mind that this isn't to identify new features but to validate what you've done and identify release issues)

- » Scaling tests

- » Internal training required to support the release

- » Tweaking performance based on scaling test results

- » Integrating the product within enterprise-wide products and services

Release plan in practice

To see how a release plan works in the real world, follow these steps:

1. **Develop a release goal.**

This goal is the target for everything else. The product owner ensures that the goal aligns with the product goal and works with the scrum team to ensure that the entire team feels comfortable with the goal.

2. **Identify the target release date.**

This date may be influenced by factors outside the control of the scrum team.

3. **Identify the highest-priority requirements (MVP) on the product backlog that support the release goal.**

   Priority is a function of value and risk. Tackle the highest-value/highest-risk items first. See Figure 5-4 for a value matrix.

4. **Refine the requirements estimates as needed.**

   Sometimes, issues and/or synergies are discovered when the developers look at the smaller package of requirements that go into a release plan. The requirements will also be more detailed and broken down (no larger than 34; see Chapter 4) than the team originally estimated at the product roadmap level.

5. **Identify the team's velocity.**

   Established velocity from previous sprints is a great starting point if the team is stable and has been working on the same product. If the team hasn't established velocity, start modestly until you have run a few sprints and velocity can be ascertained.

6. **Plan a release sprint (if needed).**

   Determine as a scrum team whether you'll need one and, if so, its length.

7. **Finalize the release scope.**

   Based on velocity, total estimates of requirements and number of sprints within the release timebox, how much functionality can you include? Which is more flexible — the date or the amount of functionality? What adjustments need to be made to the release date or scope of requirements to release as much as you can within your timebox?

   Suppose that your velocity is 20, the release timebox is five sprints, and the total estimated points for the release is 110. This puts you 10 points over what's available in the release. The product owner has a decision to make. Are the requirements that make up the bottom 10 points in the release valuable enough to include, or can the release go on without them? Or does the release need to be extended one sprint, and will that be acceptable to the stakeholders and customers? Knowing this early during release planning gives everyone time to make adjustments.

TIP

One option in release planning is to use the *release train* model. Rather than have releases of varying duration, in this scenario, each release is exactly the same length — six weeks, for example. At the end of each six-week cycle, the completed functionality from each of the sprints is packaged and released. This way, a development rhythm is created, and everyone in the organization can anticipate his workload and schedule moving forward.

Use any of the estimation and consensus-building techniques discussed in Chapter 4 to refine the product backlog items in the release, if requirements still need to be refined and estimated (see the preceding Step 4). If your releases consist of many product backlog items, use affinity estimating (the T-shirt sizing technique discussed in Chapter 4) for release planning.

REMEMBER

As with all scrum documentation, we prefer the simplest tools possible. The entire release plan can be mapped out with your trusty physical or virtual whiteboard and sticky notes. This allows for ease in change and immediate access. Also, it just plain saves time.

Sprinting to Your Goals

Finally, the heart of scrum! Sprints and their built-in inspect and adapt model are integral scrum features. Through scrum's iterative cycle, you can achieve the three pillars of empiricism — transparency, inspection, and adaptation — that we discuss in Chapter 1.

By breaking your work into tangible pieces and then using the empirical scrum model to assess your progress, you can pivot constantly while moving forward. This allows you the nimbleness and ease of adaptation sorely missing in waterfall.

Each scrum team member has the same purpose in the sprints: maximizing effectiveness in delivering desired outcomes.

Defining sprints

As we discussed in Chapter 1, sprints are the essence of scrum. They're a consistent timebox for product development by the developers. Each sprint includes the following:

>> Sprint planning

>> Daily scrums

>> Development time, including regular review by the product owner

>> Sprint review

>> Sprint retrospective

The consistent timebox of sprints allows the developers to establish a development rhythm. It also enables scrum teams to extrapolate into the future based on empirical data such as velocity. As soon as one sprint is finished, another begins. A consistent iterative feedback loop flow is created, resulting in an ideal production environment and continuous improvement.

TIP

Imagine that you're a runner. You're consistently training for the 100-yard dash and have become incredibly proficient at it, but suddenly your coach asks you to run a marathon. If you attempt the marathon at your 100-yard-dash pace, you won't finish the marathon. You need to modify your training to adjust for a marathon pace, which will require coaching, schedule, and diet changes over time. All your muscle memory and the type of endurance your body has developed will need to be relearned to run a different race length.

Planning sprint length

Because sprint goals don't change during a sprint, the answer to the question "How long should a sprint be?" depends on your product and how long your organization can go without making changes. That is the outer edge. You have no reason to discuss going beyond that in duration. For example, if your organization struggles to go a week without needing changes, don't even entertain the idea of a two-week sprint. You won't be able to maintain the integrity of the stability of the sprint, and stability is a huge driver of performance in scrum. Instead, discuss how much shorter you can make the sprint.

REMEMBER

According to *The Scrum Guide* (2020 version), sprints are "fixed length events of one month or less to create consistency."

Also, sprint lengths don't change after they begin and ideally don't change throughout development unless they're being made shorter. If a scrum team changes sprint length, it comes at a significant cost: Their earlier velocity is no longer relevant. Performance is not a straight mathematical line that can be sliced, diced, and reassembled. Just because a scrum team splits their sprint from one to two weeks doesn't mean they will automatically accomplish half their historical two-week velocity.

Shorter sprints decrease the amount of time between feedback received from stakeholders, enabling scrum teams to inspect and adapt earlier and more often:

>> With one-month sprints, you have 12 opportunities to inspect and adapt per year.

>> With two-week sprints, you have 26 opportunities per year.

>> With one-week sprints, you have 52 opportunities per year.

Longer sprints have a diminishing return because less of a sense of urgency exists due to the multiple days still available to the team. Weekends and longer sprint meetings can also have a negative effect on efficiency.

The capacity of developers during a one-week sprint may be higher or lower than half the historical two-week velocity. You don't have any idea until you run a few sprints, and you don't know for sure until you run a lot of sprints.

WARNING

While the cost of changing sprint lengths throughout development is significant, the cost of changing a sprint goal during a sprint is worse. If a sprint goal becomes irrelevant (for example, changes in company direction or changes in the market) before the end of a sprint, a product owner may decide to cancel the sprint and plan a new sprint to reflect the right priority. But be aware that canceling wastes valuable time and is quite traumatic for the scrum team and the organization. Also, the shorter the feedback loop (that is, the length of the sprint), the less likely a product owner would be to cancel a sprint.

CUMULATIVE FLOW DIAGRAMS

Cumulative flow diagrams (CFDs) provide scrum teams visibility into the patterns of their output and help them identify possible bottlenecks in their processes.

A burnup chart, shown on the left side of the figure, is a type of CFD that shows the number of requirements the team completed within a set duration of time. CFDs, shown on the right side of the figure, give a snapshot of how much work is in any given stage of the process, exposing indicators such as lead, cycle, work, and wait times and identifying points of inefficiency.

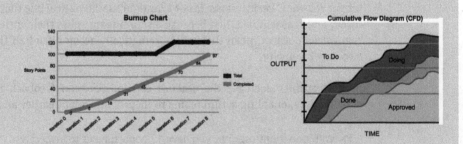

Changing sprint lengths during development makes performance indicators inconsistent over time. In addition to the loss of relevancy of the historical velocity with changing sprint lengths, CFD indicators such as lead, cycle, work, and wait times also become irrelevant.

TECHNICAL STUFF

One thing we know from science is that you can't turn off your mind. It's always working. If you can give your developers a small number of problems to solve and tell them that they'll face those problems tomorrow, they'll think about them consciously at work. Whether they want to or not, they'll also think about them unconsciously when they're away from work. This is the reason why the stability of sprints is so important. After a sprint starts, the developers must have confidence that the scope is stable so that their minds can be fully focused on what needs to be done for this sprint, whether they're at work or away from it. Have you ever had an epiphany while brushing your teeth? That's the dynamic we're talking about here. But you need two elements: a limited number of problems and confidence that you'll face those problems tomorrow. If a developer works on Product A, Product C, and Product Who-Knows-What every day, this won't happen. A developer will mentally engage only when he gets to the office and discovers what's ahead of him in reality. One reason why agile development efforts are so innovative is that they have this stability and, thus, more of the developer's mind share.

TIP

With our clients, we've found that the one-week sprint length beginning on Monday and ending on Friday is a nice rhythm. It gives the team clear time off, avoids weekend cheating to get more work done than is within the team's capacity, yet is long enough for real progress to be made every week. This shorter feedback cycle also allows scrum teams to inspect and adapt more frequently. For these reasons, scrum teams should always be looking for ways to responsibly shorten their sprint length.

The key is to run sprints that enable your developers to realistically create tangible, tested, and approved product increments every single sprint. After each sprint, you will have something real to show to stakeholders.

TAKING A QUEUE FROM MATHEMATICS

Queuing theory is the mathematical study of waiting in lines. Studies have found that when customers are waiting in a restaurant for a table, they'll wait twice as long if they are given something satisfying at the start. For example, if they're asked to sit at the bar and offered the ability to order a drink or even given a tasty sample, they'll stick around longer and wait for that busy table to be cleared.

The same principle is working for you in scrum. At the end of each sprint, you have something working and tangible to place in the hands of stakeholders. This "early and often" concept is a known technique for raising customer satisfaction.

Following the sprint life cycle

Each sprint has the same process: sprint planning, daily scrums, a sprint review, and a sprint retrospective. Sprints are developmental cycles that repeat until your desired product outcomes are achieved. Requirements (often in the form of user stories) are developed, tested, integrated, and approved within each sprint. The process continues sprint after sprint. Figure 5-5 depicts a one-week sprint life cycle.

SPRINT PLANNING

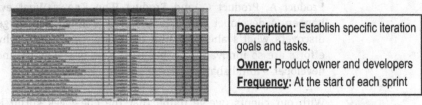

FIGURE 5-5:
The one-week sprint life cycle.

Description: Establish specific iteration goals and tasks.
Owner: Product owner and developers
Frequency: At the start of each sprint

TIP

When scrum teams are distributed offshore with team members in faraway time zones (such as the United States and India), arrangements need to be made for all team members to attend each of the sprint meetings. To account for time-zone differences, the domestic team members might join the meeting Sunday night while it's Monday morning for the offshore team members. At the end of the sprint, the domestic team members finish the sprint Friday morning and take the rest of the day off while the offshore team joins the sprint review and retrospective Friday night. Rotating each sprint might be appreciated on each end so that each team member doesn't always have to work on Sunday nights or Friday nights.

The key is that the scrum team learns new things after each sprint. Change happens; it's inevitable. Responding and adapting to it should be considered progress, not failure.

Change is easy in scrum because at the end of every cycle, what was created was done to completion. When you go into your next sprint and work on items from the product backlog, it doesn't matter whether those items have been on the product backlog for four months, four weeks, or four minutes. Old or new, each product backlog item is not prioritized by the order in which it was received; instead, it is prioritized by the order in which it will deliver the highest value to the customer.

TIP

In our experience, the Monday-to-Friday work week is a natural, biorhythmic time frame. Teams need a weekend break, which fits naturally with life patterns.

DON'T GO CHASING WATERFALLS

Scrum is different from the traditional waterfall method, in which all items are in a package and that package is matured. So, if changes come in halfway through development, the impact of those changes is nebulous and woven across multiple requirements. This unknown impact is what made *change* a dirty word in waterfall.

Some who are new to scrum and hold on to waterfall ways may mistakenly view a sprint as simply a smaller timebox than before for completing tasks, which are part of an overall upfront plan:

- They set multiple sprints upfront at the beginning of their work and identify the exact requirements and tasks that will be done during each sprint.

- They spread waterfall phases across sprints. (Requirements are gathered in the first sprint; all the requirements are designed in the second sprint; the requirements are developed in the third sprint; the developed requirements are tested in the fourth sprint; and so on.)

- They hold very brief sprint reviews as status reports about the product backlog rather than product increment demonstrations.

- They hold brief sprint planning meetings to confirm the original plan.

The increased frequency of review of the original plan seems nice to a team new to agile thinking but completely misses the point and falls short. This is still waterfall.

The sprint life cycle allows for the easy incorporation and adaptation of change based on reality. This is empiricism.

Planning Your Sprints

Sprint planning is the fourth element in the roadmap to value. All the work to be accomplished during that specific sprint is planned here. Each sprint planning session is timeboxed to no more than eight hours for a one-month sprint. Shorter sprints require shorter sprint planning meetings. For example, if you have a one-week sprint timebox, you have a maximum of two hours to plan your sprint.

Sprint goals

A goal is created for each sprint. The product owner initiates the goal discussion, identifying the business value objective that needs to be met. After the team is clear on the goal, the product owner and the team choose the requirements from the product backlog that best support the goal. As with the release goal, the sprint goal drives the requirements developed, not the other way around.

The sprint goal itself must support the release goal, which supports the product goal. This goal decomposition and alignment are essential for ensuring that you're doing purpose-driven development.

The developers are critical in creating the sprint goal. Because they're the ones doing the actual work (while the product owner establishes the direction or "the what"), the developers establish "the how" and "how much."

If your team has an established average velocity, it may be used as input for determining the amount of work they will take on during the sprint.

The team can also use velocity for stretching, testing its limits, or backing off if they're struggling to achieve the goals set. If they've been achieving 34 story points comfortably, they might push it to 38 or 40. If they've been struggling to achieve 25, they might lower it to 23 while the scrum team figures out organizational drag that can be removed.

Three topics are covered during the sprint planning meeting at the beginning of the sprint:

>> Topic one is where the product owner — with input from the developers and facilitated by the scrum master — determines why the sprint is valuable and establishes the sprint goal.

>> Next, topic two is to identify what can be done to accomplish the sprint goal — selecting product backlog items that enable the sprint goal.

>> Lastly, in topic three, the developers determine how the chosen work will get done to achieve the sprint goal by decomposing the backlog items into supporting tasks, such as the sprint goal, product backlog items selected for the sprint, and creating the sprint backlog.

WARNING

The sprint planning meeting may not always go smoothly, especially at first. You may slip down rabbit holes, discover tangents, and unearth different estimations of what's possible. This is where a strong and deft facilitator is needed in the form of the scrum master. It's their job to ensure the session stays on track and the heat stays on low.

Topic one

At the start of topic one, the sprint goal is created, and the developers must fully understand it because it will provide the boundaries and direction for the work they will do throughout the sprint. The product owner begins by proposing how the product could increase its value and utility in the current sprint. Then, the whole scrum team collaborates to define a sprint goal that communicates why the sprint is valuable to stakeholders. The sprint goal is finalized before the end of sprint planning.

Many different formats are available for communicating the sprint goal, but our preference is to begin the goal with the phrase "Demonstrate the ability to. . . ." We've found that stating the goal in terms that can be usable at the sprint review ensures the team will develop something that works. It helps the team accomplish the desired outcomes by the end of the sprint.

Radiating this sprint goal for the entire product team after sprint planning helps keep everyone's expectations aligned.

Topic two

The product owner and developers then select a portion of the product backlog that supports the goal. This won't necessarily be the final sprint backlog, but the forecasted functionality would satisfy the sprint goal if it's finished in the sprint. It's what the developers will work from to achieve the sprint goal and determine the sprint backlog of tasks in topic three.

Topic two gives the developers and product owner another opportunity to clarify existing requirements or identify new ones needed to achieve the sprint goal. This would also be the time to give the final size estimation on any clarified requirements and size any new requirements for the sprint. Remember this yardstick: If any requirements are sized higher than an 8, they're too big for a sprint (see Chapter 4).

TIP

We like to bring six to ten product backlog items into each sprint. This is usually the right balance of delivering a product increment with substantial functionality and a litmus test for whether each item is sufficiently broken down.

WARNING

The only requirements discussed in sprint planning should be those estimated between 1 and 8 on the Fibonacci scale. This isn't a scrum rule, but it aligns with our affinity estimating model (see Chapter 4). It has been an effective way for many teams to stay focused on properly refined requirements that can be completed within a sprint. For more on Fibonacci numbers, see Chapter 4.

Topic three

When the scrum team has determined the goal and the supporting requirements, the developers break down those requirements into individual tasks — how they will turn product backlog items into the working product increment. The tasks for each requirement should explicitly satisfy the team's definition of *done*. For instance, if the definition of *done* includes integration with product A, at least one task for the requirement should be "integration test with product A."

TIP

Ideally, each task should be able to be completed in one day. This gives the developers a tangible, realistic time target as they break requirements down into tasks. It also sets a benchmark for alerting the team to any development problems. If a task takes multiple days to develop, an issue might need to be addressed with the task or the developer.

Developers may choose to estimate the tasks for each requirement in hours if the organization wants that level of visibility. But many teams simply use velocity and complete/not complete product backlog items to visualize sprint progress adequately.

The developers are forced to be the most detailed here, which helps to sharpen the mind. They can really dig down and look at what needs to be done.

By the end of sprint planning, the developers should be clear on how the chosen sprint backlog items support the sprint goal and how the work will be done to complete those backlog items. This does not mean all (or any) of the tasks on the sprint backlog will be assigned now. Rather, each day the developers self-organize by having each developer pull a task and work on it to completion. (You find more on pull versus push in "Working the sprint backlog" later in this chapter.)

Your Sprint Backlog

The sprint backlog is created in the sprint planning session and includes the sprint goal, the ordered list of backlog items selected for the sprint, plus the plan or tasks necessary to achieve the sprint goal.

A sprint backlog might contain the following information:

>> The sprint goal and dates

>> A prioritized list of the requirements (for example, user stories) to be developed in the sprint

>> The estimated effort (that is, story points) required to develop each requirement

>> The tasks required to develop each requirement

>> The hours estimated to complete each task (if needed)

>> A burndown chart to show the status of the work developed in the sprint

The burndown chart benefit

Burndown charts are ways to represent progress achieved within the sprint visually. They depict the amount of work accomplished versus the amount left to go. Figure 5-6 shows an example:

>> The vertical axis represents the work left to be done.

>> The horizontal axis depicts the time still available in the sprint.

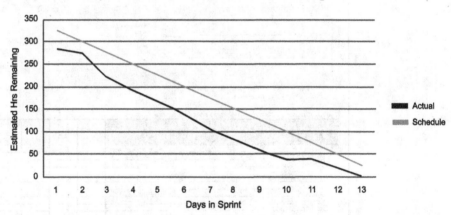

FIGURE 5-6:
Sprint
burndown chart.

Your sprints will show a diagonal trend line from the top-left corner to the bottom-right corner, representing what an even and consistent burn would look like, though you won't have a perfectly even burndown.

Also, some burndown charts have a line showing the outstanding story points. This allows you to quickly and easily see the status of your sprint from both time and outstanding business risk. The story-point line is a good indicator of whether a plummeting remaining capacity or time is appropriate.

If the story-point line is flat, but the team's remaining capacity is dropping, perhaps a team member is cherry-picking tasks across multiple user stories, or developers are completing tasks, but the product owner is not giving timely approval/rejection of user stories. The lines are helpful indicators for evaluating the team's health, product, and progress toward accomplishing their goal.

TIP

You can create your own burndown chart with Microsoft Excel or download the one included within the sprint backlog template, which you can download for free from this page: https://platinumedge.com/blog/anatomy-sprint-backlog.

The burndown chart is generated from the sprint backlog. The sprint backlog should be updated daily; only the developers can do this. At the end of each day, each developer updates their task (whether on a 3x5 card, a spreadsheet, or in an electronic tool) by entering the number of *remaining* hours (*not* the number of completed hours) left to complete the task. That's it. One number. It takes seconds, and the results are invaluable. See Figure 5-7 for a sample sprint backlog.

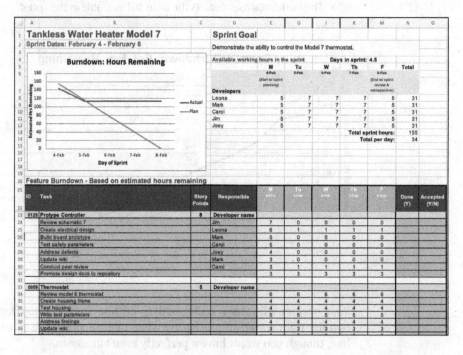

FIGURE 5-7:
A sprint backlog is a key scrum artifact.

The sprint burndown chart is an information radiator that shows anyone who wants to know the status of the sprint. Burndown charts are generated automatically as developers update the amount of time left on their one active task at the end of each day.

The burndown chart shows the amount of time remaining for the sum of all the requirements on the sprint backlog. Compared with the trend line, it provides a daily level of status detail for a scrum team that you can't get with traditional project management techniques.

Setting backlog capacity

How much capacity is in a day? If you're looking at the number of hours a developer can devote per day to their main job — developing! — allow for less than eight hours. Every organization has a certain amount of overhead. We find that for most organizations, somewhere between five and seven hours is a normal effective workday.

An average of 16 hours per week are wasted on unclear objectives, poor team communication, and ineffective meetings.

How much capacity is really in a sprint? In a one-week sprint, scrum teams will spend up to two hours in sprint planning, up to one hour in sprint review, and up to 45 minutes in a sprint retrospective. That's about four hours in sprint meetings. (Do you have to use all four hours? No. Can you go over the limit for any given meeting? No.)

That accounts for four of the five scrum events (assume that a maximum 15-minute daily scrum won't affect development time), but don't forget product backlog refinement. We find that developers will, on average, spend 10 percent of their time each sprint in product backlog refinement activities. This translates to about three to four hours in a one-week sprint.

Often, we find that teams don't need the full recommended timebox for shorter sprints, but for longer sprints (such as three or four weeks), we find they often will max out the timebox and very likely need even more. As with all things agile, barely sufficient applies even to team meetings.

Is there any buffer in scrum? Sure. We call it *slack*. Consider that the developers have 165 hours available to them for a sprint. They shouldn't take on 164 hours under the false assumption that everything will go exactly according to plan. The slack varies from team to team, but you should make it transparent.

So, the capacity for one developer for a one-week sprint would be 18 to 27 hours, depending on the organization's established effective workday. Take this into consideration when identifying the developers' capacity during sprint planning. This is assuming no paid holidays, vacations, or other time off is planned that will keep developers from developing.

Who said scrum is the Wild West? You can't get much more disciplined than this.

What an incredible impact having a dedicated and effective scrum master means to a scrum team's capacity. By removing the organizational drag (impediments) that keep effective workdays from increasing from five to seven hours, the impact can add up to an additional nine work hours in a one-week sprint per developer. For a team of seven, that's a potential 63-hour efficiency increase. Scrum masters add value.

What happens if, at the end of sprint planning, the developers find that the number of estimated hours for their tasks from the sprint backlog is more than their capacity? Do they hunker down and work overtime? No, the product owner has an early decision to make: Which sprint backlog items will be moved back to the product backlog to get the number of hours below the team's capacity? Sustained overtime leads to poor team morale, poorer quality, and long-term productivity losses.

TECHNICAL STUFF

The value of an iterative planning process is easily visible within sprint planning. By the time the work to be done is outlined and broken down to the task level, you will have done so in a way that minimizes time waste and maximizes business value and ROI (return on investment). This is because the roadmap to value, from the product goal all the way down to the sprint level, has enabled continuous prioritization and progressive elaboration of only the most important product backlog items.

Working the sprint backlog

We see developers get distracted and go off target by making some common mistakes. Follow these practices to counter those mistakes when working with the sprint backlog:

>> Make sure that requirements are broken down into tasks that accurately and completely reflect your definition of *done* (see Chapter 4).

The product owner should not accept a requirement until it completely satisfies the acceptance criteria and sprint definition of *done*.

>> Ideally, all the developers work on only one requirement at a time and complete that requirement before starting another. This is called *swarming*. Swarming can be accomplished by such activities as

- Each team member working on individual tasks related to the same requirement

- Pairing two people on one task to ensure quality

- Team members shadowing each other to increase cross-functionality

>> As developers swarm around one requirement at a time, this ensures cross-functionality, and every sprint will have something tangible accomplished at its end.

>> Each requirement must be fully developed, tested, integrated, and accepted by the product owner before the team moves on to the next requirement.

>> Don't assign multiple tasks to individual team members.

Each day, the team coordinates priorities and decides who will do what. A developer should only work on one task at a time until that task is completely done. This is called a *pull mechanism*. Don't fall back into the traditional method of a manager assigning tasks to team members.

TIP

Swarming on requirements stems from the lean concept of work in progress (WIP) limits. When a team has a lot of work in progress, it delays taking the actions necessary to finalize that work and rear-loads issue correction. Your WIP limit should ideally be only one requirement at a time for the team and only one task at a time per developer. The developers usually find that their tasks get completed sooner than if they had started them all simultaneously. Having only one requirement open at a time is also an effective way of exposing process bottlenecks, which can then be addressed and fixed for faster throughput.

PUSH VERSUS PULL

Traditional project management follows the push model of assigning tasks to individuals when they're identified. Each individual manages and focuses solely on the tasks in their personal queue. This queue builds up over time, and attempts are made to redistribute task load across team members to avoid over- or underloading. The trouble with push systems is that it's difficult to know the status of things unless everything is either unstarted or complete. This also tends to contribute to team members operating as silos rather than cross-functional teams.

Pull models, like scrum, maintain all work in a common queue, and items are pulled from the top by individual developers (which assumes proper ordering and prioritization during sprint planning). You don't need the redistribution of task load, and it provides a natural pause for developers to evaluate where they can help others on open tasks before pulling a new one. Under a pull model, developers are also more likely to work on tasks much closer, if not exactly, to the original order of priority than they would in a push system. Bottlenecks are less common, and overall workflow is more predictable.

(continued)

(continued)

Push systems encourage individual-centered (silo) goals. Pull systems support collaboration for the sake of achieving product-centered goals.

For example, at the grocery store, you can choose between a push and pull option when you go to check out:

- The push option is chosen by going through a checkout line with a dedicated clerk for that line. The line is "assigned" to you because you chose it, and you're standing in it. You're stuck with it unless another line empties, and you get to it before someone else does.

- You can choose the pull system and increase your chances of getting through as quickly as possible. Do this by selecting the self-checkout option, where four to six individual checkout stations are ready for whoever is next in line. Rather than being committed to a single checkout line for the remainder of the checkout experience, you'll be able to take advantage of the next open self-checkout station as soon as it's available.

Prioritizing sprints

Each sprint has its own life cycle, as shown in Figure 5-5 earlier in this chapter. Within each sprint, each requirement has its own prioritization and life cycle, too. Each requirement and task is developed, tested, integrated, and approved before the team moves on to the next-highest-priority item. See Figure 5-8 for a representation.

The sprint backlog items are prioritized from highest to lowest and developed in that order. The developers work on only one requirement at a time. When that requirement is finished, the team moves on to the next-highest-priority one rather than picking one lower on the list that might be easier or more interesting.

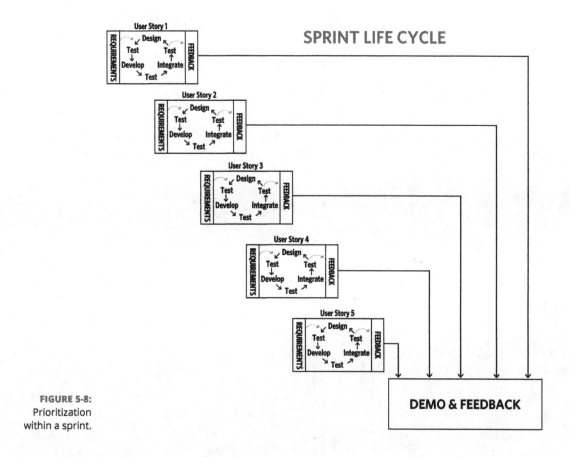

SPRINT LIFE CYCLE

FIGURE 5-8:
Prioritization
within a sprint.

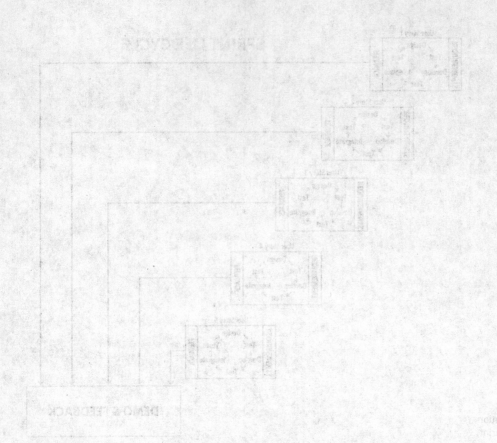

Chapter **6**

Getting the Most Out of Sprints

Sprints are the essence of scrum, so it's worth spending an entire chapter on them. You have the gist already: Sprints are fixed-length timeboxes designed so that your developers can create a development rhythm. They also nurture the inspect-and-adapt premise.

But that's not all that sprints do. In this chapter, we introduce the daily scrum — an invaluable 15 minutes every day that will focus and organize your short-term goals like never before. Facilitated by the scrum master, the daily scrum keeps your product development on track as the scrum team deals with impediments and coordinates the day's priorities.

This chapter also exposes you to the sprint review and sprint retrospective. These two meetings take the concepts of inspection and adaptation to new levels. Stake-holders review the product developed and give the product owner immediate feedback; the scrum team assesses how the sprint went and incorporates any improvements into the process.

The Daily Scrum

The daily scrum is one of the five scrum events on the roadmap to value (see Figure 6-1).

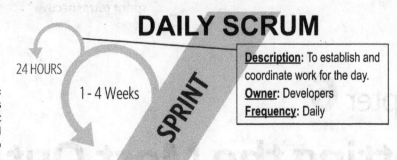

FIGURE 6-1:
The daily scrum is an integral aspect of the sprint and the roadmap to value.

REMEMBER

Planning is huge in scrum. You don't set a goal, forget it, and then gather six months later to see what happened. You inspect and adapt every single day — and even throughout the day.

Because developers swarm daily to attack a single requirement, coordination is key. Removing impediments is also crucial for developers who work closely together to deliver potentially releasable increments within short periods. The daily scrum is how they coordinate.

REMEMBER

If you manage your product development by weeks (that is, with weekly project manager status reports that may not get reviewed promptly), you slip by weeks. In scrum, you may still slip but only by a day, because scrum teams manage by day through the sprint backlog using direct interaction in the daily scrum. We look more closely at this comparison in Chapter 7.

Defining the daily scrum

As its name implies, a daily scrum takes place daily during each sprint. The time-box is 15 minutes maximum, no matter the sprint's overall length. Meetings in scrum, like artifacts, are barely sufficient. Anything longer than 15 minutes would eat into valuable development time. Besides, 15 minutes is plenty of time to accomplish everything necessary.

The purpose of the daily scrum is to inspect progress toward the sprint goal and adapt the sprint backlog as necessary, adjusting the upcoming planned work. The team coordinates the day's sprint activities and identifies impediments keeping the developers from accomplishing their sprint goals. Every developer participates, so everyone is dialed into what the entire team is working on. If an impediment comes up during the daily scrum, it's dealt with following the daily scrum. The event is a coordination meeting, not a problem- or complaint-solving meeting.

REMEMBER

The scrum master is causing the removal of impediments by facilitating the conversation about them and coaching the team, so they reflect and find a way to improve the area. Some impediments may need to be removed by the product owner or require discussion between a team member and someone outside the team.

Participants in the daily scrum are the developers. The scrum master ensures that the meeting takes place and stays within the timebox, and the developers direct the meeting. The product owner may attend and provide clarifications on prioritization as needed, and anyone else who's involved and interested can listen in but don't say anything. This way, they can enjoy the daily transparency and be involved in the daily process, but they can't hinder or derail it.

We often like to have scrum masters participate beyond facilitation by addressing the impediments identified and/or in progress.

REMEMBER

The daily scrum is how developers self-organize and self-manage. Each day, the team decides who will do what and who will help whom. Nobody dictates work from the outside, such as a project manager or another nondeveloper.

If a daily scrum starts to feel like a status-report meeting or developers start addressing one person (such as an informal team lead, the scrum master, or the product owner), the meeting has missed the point. A daily scrum should be a peer-to-peer meeting.

The key takeaway from a daily scrum is clarity about what it means to be successful that day. Then the team swarms if necessary to do the highest-priority work. The team finds value in this event only if team members achieve relevant clarity and purpose about the day's goals. Daily scrums offer an opportunity to inspect and adapt in the moment.

REMEMBER

A common misconception about the daily scrum is that it's a time for the developers to report to the product owner or a time for product owners to introduce new requirements or update a sprint goal. Don't let the daily scrum become a business-status-reporting meeting; it's a coordination meeting to enable high performance.

Scheduling a daily scrum

Because a daily scrum lasts only 15 minutes, everyone needs to be on time and ready. To reduce the complexity, the daily scrum is held at the same time and place every working day of the sprint. You'll find a direct correlation between how late a meeting starts and how loose the focus is after the meeting starts.

Many teams find starting their daily scrum a half an hour after the normal work-day begins to be ideal. This schedule gives your team time to get coffee, answer emails, discuss the previous evening's antics, and cover anything else in their morning rituals.

A key disruptor of the daily scrum is distraction. Encourage team members to prioritize the daily scrum over text dings, emails, phone calls, and even unexpected Amazon deliveries.

Conducting a daily scrum

Imagine a scrum team gathering around its physical or virtual sprint backlog or task board at the beginning of the day. Each person can see at a glance the progress made the day before; then each person proactively chooses a new task for the current day. Team members coordinate where help is needed to accomplish a task before the day ends; then, they go straight to work.

As we discussed in Chapter 5, tasks should be broken down so they can be accomplished in a day or less. Even then, when developers are left to themselves for days on end without coordinating and swarming as a team, they can get bogged down in unnecessary details or problems that could be easily resolved with help.

Daily scrums synchronize a team, and everyone goes to work helping each other do what it takes to get to *done*. Together they completely own the outcome. Come the next day, the team members are excited as they inspect their progress.

The daily scrum is not the only time developers adjust their plan. Anytime they see a need, they can address it to keep the work moving forward.

Daily scrums improve communications, identify impediments, promote quick decision-making, and consequently, reduce the need for other meetings.

Making daily scrums more effective

The following tactics can keep your daily scrum meetings quick and effective:

>> Diligently start on time. See "Scheduling a daily scrum," earlier in this chapter.

>> Conduct the meeting standing up. Studies have shown meetings conducted standing up are 34 percent shorter than those conducted sitting down. No one has a chance to slump in a chair and relax; it's as though everyone is already on the move, even if they're remote.

>> Focus the meeting on coordination, not problem-solving. Impediments get removed after the daily scrum.

TIP

When impediments are uncovered in the daily scrum, the scrum master can deal with them by hosting an after-party immediately following the daily scrum. This involves only those who need to be involved and is for addressing any issues that came up during the daily scrum. A backlog of these "team topics" can also be kept so the team can address them when appropriate, such as during the after-party or the team retrospective. Not all topics raised during the daily scrum need to be addressed that day.

>> The scrum master can be a helpful meeting facilitator, especially for newer teams. As necessary, the scrum master also keeps the meeting on time and makes sure only the scrum team participates. The scrum master's touch should be as light as possible.

>> Cover only immediate issues and priorities relating to that day and that support the sprint goal.

>> Gather around the task board — even if you're meeting virtually — to ensure the context and focus. Virtual participants will appreciate using multiple monitors so they can see their team members and the team's task board.

>> Don't assign a set speaking order because when people know the order, they tend to check out until it's their turn. Sometimes, they don't even show up until just before their turn.

TIP

During in-person daily scrums, we toss a squeaky dog toy to a random developer when that person should speak. If anyone takes too long, we switch to a timer ball with an alarm. An alternative is tossing out a five-pound ream of paper and allowing the person to talk for as long as they can hold the paper out to their side. These tactics keep the daily scrum fast, forward-moving, and fun.

>> Don't allow vague statements or rely on team members' memories of what's in the sprint backlog. (See the next section, "Team Task Board.")

TIP

The latest *Scrum Guide* states: "The Developers can select whatever structure and techniques they want, as long as their daily scrum focuses on progress toward the Sprint Goal and produces an actionable plan for the next day of work." Some teams have found this can best be done using three statements addressed by each developer, such as, "Today I plan to. . . ," and "I'm stuck and need help on. . . ."

At Platinum Edge, we also encourage our clients to include "I'm feeling . . . about where we're at today" to take a pulse of the team's morale. Happy teams build better products faster.

Team Task Board

A physical or virtual *task board* is one way to display the sprint backlog. Although it's common for scrum teams to manage their sprint backlog in digital format, it can also be done using a wall or whiteboard space, 3x5 cards, sticky notes, and tape. Digital tools that simulate a physical wall or whiteboard space and virtual sticky notes are ideal for remote teams. Figure 6-2 shows a sample task board.

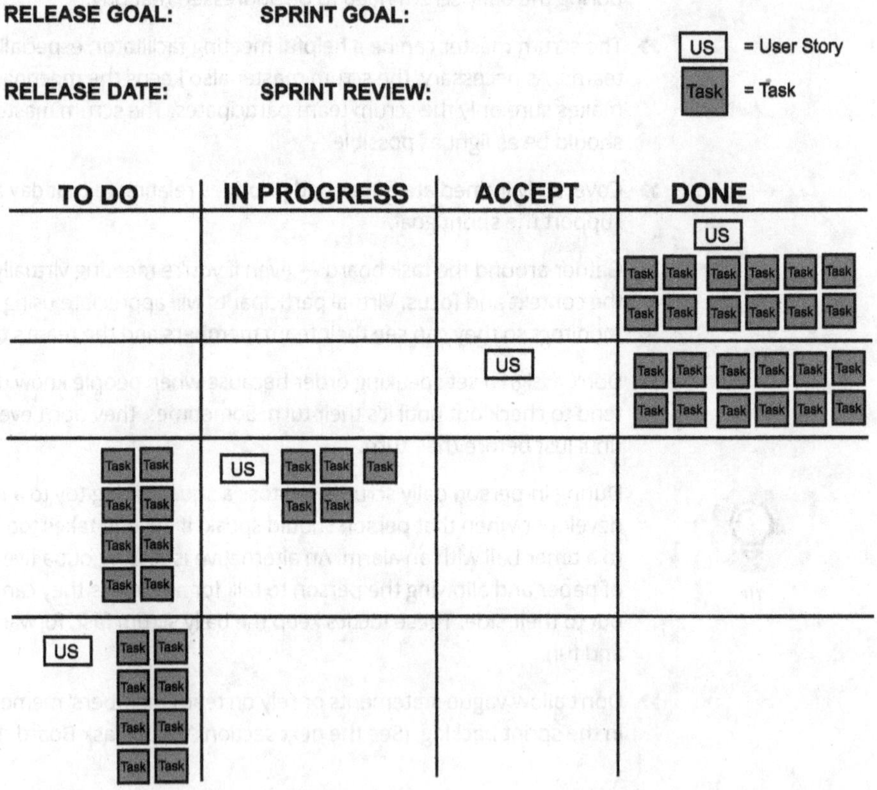

RELEASE GOAL: **SPRINT GOAL:**

                                                                    US = User Story

RELEASE DATE: **SPRINT REVIEW:**

                                                                    Task = Task

TO DO	IN PROGRESS	ACCEPT	DONE
			US
			Task Task Task Task Task Task
			Task Task Task Task Task Task
		US	
			Task Task Task Task Task Task
			Task Task Task Task Task Task
Task Task	US Task Task Task		
Task Task	Task Task		
Task Task			
Task Task			
US Task Task			
Task Task			
Task Task			
Task Task			

FIGURE 6-2:
A team
task board.

Like the product roadmap, the task board increases engagement and flexibility because it's tangible.

A task board is excellent because it's a quick, effective way to show the status of an entire sprint. Keeping the task board within sight of the entire product team ensures that everyone instantly knows what's done, what's not done, and everything in between.

Use these basic elements:

- **»** Top
  - The specific sprint goal
  - The overall release goal

  Release and sprint review dates can also be included.

- **»** Columns (from left to right)
  - *To Do:* Requirements and tasks in the sprint that have yet to be developed

    Developers pull from the top of this list to start a new task. If two developers want to take the same task, they can pair up on it, one developer can shadow the other, or they can decide who can best handle it.

  - *In-Progress:* The product backlog items and tasks that the developers are working on

    Different colors or stickers can be used for each task to designate ownership or identify tasks blocked by an impediment. If used, work-in-progress limits should be displayed in this column. After developers complete a task, they look here to see who they can help. Otherwise, they pull the next task from the To Do column and verify with the team that it's the right task to work on.

  - *Accept:* Requirements that are awaiting acceptance by the product owner

    If the requirement is rejected — and enough time is left in the sprint — it goes back to the In-Progress column. Otherwise, the requirement gets moved back to the product backlog for consideration in a future sprint. (See "Handling unfinished requirements" later in this chapter.)

  - *Done*: The requirements that the product owner has accepted as complete

Only the developers can move the tasks from To Do to In-Progress to Done, and only the product owner can move the requirement from Accept to Done. If a requirement gets rejected by the product owner, the developers create new tasks to address why the requirement was rejected.

THE KANBAN BOARD

Kanban is Japanese for *signboard, billboard, signal card,* or *card you can see.* In the 1950s, Toyota formalized this concept to standardize the flow of inventory parts in its production lines. In essence, kanban boards contain cards that represent single pieces of work. Each card acts as a status signal and indicates when new work can be pulled in.

This practice helped inspire lean thinking and manufacturing practices, and many scrum teams today use something like a kanban board system. Task boards function much like kanban boards, providing a visual status (signal) of exactly where each task (piece of work) is in the overall process. This level of visibility makes it easier for developers to be disciplined and swarm on requirements to get it to the Done column.

REMEMBER

Requirements in the Accept column shouldn't be allowed to pile up. Ideally, when a requirement card is placed in the Accept column, it should either be placed in the Done or Rejected columns for further development the same day. If a delay occurs, the product owner needs to be coached not to let stories accumulate as they wait to be accepted. You have no reason for delay if the product owner is a dedicated team member who is available at any time for clarification, the requirements have been detailed to a single action or integration, and the requirements have passed the definition of *done.* It's critical for the developers to know when their work is done and can swarm the next requirement.

Swarming

In Chapter 5, we introduced the concept of swarming in the context of the sprint backlog. *Swarming* means all developers work on only one requirement simultaneously during the sprint. Although this principle isn't specific to scrum, it's such an effective way for teams to execute their sprint backlog that it warrants discussion here.

One of the main benefits of scrum is that developers start and finish requirements to satisfy their definition of *done* to produce a potentially releasable product increment within a relatively short timebox. The team revises the process based on lessons learned and repeats that cycle again and again. The goal is to finish — not just start — as many requirements as possible.

Swarming enables teams to enjoy the following benefits:

>> Maximizing chances for success, with the skills and abilities of the entire team focused on a single requirement

- ❯❯ Completing the cycle of planning, designing, developing, and testing to completion for each requirement

- ❯❯ Resolving issues and impediments today

- ❯❯ Dramatically decreasing the introduction of defects into a product through pairing and single-tasking (versus multitasking)

- ❯❯ Eliminating single points of failure in knowledge, processes, and skill sets

- ❯❯ Finishing the most important requirements completely and first

- ❯❯ Single processing of requirements is statistically proven faster than batch processing.

When team members see all their fellow developers working on a task — and there are no other tasks left for the same requirement (the user story) — it's perfectly natural for them to think starting a new requirement is more productive than helping other developers with the in-progress requirement. However, this tendency can get out of hand to the point where teams find themselves with multiple requirements started but none of them finished. Developers can avoid this risk by shadowing, pairing, researching, or helping in whatever way necessary to get the task to the Done column.

This process ensures that something gets completely developed in every sprint and is available to show to stakeholders. Every sprint produces shippable results. The developers' efforts are focused, teamwork is enhanced, and the iterative process of scrum is put into play.

TIP

Stay focused. Stop starting and start finishing.

Dealing with rejection

If the product owner rejects a requirement placed in the Accept column, the developers have two options:

- ❯❯ **Finish their current tasks and then swarm the rejected requirement:** This option might be better if plenty of time is left in the sprint to complete both the current tasks and the rejected requirement.

- ❯❯ **Abandon their current tasks to swarm the rejected requirement:** This option might be better if not enough time remains in the sprint to finish both the current tasks and the rejected requirement.

MULTITASKING AND THRASHING

Microsoft conducted a study entitled "Executive Control of Cognitive Processes in Task Switching" led by Joshua Rubinstein, David Meyer, and Jeffrey Evans on the effects of multitasking, showing that multitasking doesn't work. On average, it takes 15 minutes to get your brain back to the level before you answered that phone call or email. Studies have also shown that an interruption as short as 4.4 seconds triples the number of errors made on subsequent tasks that require sequencing. Developers who reduce multitasking get a sound head start on achieving the 30 to 40 percent increased product-to-market time we've seen so often.

Thrashing occurs when developers jump back and forth among products, requirements, or tasks, switching context in the process. Thrashing increases the time required to complete tasks by a minimum of 30 percent. If you don't have enough people to take on the workload that can be handled by dedicated, swarming developers, you definitely don't have time to thrash them.

The product owner decides the priority when faced with this decision. Variables other than time left in the sprint may influence the product owner's decision. As the team inspects its learning and adapts throughout a sprint, the rejected story may become less valuable to achieving the sprint goal than the next require-ment in progress. So, even though time is left in the sprint to do both, the risk of not finishing the in-progress requirement may be higher than the risk of not finishing the rejected requirement.

In any case, attention to priority and close daily coordination with the product owner throughout the sprint keep the entire scrum team focused and on task.

REMEMBER

Scrum teams should always push themselves. If developers accomplish 100 percent of their sprint backlog every time, they may not be stretching themselves. A high percentage of sprint backlog completion should be the goal, but you shouldn't expect scrum teams to hit 100 percent every time. Even if a low-priority item on the sprint backlog doesn't get completed, good scrum teams plan a sprint that can accomplish their sprint goal with the higher priority items. And good scrum masters, like aeronautical engineers, help the scrum team find ways to reduce drag to become more efficient. This is how scrum teams realize the continuous-improvement benefit of scrum.

Handling unfinished requirements

Even high-functioning developers who estimate well, swarm, and stick to a work-in-progress (WIP) limit of one item at a time throughout each sprint may end up with incomplete or unstarted requirements left on the sprint backlog at the end of a sprint. This result may be okay if team members swarmed the higher-priority requirements to completion and have working product increments that can be shipped.

But what does the team do with those remaining requirements?

If a requirement isn't started or was started and not completed, the product owner puts it back in the product backlog in its entirety (keeping all notes, tasks, and documentation intact, of course) and then reprioritizes it against the rest of the product backlog. Potentially, the product owner may pull the requirement into a future sprint according to its new priority.

Based on what was completed during the sprint, the unstarted or unfinished requirement may no longer be necessary or may not have as high a value as before. The work done in the sprint to achieve the sprint goal may be enough; the next sprint may focus on a different goal or feature.

Because it wasn't finished, any effort made on the requirement isn't included in the team's velocity for that sprint. If the requirement does make it into a future sprint, it needs to be refined, clarified, and reestimated based on the remaining work to be done. You can't bank or cache story points.

An exception may occur when, after working on an unfinished requirement, you find that you can split it. You finish one part of the requirement that is valuable and releasable during the sprint; the other part goes back into the product backlog to be reestimated and reprioritized.

The lesson here is that you should swarm to get to *done* during the sprint.

The Sprint Review

The sprint review is the next stop on our roadmap to value (see Figure 6-3). This scrum event is integral to the inspect-and-adapt nature of scrum and takes place at the end of each sprint.

The purpose of the sprint review is to inspect the outcome of the sprint and determine future adaptations. The product owner needs organizational feedback on whether the product is moving in the right direction. This review is also a great opportunity for the developers to stand up and show off their accomplishments.

This meeting at the end of every sprint is a working session, ensuring the stakeholders are up to date on what was accomplished in the sprint. This meeting is a forum for delivering feedback directly to the scrum team. Also, stakeholders have a working, releasable product increment in their hands. Progress toward the release and product goals are discussed, including the remaining budget.

SPRINT REVIEW

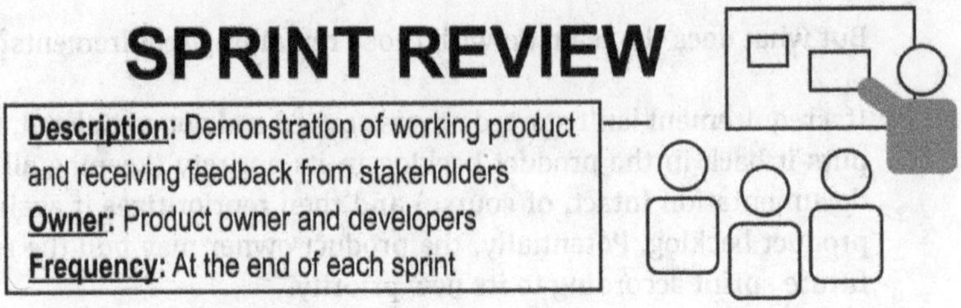

FIGURE 6-3:
The sprint review is a scrum event on the roadmap to value.

Description: Demonstration of working product and receiving feedback from stakeholders
Owner: Product owner and developers
Frequency: At the end of each sprint

The sprint review process

The sprint review, which is timeboxed to a maximum of four hours for a one-month sprint (shorter for shorter sprints), takes place at the end of the last day of the sprint. Therefore, allow for this time expenditure during the sprint-planning session.

The participants in the sprint review are the entire scrum team and the stakeholders in these roles:

>> **Scrum master:** Facilitates the meeting, ensuring it stays focused and on time.

>> **Product owner:** Briefly reviews the sprint goal and how well the scrum team met the goal, fills in the stakeholders on what items from the backlog have been completed, and summarizes what's left to go in the release, including the remaining budget or financial information. The product owner will also lead a collaborative discussion with all participants to determine what might be the next thing to work on.

REMEMBER

The sprint review isn't the time for the product owner to provide feedback to developers on the completed functionality; the product owner does that every day throughout the sprint. This event is for the scrum team to receive feedback from stakeholders on the direction in which they're taking the product.

>> **Developers:** Demonstrate and explain the completed requirements.

>> **Stakeholders:** Ask questions and provide feedback.

The process begins with the developers preparing for the review. Consider the following guidelines for sprint-review preparation:

>> The developers spend minimal time (probably no more than 20 minutes) preparing beforehand to showcase completed requirements.

>> No formal slides should be used in a sprint review. Rather, the developers should spend their time developing the product instead of preparing a presentation.

>> Only the requirements that have been deemed done (according to the definition of *done*) and approved by the product owner are demonstrated.

>> The developers showcase the shippable functionality of the requirement — that is, how it works in the real world.

WARNING

If you spend your time showing stakeholders what could or should have been done, you're giving a rigged demonstration and haven't done anyone any favors. Stakeholders never expect less; they always expect more. By making it look like your product increment works when it really doesn't, you increase your workload for the coming sprint because you'll have to make the work you showed (and the new work you plan for) actually work. Demonstrate only working, releasable product increments.

Stakeholder feedback

Critical to the success of the sprint review is stakeholder feedback. A constant communication cycle keeps the product development on track and produces what stakeholders want. Although stakeholders can't tell developers how to develop requirements, they can give feedback to the product owner about the requirements and features they want to be developed and how well the implementations serve customers' needs.

This feedback loop also serves another purpose: It keeps the developers involved and emotionally engaged in the work.

Feedback is a common theme throughout scrum. Figure 6-4 shows how many layers of feedback are involved in the scrum framework. Each time feedback is received, it gets cycled back into the product backlog and sprint-planning sessions — truly inspection and adaptation.

Product increments

The product increment is the third of the three scrum artifacts. (We discussed the product backlog in Chapter 3 and the sprint backlog in Chapter 5.)

FIGURE 6-4:
Multiple layers of
feedback exist in
a typical scrum
product
development
effort.

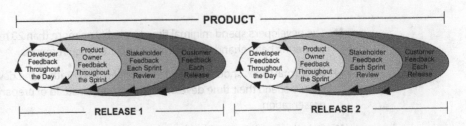

Within a single sprint, the product increment is a working product deemed *done* by the product owner and now potentially releasable. It's *potentially* releasable because the product owner may not decide the product is ready to release until later. But it's ready to release as soon as the product owner is ready.

A product increment has been

>> Elaborated

>> Designed

>> Developed

>> Tested

>> Integrated

>> Documented

>> Approved

During the sprint-review meeting, this product increment is demonstrated to stakeholders. The inspect-and-adapt sprint life cycle continues as feedback is taken and translated into requirements. Then these requirements may be enhanced during product-backlog refinement; they may rise in priority for consideration in future sprints and eventually become new product increments.

The sprint review is about improving the product. The sprint retrospective is how scrum teams can make this continuous improvement happen for their team and process.

The Sprint Retrospective

The sprint retrospective is the last scrum event in the sprint on the roadmap to value (see Figure 6-5). This scrum event takes place after every sprint.

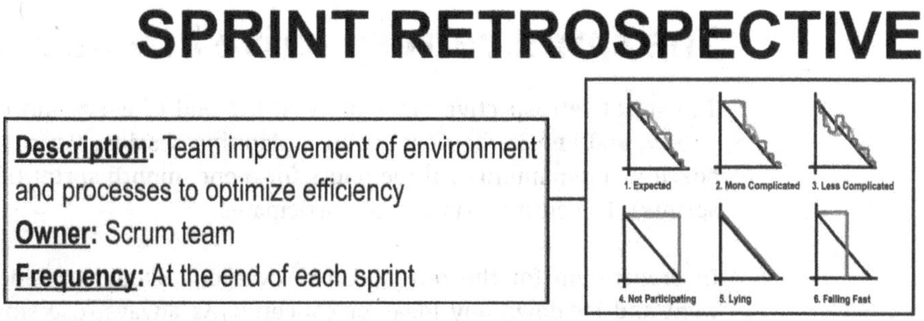

SPRINT RETROSPECTIVE

FIGURE 6-5:
The sprint retrospective — the final element on the roadmap to value.

Description: Team improvement of environment and processes to optimize efficiency
Owner: Scrum team
Frequency: At the end of each sprint

1. Expected   2. More Complicated   3. Less Complicated

4. Not Participating   5. Lying   6. Falling Fast

The sprint retrospective aims to review and improve the team's practices, environment, quality, and effectiveness. It's an opportunity for the scrum team — scrum master, product owner, and developers — to assess what went well in the unfinished sprint, the problems it encountered, and what can be improved. The process is inspection and adaptation — one more time — focusing on the people, interactions, processes, tools, and the definition of *done* used by the scrum team.

The outcome of the retrospective should be plans of action to continuously improve scrum, people, interactions, processes, and tools in every sprint. Although the scrum framework is simple — three accountabilities, three artifacts, and five events (see Chapter 1) — and doesn't require tweaking, each scrum team has quirks and nuances because of their product, organization, and development methods. Through the process of inspection and adaptation, you can aim those individualities toward the product goal.

Because the sprint retrospective asks for input and feedback from all scrum team members, it increases ownership through engagement and a sense of purpose. Team spirit is enhanced, which, in turn, leads to an increase in productivity and velocity — self-management.

REMEMBER

It's critical in sprint retrospectives to create a trusting environment. Each person's view is listened to and respected, and nothing is taken personally. Trust is the key to keeping the retrospective from being a labyrinth of euphemisms or politics. The scrum master plays a pivotal role in creating an environment of trust.

WARNING

The sprint retrospective may unveil problems within the team. An adept scrum master can facilitate the event to deal with these issues in an equitable, low-intensity environment. A sprint retrospective isn't for venting; it's for actionable improvement plans. Be on the lookout for passive-aggressive speech and personal agendas.

The sprint retrospective in a nutshell

The sprint retrospective takes place at the end of every sprint, after the sprint review, and before the next sprint's planning session. Retrospectives are time-boxed to a maximum of three hours for a one-month sprint (shorter for shorter sprints). The entire scrum team participates.

In preparation for the retrospective, everyone should consider how the sprint went and jot down any ideas or concerns. As always, use simple tools such as sticky notes; avoid formal presentations.

Although the scrum master may facilitate the meeting, everyone participates at a peer-to-peer level. The purpose of the sprint retrospective is to inspect the sprint that just ended to

>> Identify what went well in the sprint with the processes, tools, and team dynamics.

>> Discuss and discover opportunities for improvement.

>> Define an action plan for implementing the improvement(s).

Remember to emphasize and give equal air time to what went well during the retrospective. It's important to focus on the positive and identify what's working well so you can keep doing it. Rejoice as a team in successes. Especially during initial scrum implementation, it's important to recognize the wins — big and small.

TIP

The sandwich technique is an effective way to keep things positive and avoid isolating people during a retrospective. Start with positive, work through negative, and end with more positive.

A retrospective discussion is action-oriented and doesn't focus on justifications. When you hear the word *because*, that's a good indication the discussion has turned to a justification of why someone did something a certain way. Keep moving forward by saying something like, "This is what I experienced, and this is what might work better going forward." Don't say, "I did it this way because . . ."

REMEMBER

The sprint retrospective is an opportunity for the entire scrum team to improve continuously. So, it may not be best for the scrum master to always be the one doing the facilitating. Bringing in an experienced neutral third-party facilitator can benefit the entire scrum team (including the scrum master) to figure out ways to improve together as peers and equals.

Engaging sprint retrospectives

Esther Derby and Diana Larsen wrote an excellent book called *Agile Retrospectives: Making Good Teams Great* (published by Pragmatic Bookshelf). Check it out for more tips and techniques on sprint retrospectives and other agile practices.

In *Agile Retrospectives*, Derby and Larsen point out that there is more to finding out what went well and what improvements need to be made than simply asking the same three questions at the end of every sprint. Retrospective facilitation takes preparation and strategy to get maximum participation, candor, and useful data from team members. The Derby and Larsen model for structuring a retrospective consists of a playbook of engaging techniques to help answer these questions:

>> What do you think went well?

>> What would you like to change?

>> How should we implement that change?

To maximize retrospective effectiveness, we recommend the variety of techniques described by Derby and Larsen for each of the following aspects of a sprint retrospective:

1. **Set the stage.**

   You want to establish ground rules for productive communication and clarify expectations and purpose from the beginning. Prepare the team for open and honest discussion.

2. **Gather data.**

   Making decisions based on superficial, bad, or incomplete data can do more harm than good. You want to uncover important topics, jog memories, and correlate experiences that need to be addressed. You want to know what people think and how they feel about it.

3. **Generate insights.**

   Many teams gather data but do nothing with it. Just as the best designs come from self-organizing teams, the best insights come from teams that take the time to explore what the data means.

4. **Decide what to do.**

   Change and adaptation can only take place with time. Action requires a plan. Deciding what to do shifts the team's focus to moving forward — to the next sprint.

5. Close the retrospective.

Closing provides the opportunity to scrum the retrospective through activities that evaluate the effectiveness of the retrospective experience and identify ways to improve it. It also encourages expressing appreciation.

TIP

To stimulate discussion in retrospectives, organize activities around specific questions, such as the following:

>> What is keeping us from increasing our velocity from 36 to 38?

>> Does everyone have the tools needed to do the job?

>> Do any impediments keep repeating?

>> Is our daily scrum effective in identifying impediments and coordinating daily priorities?

>> Is our team lacking certain skills, and if so, how can we gain them?

Some scrum teams need to be coaxed and prodded to get engaged. They may be hesitant at first to say what they truly feel. Others may want to talk at once and are bursting with ideas and input. A perceptive, proactive scrum master adapts to work with either type of group — or anything in between — to achieve the best results.

TIP

Find only one action to take each sprint. Initially, it may be tempting to address all issues the team discusses. Instead, find an action that is both high-impact and feasible to implement.

TIP

The action items from the retrospective should be put into the product backlog as process improvement items. The scrum team should agree that at least one improvement action goes into every sprint. Bring at least one priority retrospective item into the next sprint, perhaps from the latest retrospective. After all, why wait? The purpose is to inspect and adapt, so don't delay the adaptation part!

Hundreds of helpful sprint retrospective techniques with engaging team activities are available for teams wanting to improve. Try searching the Internet for *Triple Nickels, Five Whys, SMART Goals, Temperature Reading, Team Radar, Mad Sad Glad, Liberating Structures,* and *Random Retros.* These are good activities to use during a retrospective (most of which are also outlined by Derby and Larsen in their book, *Agile Retrospectives: Making Good Teams Great*). If a team sprints weekly, they'll hold up to 52 sprint retrospectives a year, so adding variety to their inspection discussion can help with ongoing engagement.

Inspection and adaptation

Scrum is about planning the right things at the right time. It's about responding to changing markets and lessons learned. It's about continually learning, assessing, minimizing risk, and maximizing value at every step.

The inspecting and adapting perspective provided in the official *Scrum Guide* (http://scrumguides.org) is a good way to wrap up this chapter. We've added the italic formatting for emphasis:

>> **Inspection:** The scrum artifacts and the progress toward agreed goals *must be inspected frequently and diligently* to detect potentially undesirable variances of problems.

>> **Adaptation:** If any aspect of a process deviates outside acceptable limits or if the resulting product is unacceptable, the process applied or the materials produced must be adjusted. The adjustment *must be made as soon as possible* to minimize further deviation.

Inspection enables adaptation. Inspection without adaptation is considered pointless. *Scrum events are designed to provoke change.*

Also, the *Scrum Guide* states that adaptation becomes more difficult when the people involved are not empowered or self-managing. A scrum team is expected to adapt the moment it learns anything new through inspection.

IN THIS CHAPTER

» **Understanding the feedback loop**

» **Maintaining transparency and correcting the course**

» **Dealing with antipatterns and external forces**

» **Establishing a culture of innovation**

Chapter **7**

Inspect and Adapt: How to Correct Your Course

O ften during product development, you find your product in a different place from what you expected. In this chapter, we explore how scrum facilitates continuous learning and improvement. We also look at how you can work in the presence of uncertainty instead of hoping you can plan it away. After all, being agile is learning and adjusting as you go — being flexible enough to build the best product with the right features and quality.

Need for Certainty

Management's need for certainty of outcomes may well drive the downward spiral or decay of many products and great ideas. They could refuse to accept the basic reality of uncertainty, settling for the relative safety of the known at the expense of the better. The power of empiricism is being okay with uncertainty until you've learned the information you need to have more certainty about the outcome of your product or goal. For example, it will be difficult to know six months from now if a needed component being built by another team will be finished on time if the other team won't begin development for three months. But two weeks before its expected delivery, you can have a much clearer expectation of its readiness.

REMEMBER

Empirical means to learn or verify by means of observation. So, scrum is, by definition, an empirical process control model because each step of the way, you inspect your results and adapt immediately to a better outcome.

Figure 7-1 depicts the forecasting tool known as the Cone of Uncertainty. The basic principle is that outcomes are hard to predict across a span of time, but as you arrive closer to your goal, certainty increases.

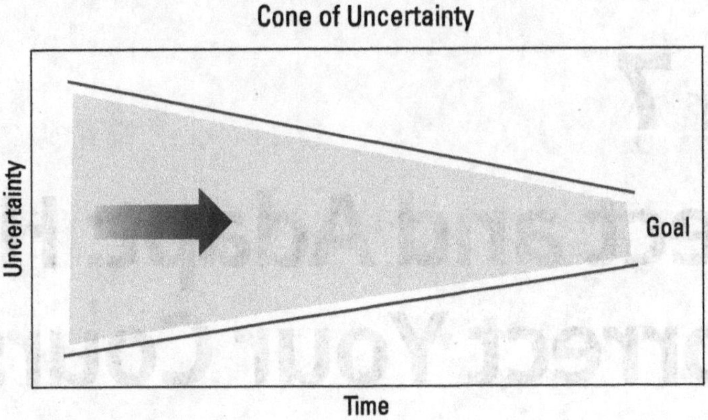

Cone of Uncertainty

FIGURE 7-1:
Cone of
Uncertainty.

Weather forecasters use the Cone of Uncertainty to depict the path of hurricanes over several days. Empiricism embraces the reality of some uncertainty and provides a framework for managing the associated risks by continually improving and adapting.

The Feedback Loop

In economics, a *feedback loop* is defined as the outcome or results of one process or one cycle used to inform the next. This feedback loop is what feeds the data to the empirical inspection process. Figure 7-2 looks at the feedback process of scrum teams.

The idea behind a feedback loop is that you can continually improve from the information learned from experience if you have a way to apply the lessons learned to future situations. An inherent part of the scrum process is recognizing that the knowledge and experience gained during each sprint need to be reintroduced in later sprints to inform the evolving plan. At the outset of a product, product roadmap and sprint plans are always made with the best information available at the time. The plans are accepted by the whole team and socialized among stake-holders. Rigid adherence to an exhaustive initial plan can ignore lessons learned during the process and stifle innovations from within the team. Instead, scrum uses customer and team feedback to improve the plan.

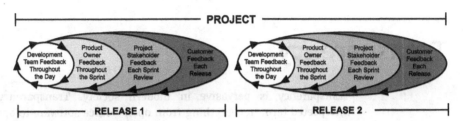

FIGURE 7-2: Feedback process.

You may wonder why you should plan at all if you know that an initial plan is likely flawed. You establish a plan as the first step in your learning process. Much as a flight crew files a flight plan based on the expected conditions, so crew members and air-traffic controllers know what to expect, product roadmaps lay out the scrum team's preflight expectations. After a flight crew takes off, the members evaluate actual conditions such as weather, winds, and scheduling to adjust the flight plan as needed. Likewise, in scrum, you provide feedback daily, and as you learn more information, you adapt your ideas and plan.

TIMING OF DECISIONS

We don't necessarily advocate making all decisions at the last possible moment. A Lean development concept states that because developers are always learning, they should wait until the last responsible moment to make decisions. Others argue that there's little value to be gained by waiting. One simple heuristic idea is to put decisions into three buckets:

- Things that are *known*

- Things that are *knowable*

- Things that are *unknowable*

Choosing to delay decisions for the known may bring no value. Likewise, a delay won't add value if a decision can't be moved from unknowable to knowable. However, delaying is appropriate when a thing is knowable. Waiting until more is known about that thing will likely result in a better decision.

Feedback loops can be positive (resulting from successes) or negative (resulting from failures). Success can breed success, but failure can inform success if you learn from it. This concept is why we ask both what worked well and what can be improved during each sprint retrospective. It's important to continue to support scrum successes and look for changes that can have a positive effect.

Transparency

Transparency is pervasive in modern society. Transparency is a broadly interpreted term in everything from open-source software to open collaboration on ideas. In Chapter 1, we define why transparency is a basic pillar of improvement. It's important not to miss the critical value of transparency within the inspect-and-adapt process. Without a transparent culture, decisions are made with inaccurate data. Far too often, we see organizations value good news more than accuracy and end up making decisions based on bad information.

Following are some basic principles of employing transparency during product development:

>> Just the facts. Display what is fully true to stakeholders specifically by only showing as complete work that is fully done according to your definition of *done*.

>> Be open and clear about the plan, design, process, and progress.

>> Make all information easily accessible to everyone.

>> Post the product goal, roadmap, release plan, sprint goal, and the definition of *done* on the wall where everyone involved can see them.

>> Encourage an environment of factual measurements and outcomes.

>> Have potentially awkward conversations early.

It's common to want to avoid having honest and awkward conversations, but avoiding uncomfortable situations can cause problems. (In fact, whole books and courses have been written to teach people how to deal with these situations.) We want you to understand the importance of knowing the hard costs associated with avoiding or delaying awkward moments. The most direct of these costs is time wasted going in the wrong direction and delaying a better course of action. Don't put off those uncomfortable conversations; have them as soon as you realize something needs to be addressed.

BEWARE OF OBFUSCATION

Some organizations we've trained and coached had a work culture that prevented team transparency. Watch out for antipatterns that force teams to hide reality as a means of self-protection. Additionally, be aware that some outside or contracting organizations have made an art of avoiding factual reporting. As a leader, you need to value and trust the specific knowledge of your scrum teams. Enable team success rather than second-guess its progress.

As the chief executive officer of a boutique software development company, David learned this lesson the hard way. While believing in the concepts of autonomous teams, he had a hard time trusting the team's progress when the stakeholders asked for assurances of success. Because the only answer David wanted to hear when he asked the team about product quality or timing was, "Yes, we will be on time," the scrum team couldn't ask him for help or clarity because they feared his wrath. The answers, in truth, were available via the scrum artifacts, but David was too busy to look. After realizing that he wasn't creating an environment that enabled the team's success, he changed. He learned to follow the team's visible scrum artifacts instead of asking for a status report, which enabled him to see the truth and join the team in being successful instead of withdrawing from any potential failure. Then he facilitated awkward conversations with stakeholders as early as possible. His change of approach to ownership was a huge win for his teams. Over time, the teams began to trust him to enable their success again. As a result, team quality and timeliness made a major leap forward. David initially exhibited several familiar antipatterns that hinder the inspect-and-adapt process.

Antipatterns

The term *antipattern* has been used to describe a well-intentioned solution to a problem that instead causes unintended negative consequences. It's important for an organization that's adopting or maturing its scrum practice to allow scrum to expose antipatterns as part of the inspect-and-adapt process. It's also important not to customize scrum to match a flawed culture or practices. Instead, make changes in the culture to facilitate the success of your scrum practice.

You may be familiar with some of the following antipattern examples that occur:

>> **Analysis paralysis:** Being unable to move forward due to continual analysis and unwillingness to accept uncertainty

>> **Smoke and mirrors:** Creating the illusion of further accomplishment, such as overstating quality or completeness

>> **Seagull management:** Swooping in as a leader and making a bunch of noise and then flying away, hoping to have motivated everyone with a sense of urgency but instead causing fear and panic

Scrum teams and agile leaders need to look for the root causes and cultural antipatterns that block the feedback loop. Once the antipatterns are identified, they should be escalated to leadership as an impediment to the scrum team. Removing these cultural impediments needs to be a priority because they may hinder multiple scrum teams within the organization.

External Forces

A team can be affected by things outside the team that affect the team's ability to deliver the product. These forces act like a headwind or crosswind that forces an aircraft off course or behind schedule.

For scrum teams, these forces may be changing regulations, evolving architecture, or reprioritized features. A team may be powerless to change these realities, but scrum exposes the effects of the forces and often exposes alternative courses of action.

One common excuse for saying that scrum can't work in an environment is that external forces make it impossible for scrum to be successful. But scrum can succeed anywhere as long as there are sufficient buy-in and effort from the people involved to make it work. In later chapters, we give you some examples of successful scrum organizations that likely had more constraints than your organization does.

In-Flight Course Correction

In this section, we go back to the analogy of the flight crew and the flight plan to explain the dynamics at play in planning and replanning based on empirical data. A flight crew always plans the details of an upcoming mission based on the parameters assigned for that mission. The crew estimates fuel use, time in flight, and execution details based on all known and expected details. On the day of the mission, the crew members gather any updated weather reports and mission changes.

When the aircraft is airborne, members of the flight crew continuously evaluate speeds and headings and compare the plane's actual position with the flight plans. Figure 7-3 shows a planned route and a measured location in flight.

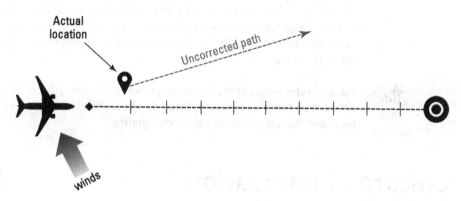

FIGURE 7-3:
Flight path.

Each time crew members measure the location while in flight, they evaluate why they're moving away from the plan. They look at the data to determine possible causes for the course adjustment, such as unexpected wind directions or velocities or a difference between the planned heading and speed and the actual heading and speed. Next, they use the new information to adjust the plan to achieve the mission objectives — all while going faster than 400 miles per hour. The flight crew repeats this inspect-and-adapt process over and over to ensure a mission's success.

In scrum, sprints serve as perfect times to reevaluate and improve plans. New information is welcomed and applied in a transparent organization to achieve product success.

WARNING

Avoiding the costly overhead of redundant or bureaucratic parallel processes is important. We've worked with well-intentioned organizations that expend more effort in measuring status and producing status slides than they expend building products, hoping to maintain control or avoid uncertainty. Creating status reports is an unnecessary parallel activity. An organization that has transformed to being agile and has fully adopted scrum lets go of these artifacts and embraces the new way.

Testing in the Feedback Loop

In scrum, you test during every sprint, doing component tests, functional tests, and tests for user feedback. Contrast that type of product development with a typical waterfall project, in which testing happens only at the end of a project.

Finding errors at the last minute causes either heroic and expensive fixes or pushing out the timeline. Like an aircraft whose path goes uncorrected, a product that is not validated ends up way off course.

The daily priority is informed by the feedback received during testing and customer validation as the sprint progresses. Corrections in the product are usually made the same day, while they're easiest and least expensive to fix and don't hold up further progress.

REMEMBER

On a scrum team, everyone is responsible for everything. It isn't up to one specialized tester to test everything for everyone else. The entire team owns the outcome, and all members care about quality.

Culture of Innovation

Many companies, from the newest to the oldest, say they want to be innovative. They likely see the market advantages of creative approaches. Yet, the command-and-control structures they use to manage products and processes impede the innovations they seek. Organizations' fundamental beliefs about purpose determine whether their teams work in a culture of innovation.

The scrum framework functions best in a culture of self-organization, purpose, and innovation. Product and process innovations are encouraged via the inspect-and-adapt model, and the idea of innovation is at the heart of working as a team. Using the feedback loop is a great way to encourage innovation.

Following are some ways that you can create an innovative culture:

>> Empower teams to challenge conventions or constraints.

>> Remove organizational barriers to creativity.

>> Rethink how you motivate.

>> Seek out creative lateral-thinking people.

TECHNICAL STUFF

Psychologist and philosopher Edward de Bono is credited with coining the term *lateral thinking*, which he defined as a mindset of challenging conventions and constraints. A lateral thinker can overcome his previous beliefs about limitations and conventions. A person who engages in lateral thinking doesn't ignore the existence of constraints; instead, he searches for ideas and solutions that aren't immediately obvious.

MOTIVATING CREATIVITY

In his TED talk (www.ted.com/talks/dan_pink_on_motivation#t-1094472), business author Dan Pink challenged previous ideas about motivating creativity. Using recent social-sciences research, he laid out a case that challenges the effectiveness of carrot-and-stick or extrinsic reward-based motivators. Intrinsic motivators such as autonomy, mastery, and purpose are more effective for encouraging team members to engage in lateral-thinking tasks.

A popular modern narrative seems to be that engineers and developers are robotic, logic-based, or linear thinkers. In our experience, that isn't the case for most highly effective knowledge workers. They're creators with well-honed cognitive skills who can't be replaced by the complex algorithms they create and thrive in a culture of innovation. As we trend toward replacing business functions with automation, we need to make space for lateral thinkers who can go beyond perceived constraints. Without creativity, we get stuck making the same mistakes.

3

Scrum for Any Industry

Chapter **8**

Software Development

You don't actually do a project; you can only do action steps related to it. When enough of the right action steps have been taken, some situation will have been created that matches your initial picture of the outcome closely enough that you can call it "done."

— DAVID ALLEN

Software development is the context within which scrum's creators formalized agile values and principles and within which the scrum framework was born. Therefore, it's no surprise that scrum is easily applied to this industry.

As technology advances, so do its complexities. New challenges arise, and project management frameworks that endure will be those that allow for and enhance change.

In this chapter, we show you some of the software industry's challenges and describe how scrum helps address them. You see scrum applied in contemporary examples and understand how the framework allows you to be as nimble and fast as this exponentially growing world of technology.

Scrum and Software Development: A Natural Fit

Software development is creative in nature. The sky isn't even the limit, as ideas, concepts, and reality go way beyond that now. Necessarily, the design solutions employed often are as creative as the products they serve.

Given its empirical nature, scrum fits this environment perfectly. Scrum doesn't tell you how to do anything. It simply lets you see clearly (that is, exposes) what you're doing and assess from there.

A huge variety of languages, tools, methods, and platforms exist to solve these complex problems. Scrum doesn't tell you which ones to use. Rather, this framework lets teams self-manage to decide which ways are best for their circumstances. Scrum does this through unfettered transparency, frequent inspection, and immediate adaptation.

The very nature of scrum allows you to find solutions every day, in every sprint, and with every release. Both the product and the process are nurtured for creativity and excellence.

Traditional project management methods and frameworks are predicated on accurately predicting the future. They're linear and sequential. They act as waterfall. (You can read about waterfall approaches in *Agile Project Management For Dummies*, Third Edition, by Mark C. Layton, Steven J. Ostermiller, and Dean Kynaston [published by John Wiley & Sons, Inc.].) What's important to understand is that technology and design needs have far outgrown this change-averse framework.

Waterfall project management entails progressively maturing a set package of requirements in different stages. One stage is completed before moving on to the next, such as designing all requirements for the entire product before doing any development and completing all development work before doing comprehensive testing, which is left to the end. With scrum, these phases are cycled repeatedly throughout product development so that a continuous circle of design, development, testing, integration, and feedback is achieved each day, sprint, and release.

As products became more complex, the natural boundaries of waterfall became abundantly clear. Multiple phases and long delays existed before coding even began. Early performance was no indicator of later performance because each phase's tasks were fundamentally different. Code testing was loaded toward the end of development when the team had the least amount of time or money. Customers didn't interact with the product until it was too late to incorporate their feedback. Product development was delayed or never completed, and often, they came up short.

Scrum emerged from the need to find better ways to build software. Keep in mind, however, that the scrum framework can be applied to any product development in which you can encapsulate the work and prioritize an item against other items.

WINSTON ROYCE HAD IT RIGHT

In a strange quirk of history, the man mistakenly attributed with introducing the waterfall framework to large software projects emphasized the basic agile and scrum principles: inspect and adapt.

Winston Royce was a computer scientist and a director of the Lockheed Software Technology Center who published a paper titled "Managing the Development of Large Software Systems." He described several methodologies, including waterfall and an early iteration of agile, as shown in this figure.

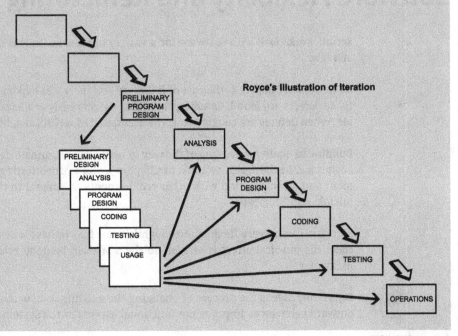

(continued)

(continued)

Royce clearly warned about the pitfalls later to be endured with waterfall. Strangely, the very system he's mistakenly credited with inventing is the same system he warned us about. He wrote:

"The testing phase which occurs at the end of the development cycle is the first event for which timing, storage, input/output transfers, etc., are experienced as distinguished from analyzed . . . . Yet if these phenomena fail to satisfy the various external constraints, then invariably a major redesign is required. A simple octal patch or redo of some isolated code will not fix these kinds of difficulties. The required design changes are likely to be so disruptive that the software requirements upon which the design is based and which provides the rationale for everything are violated."

Royce said leaving testing as a separate phase at the end was "risky and invited failure." He suggested an iterative approach that used frequent testing and adapted based on the results. Every step linked back to the previous one.

Software Flexibility and Refactoring

Scrum works well with software for a variety of reasons. In this section, we look at a few.

As we said in Chapter 4, the cost of fixing defects increases exponentially the later those defects are found. Catching and fixing defects early is a hassle, but it's doable. When defects are caught later, the accumulated technical debt can be costly.

Building in quality every step of the way to reduce and eliminate defects is a scrum advantage. In the sprint sections of Chapter 5, you learned testing every requirement and its integration with other requirements is integral to the process. Yet, mistakes still happen.

Software can be very flexible. Although it's not free to have a developer refactor code, the physical effect is virtual, so the work can be done relatively easily in many cases.

REMEMBER

Refactoring code is the process of changing the existing code without changing its outward behavior to improve nonfunctional aspects of the system.

Refactoring is inevitable in scrum (in a good way), and you'll do more of it than ever before because you're responding to and embracing change. Fortunately, scrum's empirical approach disciplines teams to continuously inspect and adapt to improve the health and quality of their product. Identifying needs for technical improvements and prioritizing them against new development are part of this ongoing maintenance.

Refactoring code is like maintaining your car. You hear the rattle, see the little red light, or smell something electrical. You know that if you don't do something, those problems will get bigger. You can pretend to have a choice, but you don't. As in refactoring code, you take the necessary little steps to ensure your vehicle is running smoothly. Maybe the car simply needs more oil or a bolt tightened. But if you wait, your engine could seize, or a part could break, leading to a much higher expense and more time wasted.

Refactoring enables you to make a working module that's scalable, extensible, and stable. In today's world, in which the one who's first wins, this type of efficiency in quality control is priceless. Refactor early and often.

Release often and on demand

Deploying new products to the market no longer requires packaging and shipping. Thanks to the Internet, the cloud, app stores, automated testing, and continuous integration, you have the flexibility to plan your releases on demand and as often as needed to suit other factors, such as market readiness, customer expectations, and marketing campaigns.

You now have a much higher degree of flexibility in the product you create and the timing by which you release it to your customer. Money previously allocated to hard-copy products is now diverted to more pressing and profiting needs. The Download Here button makes life easier in many ways. In many cases, such as Software as a Service (SaaS, covered later in this chapter), updates are pushed out automatically, eliminating the downloading step.

With scrum's emphasis on producing shippable products after every sprint, or even within sprints, you have even more flexibility in planning product releases. You don't have to wait until the end of a project to release. You can release incrementally in stages and continuously, with tested, integrated, and approved functionality.

TECHNICAL STUFF

Behemoth tech companies such as Facebook, Amazon, and Google deploy code to production multiple times a day — in the case of Amazon, 7,400 times a day (every 11.7 seconds). That's fast!

Customize your release sizes

No matter how often you release, smaller is generally better. As with the flexibility of releasing often and on demand, the size of the product you release is incredibly flexible with scrum, based on functionality, target dates, and market conditions. Scrum works with everything from one tiny enhancement that rounds out a larger, previously released requirement to a huge new generation that's about to be birthed.

Whether you're releasing a change in a single line of code or a full bundle of functionality, the product has been through a thorough process. Quality is the essence of flexibility — and the essence of scrum. Making the cost of change and improvement too high limits quality.

Inspect and adapt as you release

With the ability to customize both the timing and size of your releases, you can receive immediate customer feedback. Each time you release an increment of your product to your customer, you can assess the results and make any necessary changes. Analytics and customer service can collect data quickly, and you can fine-tune future development and enhancements from this input.

With scrum, you inspect and adapt daily, after each sprint and every release. In fact, the more often you release, the more often you can inspect and adapt.

You can even tailor the quantity and focus of feedback. Smaller releases may have more targeted feedback. Larger releases may receive a broader evaluation; you can set smaller targeted future releases from this evaluation.

REMEMBER

The sprint retrospective (see Chapters 6 and 7) idea of inspecting and adapting your process is important in releases too. You adapt your process at every iteration rather than only once in one sweltering meeting at the end of the project when everyone's relieved that it's over and ready to start on different products.

Customers have many choices because new products hit the market daily. To survive and excel, you must be at least as nimble as — and certainly faster than — the next guy. Scrum provides the framework for just this purpose.

Embracing Change

Although scrum's effectiveness and speed make it a natural fit in many situations, hierarchically structured organizations make it difficult. Incorporating new ideas and breaking away from old habits can be challenging. Some corporate cultures are open to change; others have more difficulty. It's human nature to find comfort in habits, and it takes effort and energy to break them.

To get people in the organization to embrace the change, you must reveal the value of the change to them. When the parties involved clearly understand what's in it for them, they accept the changes more readily. As the parties begin to experience the benefits of early release and adaptation, the conversion will go more quickly.

To help ease your organization's transition to scrum, we look at some specific issues in the following sections.

Developer challenges

In traditional, top-down management cultures, implementing scrum while maintaining the status quo won't work. The developers can be frustrated with double work if they're required to maintain traditional processes on top of implementing scrum. Managers can get off kilter moving forward, developing products that aren't planned upfront and don't provide the reams of reports and analysis they're used to.

With scrum, organizations can ease into inspection and adaptation one sprint at a time. Getting managers to participate appropriately (as stakeholders) in the first sprint reviews may be difficult. Equally challenging is getting people to see working software as the new benchmark of success (see the "Spotify versus Healthcare. gov" sidebar later in this chapter).

Scrum is a different way of working for the team and all its stakeholders and influencers. If the organization perseveres and allows scrum time for benefits to manifest, it sees immediate, practical, and quality results. The organization discovers that it has something real to work with after each sprint and that progress accumulates logically and rapidly. Time spent writing reports and managing status has been replaced by time spent creating real, usable products. The status is clear because it's *real*.

Business alignment with technology

Traditionally, the business side of an organization and software engineering are separate, and often, they're at odds. For decades, these groups have operated as silos within the same organization:

>> The business serves the market and the shareholders and is under extreme pressure to deliver value quickly and adapt to a constantly changing marketplace.

>> The technologists want sustainable architecture and foundations with as little technical debt accumulation as possible.

Scrum brings these two sides together. A representative from the business (product owner) and developers are involved together, providing feedback throughout the sprint. At the end of the sprint, the whole team collaborates with business stakeholders aligning the entire product team. You'll never find a more beautiful alignment and facilitation of collaboration and joint ownership. Thanks to scrum, the right people are making the right decisions about the right things at the right times. Finger-pointing is no longer relevant. Progress is exposed at all times to all parties. Inspection and adaptation points exist along the way. Self-organization and self-management mean that everyone is in it together.

REAL-WORLD CHANGE

Not long ago, we provided scrum training for one of our software clients. The client was working on a research and development product involving new technology and was given a deadline by senior management to complete a comprehensive range of features.

The team initially came up with proof of concept of features and requirements fairly quickly, which won buy-in from management to proceed with the full-scale development. However, the product backlog was vague, and the team spent unbudgeted months developing a demo version for management.

The development process was slow and fraught with technical surprises. The team missed both the first release date and the next several rescheduled release dates. At this point, we trained the team and implemented the scrum framework.

At first, the entire product team held on to traditional practices (upfront design, fixed scope and schedules, and renaming waterfall artifacts and events as scrum). But it pushed ahead, held consistent sprint reviews with stakeholders, and survived a series of tough, uncomfortable conversations about missed deadlines and how the aspects of scrum could help resolve these challenges.

The transparency in scrum began to shine through after a few sprint reviews, clarification of roles (especially getting a dedicated and fully trained product owner), and the removal of some impediments. Walls were broken down between the scrum team, stakeholders, and customers (actual users were involved in every sprint review); communication improved; and the product development was replanned with a proper product goal, roadmap, and product backlog. A release schedule was re-created based on the team's new velocity and product backlog estimates. Long story short, from that point, it took months, not years, to release the minimum viable product (MVP). The new product development plan was based on priority, customer feedback, and empirical data (such as velocity).

During initial sprint reviews, the team identified a key stakeholder (a customer who would be using the product) who hadn't been attending the sprint reviews. She was invited, and her involvement provided crucial feedback on the product. As the other stakeholders observed the scrum team's willingness and speed in inspecting and adapting, trust skyrocketed, and ownership and collaboration (including stakeholders) improved amazingly.

- In the end, the product much more accurately reflected what the customer wanted.

- Extra features were removed from the product backlog (something that a stakeholder and the product owner decided, not the developers).

- An MVP was released in full working order.

The stakeholders were fully engaged and involved with training users on the software. In fact, stakeholders ended up collaborating with the product owner on every aspect of the rollout.

Upfront engineering

The propensity of development managers, project managers, and developers to plan everything has deep roots:

>> Most schools still teach upfront engineering (see "The Marshmallow Challenge" in Chapter 1). Fresh out of class, engineers plan first and develop second.

>> Waterfall enforces the "plan all and then develop all" mindset. This process is built around completing one phase, such as designing, before moving to the next, such as developing. In waterfall, upfront engineering is part of the foundation on which everything else rests.

Given this background, you'll find there's a stigma in changing something after development starts. Traditionally, when management and developers have invested time and energy in planning something, it's hard to drop those plans and potentially suffer sunk costs. But in our mindset — and within the framework of scrum — change is ideal. All changes are a result of learning. You incorporate change every day, after every sprint, and in each release. You find out how to seek out change. In scrum, change is progress.

TECHNICAL STUFF

Sunk costs are funds spent on development that can't be recovered. In waterfall, sunk costs were more common, as projects were planned and funded upfront. If they failed along the way, companies had nothing to show for their efforts. With scrum, you can fail fast or incrementally accumulate fully built functionality.

Instead of sinking a lot of money into product development upfront, you can allocate funds along the way. If development ends earlier than intended, you lose less money in the form of sunk costs or make a great business decision that maximizes the return of your limited investment. With scrum, your days of catastrophic failure are gone.

If 80 percent of software features are never or rarely used (as referenced in the latest Standish Group study in Chapter 5), think of the wasted time, energy, and resources involved in planning, designing, developing, testing, and documenting those features. With scrum, the dominant paradigm of planning everything in advance is dispelled.

We've seen developers using waterfall spend weeks and months on planning and still not get it right. We've seen scrum teams plan features and systems of the same magnitude in hours.

Because scrum teams understand that they don't know everything upfront, they don't plan what they don't know. They assess and adapt along the way as new information is garnered and priorities are reassessed. Because transparency is continuous, management is less likely to overreact.

Emergent architecture

Emergent architecture is the progressive elaboration of your application or enterprise architecture based on requirements currently in development to achieve and maintain stability and scalability. The goal is to refactor the architecture based on the reality of working software rather than to develop the entire system based on guesses.

Many programmers see emergent architecture as a risky approach. They want the entire product to be planned upfront, leaving no code (or stone) unturned. But this approach isn't realistic or practical.

You begin with macro-level architecture decisions based on the holistic view of your requirements from the product roadmap. Then, in your first sprint, ask what the requirements and architecture are for this sprint. Let the sprint goal drive the sprint, and if that goal requires code refactoring, don't wait. Your product should work in every sprint. With scrum, you refactor more often, but that's what you want. Requirement change isn't the enemy, and neither is code refactoring.

The beginning of development is when you know the least. At that point, you shouldn't do detailed planning or build parts of the system that won't be used. You can aptly apply a Lean principle to this scenario: Decide at the last responsible moment. The sooner you start development, the higher your risk of being wrong and doing throwaway work. The later you decide, the more information you have to make that decision, lowering your risk of making a mistake.

REMEMBER

Refactoring should be built into every requirement estimation. As new requirements come to the top of the list and are refined, architecture emerges in the minds of the developers. As team members estimate and plan, they plan for refactoring.

TIP

If your sprints are one week long, you'll be refactoring small batches of architecture. If you wait until the end of development, as in traditional frameworks, you're refactoring for months or years of architecture. Refactor often. Refactor early.

A SCRUM LESSON LEARNED

7Shifts is a restaurant scheduling company founded by Jordan Boesch and his wife, Andrée Carpentier. As they were building their business, they ran into a client who, unintentionally and without spending a cent on their products, helped them convert a waterfall habit to a scrum solution.

This prospective client, a restaurant owner, asked for some features in his app, one of which was a budget tool. Jordan designed all the features to completion, including the budget app, and presented them to the client. Unimpressed, the client said, "No thanks," and was never heard from again. The result was lots of upfront planning and development without any feedback from an actual user.

Mystified, Jordan plugged along with his business, including the budget-tool app but never inspected it further. One day, he ran some analytics on the tool to see how much his clients used it. The data showed that only 2 percent of his clients used it.

Jordan set out to fix the app, starting by asking existing clients why they weren't using it. They explained that his program required them to manually enter an estimated dollar amount, which could have easily been calculated automatically with some tweaks.

Jordan released an update to the app with amazing success. He learned to plan only what you know, talk to your customers early, inspect, and adapt until customers are happy.

Scrum Applications in Software

Many technology companies are already using scrum to great success. It allows them to be faster and more flexible to stay competitive.

It's one thing to understand the theory of scrum's success; it's quite another to see scrum in action. Although we can't take you into the field with us, we can bring the field to you in the following sections. In this section, we show you some of the challenges that companies face and describe how scrum's unique adaptability comes into play.

Video-game development

This hugely popular, complex area of software development can use scrum with great success for four reasons:

>> **Flexibility:** With scrum, you start with basic features and grow the game into more complexity. This evolution happens organically; therefore, you're always developing what's most important next.

>> **Finding the fun:** Developers can add fun in small, iterative doses. The features that add the most value in terms of fun (a critical element of any game) get added first.

>> **Cost savings:** Most games fail to break even financially. Scrum's cost-saving nature is a company-saver. Even if funding is cut halfway through development (assuming the minimum play time is met), you still have the most important 50 percent of the features fully functioning and, if not yet marketable, at least reusable.

>> **Regular feedback:** This feedback may come daily, from the product owner, and at each sprint review, from the stakeholders (such as the publisher and marketing).

Gaming is about keeping customers happy and engaged. Feedback within scrum is incorporated quickly, so the result is what users want.

Development flow

Technical development generally follows the three stages for games, as shown in Figure 8-1.

>> **Preproduction:** This stage is where artists, directors, and engineers come together to find the fun. This prototyping and proof-of-concept phase aims to

determine whether the game is a good, fun idea before the company enters production and spends more money.

Especially for mobile games, engineers can prototype without art quickly. For all games in this stage, teams can validate the idea of the game, define it, develop concept art, ensure funding, and assemble developers.

>> **Production:** The proof of concept is developed by directors, artists, and engineers.

>> **Postproduction:** Professional testers test the finished product; beta testing follows; and sales, marketing, and support activities begin.

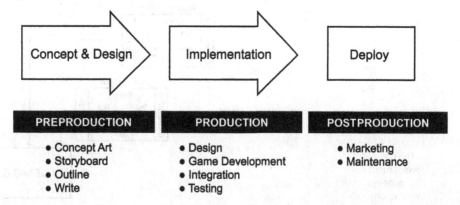

FIGURE 8-1:
The historical flow of video-game development.

As this process implies, publishers typically engage with studios under traditional waterfall contracts and structures, paying the studio only at certain long-term milestones. This arrangement often implies that the publisher goes long periods without seeing progress.

In a scrum model, game development looks more like Figure 8-2, which shows the ongoing testing necessary for quality assurance. After each task — such as concept art, storyboarding, writing, or prototyping — the task is tested and either moved on or further developed.

With scrum, publishers can identify and kill the nonfun stuff faster and have greater quality control because they regularly participate in sprint reviews and pay studios incrementally, in line with the delivery of working game increments.

Short sprints maintain a flow of outbound content that attracts and retains consumers. Scrum provides faster delivery of playable games to stakeholders, such as publishers and focus groups. This process allows developers to emphasize the fun factor and quickly eliminate the game-play elements that aren't entertaining (which can also save wasted art-creation costs).

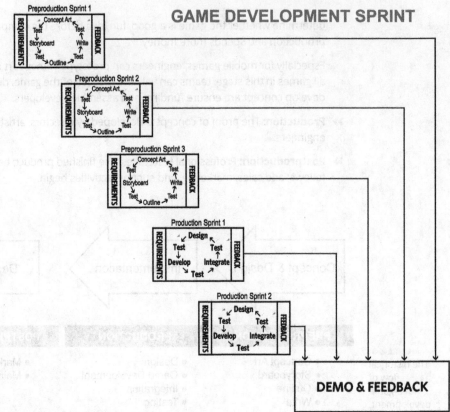

FIGURE 8-2:
The game-
development
process
with scrum.

WARNING

The definition of *done* may differ between preproduction and production. Be sure to clarify both stages upfront. A preproduction sprint's definition of *done* may include different types and levels of documentation and artwork standards from a production sprint's definition.

TIP

Ideally, games can't ship with fewer than ten hours of play time for a single-player game. Although this amount of play time may be the release goal, publishers can review the working software after every sprint and provide invaluable feedback.

Marketing

Games have traditionally been sold as retail products, but online and digital distribution are shifting the emphasis from retail to digital delivery. A huge need exists to constantly and quickly update, add, and push content to a game. This capability is the difference between surviving and not surviving. Speed to market is critical.

Game sales are overwhelmingly seasonal, with more than 50 percent of the industry's revenue coming during the Christmas season. This is a major factor in the crunch time faced by many teams because the holiday season imposes a hard deadline.

Scrum's priority-driven product backlog ensures that the highest-priority fun will be delivered in minimal crunch time, making management happy and reducing employee burnout.

Art

Art is a significant portion of the development work required in video games. Console and computer games require a lot of art and animation assets, adding up to 40 percent or more of the cost of a game title. Technical and game-play issues late in production are costly.

Art, being the costliest element, is tempting to outsource overseas. But troubles with time zones and communications almost always lead to delays, rework, and customer dissatisfaction with the quality of the finished product.

Scrum allows artists and developers to work on the same team rather than in silos, with the same goals and real-time communication about what works and what doesn't. To optimize collaboration, teams should be onshore and in-house (co-located). Onshore and co-located teams keep delays and rework costs down.

Timeboxed delivery (sprints) of art assets keeps everyone on schedule with deadlines set as a team and a steady flow of deliverables to market, keeping waste to a minimum.

Many large game titles require large teams with 15 or more developers, 10 or more artists, and 30 or more quality assurance members. For a thorough discussion of how scrum scales across larger product development efforts, see Chapter 13.

Services

"As-a-Service," development companies use scrum to get their products out the door quickly and effectively by leveraging the power of the Internet.

SaaS

Software as a Service (SaaS) is a model of distributing software applications hosted by a service provider and made available to users over the Internet. No installation on personal computers or devices is needed. Customers usually pay a monthly fee or subscription.

SWARMING SOFTWARE DEVELOPMENT

Work in progress (WIP) is the term used to describe partially completed goods, which are typically turned from raw materials to finished products within a short period. In manufacturing, WIP is minimized to reduce inventory and bound capital. WIP also occurs in software development to focus on delivery and minimize multitasking. When a feature is only partially completed (developed but not tested) or a team works on multiple items at once, leaving each item partially completed at the end of the sprint has no use to customers.

A partially completed or unavailable software feature has absolutely no value. In software development, WIP increases the complexity and risk and violates Agile principle 10 — "Simplicity, the art of maximizing the work not done — is essential." Worse yet, multitasking results in lower quality and creates the potential for lower priority work to be completed at the expense of higher priority customer needs.

Scrum teams minimize their WIP by setting limits for the number of items in progress at any one time. High-performing teams set this limit to one in-progress requirement at a time. But how can this be done?

Jason Gardner, one of our esteemed agile coaches, shared an example of swarming used by many software development scrum teams in his article, "Uncovered the Hidden Priorities that Make you Ineffective."

- The team elaborates the user story together, which might include the initial design exercise.

- One person writes the code.

- A second can be writing the unit tests — that's a separate file, so no stepping on toes there.

- A third can be writing integration or system tests — that's three people already working on one user story.

- A fourth can be writing automated user acceptance tests.

- Two classes to write? You can add two more people to write code and unit tests.

- Documentation updates (wiki, training, user, and so on).

- Consider pair programming to front-load peer review for quality.

- Writing database upgrade scripts and more!

This team swarmed on the design, development, testing, and documentation, simplifying the process through their collaboration and inspection of each other's work. They focused on the single customer need. Imagine how quickly they built a releasable product increment!

The key to team swarming is building team capability or skills. Instead of moving to the next user story and putting more work in progress, they pull the next available task from the current user story even if they don't know how to do it. They learn by shadowing their teammates and from the work itself. High-performing, WIP-limiting teams encourage each other to ask two questions: "Who can I help get to *done*?" If no one needs help, they ask, "What can I learn by shadowing?" They understand that idle work is worse than an idle worker.

Swarming requires collaboration daily during development. That is why scrum is called scrum — it's a rugby metaphor for team collaboration. This may also require a developer to work on something that isn't their strongest area. But what you get is a focus on delivering the highest priority work, earlier and more often, instead of ensuring that a worker can show they are busy 100 percent of their day doing something. Collaboration and focus prevent siloing and lead to a team of versatile, skilled developers.

Even mobile apps, which require a download, have quick downloads that can be done on the go, over Wi-Fi, or over a mobile network while roaming. Installation discs, manually entered license keys, and hours of installation steps with your device plugged in are things of the past. The cloud enables scrum teams to inspect and adapt to real live data and redeploy quickly to address feedback.

IaaS

Infrastructure as a Service (IaaS) is a cloud-computing model for providing organizations with the outsourced equipment necessary to support IT operations, including hardware, servers, storage, and other networking components. IaaS providers own the equipment and are responsible for sourcing, running, and maintaining it. Clients typically pay per use based on data volume or equipment size. These same products enable other companies to manage their IT departments and operate their infrastructure more scrum-like.

Installing a new database server, for example, used to take weeks or months. The in-house engineer had to procure the equipment and then build, configure, and install it before the database engineers could start installing it and migrating data. IaaS solutions now allow this process to be done virtually and completed in minutes.

PaaS

Platform as a Service (PaaS) is a cloud-computing model that provides solutions for the computing platform and stack (a set of software subsystems). Typically, clients pay license fees and/or per-use fees.

With IaaS and PaaS services such as Amazon, IT organizations can spin up a new server in minutes, and it's immediately ready for data and installation.

SPOTIFY VERSUS HEALTHCARE.GOV

To understand the effects of agile and scrum-based frameworks within services computing and SaaS, compare two examples: Spotify and Healthcare.gov.

Healthcare.gov was a massive rollout of cloud computing with myriad problems requiring extensive fixing. Jeff Sutherland, one of the founders of scrum, called the rollout "waterfall gone bad."

Healthcare.gov appeared agile on the front end, but the developers missed the second agile value: working software. The people on the front end did their part, but the lack of load and performance testing and optimization rendered the software useless.

Although the plan had dozens of reputable consultancies working on development, minimal coordination existed among them. The program was rolled out nationwide, but if it had been tested state by state (true to scrum and agile), many issues could have been dealt with early and quickly.

In contrast, Spotify, the online music source, did things differently and saw remarkable success. Spotify's competitors are Google, Amazon, and Apple, so Spotify had to be nimbler, faster, and cheaper to even think of competing. The company has locations and scrum teams around the world, and each team is responsible for a single piece of product. But even this setup wasn't fast enough, so the company developed continuous deployment, deploying product increments several times during a sprint.

When you compare these two huge cloud-computing services — one done through waterfall and the other through iterative and incremental development — you see the need for delivering, inspecting, and adapting working software frequently.

Customization products

Some software comes off the shelf; some is customized to meet individual customer needs. How do you handle customization with scrum? Do you need individual teams for each client?

We worked with a client that provides logistics software, which comes with a fair share of customization to work with unique equipment configurations and third-party/legacy software integrations. Before scrum, the teams that provided the customization service to clients were so far behind the curve that the lead time to get a new client running was costing the company business.

The solution was to invite the customization teams (which had not yet adopted scrum) to attend the core product scrum team's sprint reviews as stakeholders. This change allowed these stakeholders to anticipate the product well in advance. They provided feedback based on key customer use that allowed the scrum team to engineer the core product, requiring less customization for each client, as the team saw ways to use certain features and collaborate with other client representatives.

Chapter 9

Tangible Goods Production

Even a mistake may turn out to be the one thing necessary to a worthwhile achievement.

— HENRY FORD

G iven the origins of agile and scrum, it's not a far stretch of the imagination to think they should be used only for developing software. The fact is that nothing could be further from the truth. The 1986 *Harvard Business Review* article, "New New Product Development Game," mentioned in Chapters 1, was written in response to experiences in the manufacturing industries. The article used as case studies hardware, electronics, and automotive products engineered and built by companies such as Fuji-Xerox in 1978, Canon in 1982, and Honda in 1981.

The development and production of tangible goods works beautifully with scrum, and we show you how in this chapter. Situations and products may vary enormously, but the tools and techniques remain the same. By following the framework we've been writing about, you'll easily see how scrum can fit almost any product development effort. All you need is a list of requirements that can be prioritized.

The Fall of Waterfall

As we state in Chapter 8, product development is occurring at accelerating speeds, and it's not only the software sector that's seeing fundamental shifts in what's developed and how long it takes. Long-term manual manufacturing activities are changing, too. Development cycles in most industries are shorter and faster because of the time and cost savings accrued through technology. Companies such as Apple, whose products are certainly tangible, release next-generation, cutting-edge products multiple times a year.

Some argue that the scrum framework can't be applied to physical products, saying, "We can't be building the tenth floor when we realize that we need to make a change on the fifth floor!" Sometimes, they're right.

People make objections like that one all the time in software development as well. A change in design may be so costly that it can't be realistically implemented, and other options must be considered, including moving forward with no change. Maybe a different database would be preferred, but it's too costly, so the product owner decides to nix the idea and keep going as is.

Scrum is about exposing reality and making good decisions based on empirical evidence, not about swapping out requirements at a customer's every whim. Whether the industry is developing software, or manufacturing planes, trains, or automobiles, the scrum foundation applies: organizing a scrum team with appropriate roles, holding frequent inspection and adaptation points, and forcing decisions to happen at the last responsible moment (that is, planning at different levels of detail for the right things at the right time).

REMEMBER

The product owner filters out the business prioritization noise from all the stakeholders so that the developers spend their time on only the highest-priority requirements. Product owners and developers work as a team to implement the solutions to problems presented by the product owner. When everyone works toward the same goals, finger-pointing is reduced, and accountability is shared.

Engaged customers are more satisfied customers who end up getting what they want. With scrum, feedback loops are regular, consistent, and as frequent as possible, so customers get what they want at the cost they're willing to pay for it, which keeps customers involved and developers on track. Impediments can be identified and resolved early, and accountability is taken on by those who do the work *and* those who make decisions, including customers.

Construction

Uses for scrum within the vast world of tangible goods are enormous. The speed-to-market increase and cost savings that can be achieved in software are also possible in other areas. Construction with scrum is an excellent example.

Scrum works with any project, provided you can list and prioritize the work to be done. Obviously, construction projects have these qualities. They also have challenges specific to the industry. Every segment of an industry does. Instead of saying, "Oh, scrum won't work with this because of X and Y and Z," say, "These are the challenges we face, so let's look at how scrum will solve them and get us faster and cheaper to market."

In the following sections, we outline specific issues in the construction industry and describe how scrum helps solve them. By using scrum, you see how to deal with traditional problems — those you've been dealing with your entire construction career.

SCRUM AND LEASE MANAGEMENT

A leader of the Facilities Management technology organization for a multibillion-dollar nonprofit was in trouble. His team of experts worked to upgrade an expensive ERP (enterprise resource planning tool) but had very little to show for it. His budget was running out, and his business partners wondered where all the money was spent. He wondered if there was a better way. And there was.

How did he do it?

He found scrum through research and signed his team and business partners up for training. Post-training, they began forming a small, cross-functional, co-located team. The team moved from their cubicles to an unused conference room where they could more easily collaborate and work together. The first product tackled using scrum was leasing management in support of the organization's strategy to centralize worldwide leasing while reducing headcount.

The conference room walls became the team's workspace, where they transparently hung the product goal supported by cards describing the product roadmap divided into four balanced quadrants. The highest priority cards were progressively elaborated into sprint candidates and pulled into a sprint backlog taped on another wall with painter's tape. The team planned their sprint, held daily scrums, and gathered feedback from stakeholders during sprint reviews and improvement ideas during sprint retrospectives.

(continued)

(continued)

The journey was not easy and exposed many challenges. To highlight a couple, the vendor intentionally designed the ERP platform to be manually configured. The team had to figure out how to migrate their changes consistently from a development environment to a test environment and finally into production, avoiding user downtime. They also had to integrate and collaborate with teams developing other modules in parallel using traditional project management practices (waterfall).

To overcome the platform constraints, the team adhered to a strict sprint definition of *done*. They created user stories with acceptance criteria as the starting point, collaborated on the process or workflow needed by the users, configured the workflow in Development, manually tested it, configured in Test, and then manually tested it there, too. They kept a change log, documentation, test cases, and a roles and responsibilities matrix updated for every story. The definition of *done* ensured a releasable product increment could be demonstrated every sprint.

To collaborate with the other teams using waterfall, they made an extra effort to provide transparency in their work. They published their sprint goal after every sprint planning session along with the supporting sprint backlog for all to see. They invited the other teams to listen in on their daily scrum and to participate in their sprint reviews. When dependencies were identified, the product owner worked to prioritize the team's work navigating around or addressing the dependencies. They found open communication between the product owner and the other project managers was key.

The biggest breakthrough, however, came during a team retrospective when the team discovered keystroke automation tools existed, which created scripts that could be deployed in each environment. The automation discovery was HUGE, decreasing the time it took to promote changes from one environment to the next from multiple hours to seconds!

The results were astounding! The product was completed in three languages in half the expected time for a little less than half the remaining budget. The former project manager attended one of the team's first sprint reviews, and their jaw dropped in amazement when they saw how much was accomplished in such a short period. More importantly, the business partner's managing director was very pleased after the product's iterative release and said, with a big grin, "I can't wait to see what's next!"

The best in bids

Competition in the bidding process for construction projects is fierce and shows no signs of trending toward easy. Combine this fact with a steady increase in construction cost, and you have a formula for cutting corners and the potential for skipping essential steps.

None of this is news to anyone in this industry. Your bid may be pristine, providing everything the client needs at a reasonable price, but you know that your competitors' bids may undercut you by leaving things out that you know the client needs. Scrum can help both you and the client. After all, the better the client is served, the better the result, the better for your business, and the more potential for referrals.

Scrum provides the following:

>> **Transparency:** Let customers decide where they want their money to go. They can make changes, inspect, and adapt as the project progresses. But they'll be fully informed each step of the way as they participate in regular progress review sessions in the sprint review, provide feedback, and ask questions.

>> **Adaptability:** Scrum allows the team to identify course-correcting issues early. Even when you're building to completion, it's better to resolve problems identified by completing a single house than to find out about them when ten houses simultaneously reach the same point of completion. Taking this example a step further, adapting to customer feedback about a nonload-bearing wall that's misplaced is much easier to fix before electrical systems, plumbing, and drywall are installed.

>> **Daily scrum team coordination:** Having an established forum for raising issues limits bottlenecks and prevents small issues from turning into big problems. If Acme Pipe Co. fails to deliver the materials you need, the scrum master addresses the issue now and ensures it doesn't happen again — not at the end of the week, when it comes up in a weekly status reporting meeting.

In Chapter 1, we talked about the three pillars of empiricism: transparency, inspection, and adaptation. Although all three pillars serve you well throughout scrum, the transparency issue is clearly (pun intended) key in the bidding and building process.

Scrum roles in construction

In traditional project management, the project-manager role carries huge responsibilities, which are broad, all-inclusive, and often too much for one person to bear alone effectively. The project manager wears so many hats — coordinating among everyone involved — that efficiency and quality can suffer the consequences.

Scrum provides different, clearly designated roles to help the project manager shoulder the burden. Balance is restored as scrum team members take on new responsibilities:

>> The project-manager role disappears.

>> The product owner represents the funding customer and the stakeholders. Depending on how those roles are implemented in each organization, the product owner could be the person who was traditionally the project manager or the project architect or engineer. Regardless of the product owner's previous role, their scrum role is providing the "what" and "when" for the product being built.

>> The scrum master role facilitates communication and interactions, removes impediments for the developers, makes sure that each person involved understands the process, and makes sure that the team is set up for members to succeed in their jobs. This role sounds a lot like a foreperson or superintendent, doesn't it?

>> The developers consist of subcontractors, engineers, architects, and individual tradespeople.

Customer involvement

The traditional view holds that change in product development is bad. In scrum, however, change is embraced as a sign of progress. You seek change as clear evidence that you're building a better product more directly in line with what your client wants.

In traditional construction projects (as in so many other fields), you tend to involve customers as little as possible to keep changes to a minimum. Construction companies are still in the change-is-bad mindset. However, the earlier and more frequently the customer is involved, the cheaper changes are and the more likely you are to build something that the customer loves.

At the other extreme, you don't want scope creep. As customers see things take shape, they want to add more features, which builds additional scope into the project. This scope adds costs that may not have been budgeted for. In scrum, you want to reduce costs, not raise them.

Scrum prevents this situation by restricting scope by cost — and, thus, time — rather than by arguments about a written requirement's meaning. The customer can have any new requirement that aligns with the product goal, and the loss of a lower-priority requirement offsets each new requirement unless that lower-priority requirement is funded by additional budget.

Scrum facilitates the customer involvement process by

>> Structuring customer feedback within sprint cycles at natural breaks and milestones in the project, such as inspecting rough electrical or plumbing before hanging drywall to ensure that fixtures are lined up where the customer intended. This practice allows you to make any necessary adjustments before it's too late. The customer inspects completed work at the end of each sprint and provides valuable feedback then.

>> Gaining project ownership by making decisions driven by cost and return on investment within these feedback loops.

>> Giving customer change requests visibility throughout the project by showing how those requests will affect the remaining schedule and cost.

In the end, the transparency, inspection, and adaptation process allows for better communication. When everyone involved has the information they need, an environment for excellent decision-making is created.

The subcontractor dilemma

Since the Egyptian pyramids were built, project managers and subcontractors have struggled to stay coordinated and on track. Issues still arise far too frequently due to the structure within which these valuable parties operate.

The challenges are severalfold. Traditionally, the project process has been difficult to coordinate because subcontractors are numerous and contractors are few. Through a lack of coordination, communication, outcome ownership, and human nature, the parties involved focus on their own benefits and outcomes rather than on the whole project.

Each subcontractor is hugely specialized; therefore, a high degree of coordination is needed among subcontractors, the responsible party, stakeholders, and potential users. The waterfall method simply doesn't provide this environment. Fortunately, scrum does.

Here are some ways that scrum facilitates the contractor–subcontractor relationship:

>> Through regular, structured scrum events (daily scrums, sprint reviews, and sprint retrospectives), communication is enhanced, and vital feedback from all parties is encouraged.

>> Sprints and releases are timeboxed and frequent, and each party knows exactly what is expected at each increment.

>> Subcontractors have input into how much work they can accomplish in a sprint (that is, empirical data from what they accomplished in previous timeboxed sprints). Contractors can give their input on priorities, but the final decisions are with the people doing the work.

>> Subcontractors are given a big-picture perspective of their roles and encouraged to share their knowledge and experience to make the process more efficient (that is, self-organized teams contribute their specific knowledge to come up with the best designs).

>> Contractors receive knowledge and experience from the people who do the work: subcontractors.

>> Subcontractors can bring up inefficiencies and problems early (through sprint retrospectives). This feedback is critical for removing impediments.

>> Supply and procurement issues are easier to coordinate because everyone is looking down the road together through active, in-person discussions (product backlog refinement, daily scrums, and daily feedback from the product owner).

>> Quality is improved through increased coordination.

>> Material flow and staging are easier to coordinate via product backlog refinement and sprint planning, including task planning of requirements.

The key is that otherwise disconnected roles and jobs are combined into one communicating, coordinated scrum team. With scrum, you have a living organism. Each part relies on and enhances the others.

TIP

Individual subcontractor teams do well using scrum to organize themselves and their work. But the overall project team is made up of multiple subcontractors. How do you get all these teams to work as one? Well, it may not be realistic to get all teams in the same room every day, but it would be possible to get each foreperson in the same room every day to coordinate the day's priorities, identify impediments, and go to work removing them to ensure that the job moves forward unhindered.

Worker safety

Safety concerns for workers are always important, especially now, with the increased number of projects in areas with high traffic volume and large populations. Therefore, clear communication of risks and solutions is more important than ever. Lives depend on it.

Scrum facilitates increased worker safety through the following means:

>> Safety-compliance regulations are relevant and thorough. Adding these regulations to the definition of *done* means documented, validated safety measures can be in place and ready for perusal during audits.

>> Frequent sprint retrospectives allow workers to come forward with safety concerns and solutions. Good scrum masters can facilitate this process to ensure appropriate safety subjects come up.

>> Experienced workers can share their expertise in providing solutions.

>> Daily scrums provide a forum for urgent issues.

It's likely that these things are already being done in various ways, just not with scrum terms. Transparency of safety concerns is needed and provides a mechanism to inspect and implement actions to adapt.

FLYOVER CONSTRUCTION IN BANGALORE

A Scrum Alliance article titled "A Real-Life Example of Agile, Incremental Delivery of an Infrastructure Project in Bangalore, India" (https://www.scrumalliance.org/community/member-articles/754) provides an example of the scrum process in action in construction. The project was building two flyover roads at a hugely busy intersection in Bangalore, India. Many high-tech companies had major facilities at this intersection.

How did they do it?

Normally, a flyover project of this magnitude would take 18 months to complete. In the process, temporary roads would be created on either side of the main thoroughfare while both flyovers were built simultaneously. Naturally, traffic would be delayed during construction because temporary roads are used, and no flyovers are available until they are opened at the end of the project.

This project, however, was conducted with an incremental approach:

• The highest-priority requirement was identified as one side of the flyover for the first release. Therefore, a temporary road was constructed using one side of the main road. Simultaneously, construction of the flyover on the first side of the road began.

(continued)

(continued)

- Upon completion, the first flyover was opened for traffic in both directions, and construction on the opposite flyover began. Although traffic was still delayed, the delay was reduced because at least one flyover was functional. The completion of the first flyover also created a shippable product increment. Swarming was done on that side of the flyover only.

- The same temporary road was used during the construction of the second flyover. Time and money were saved because no new road was required. Perhaps a second temporary road could have been planned upfront, but the first temporary road was useful during the second phase. Inspection and adaptation eliminated waste.

- When the second flyover was complete, both flyovers were open; traffic was returned to the main thoroughfare, and the temporary road was closed.

The process seems to be simple, doesn't it? Here are some of the results:

- Using incremental delivery of one flyover at a time reduced overall construction time from 18 months to 9 months (a 50 percent time-to-market decrease).

- Traffic congestion was reduced as first one flyover and then the other flyover opened.

- Only one temporary road needed to be constructed.

- As soon as one flyover was operational, the risk of failure was reduced. If funding had been cut halfway through because one side was fully functional (that is, a shippable increment had been created), that cut wouldn't have been a disaster. The highest-risk issues had been dealt with upfront.

- Overall efficiency was improved because there were fewer moving parts at any time.

Scrum in Home Building

Scrum in home building is real, it's becoming common, and its benefits are just as strong as in other industries. A home can be defined, planned, estimated, and built using the scrum framework.

For example, the first meeting with the builder is to learn about the type of home you're looking for — features such as the number of bedrooms, type of property, number of garages, quality of finishes and flooring, landscaping, the approximate amount you want to spend, and your time frame. This meeting, which takes about an hour, gives the builder a high-level understanding of what you're looking for (the product goal and roadmap).

Over several weeks after the initial planning meeting, buyers meet with an architect to get more specific details about the plans, such as desired room layouts, floors, basement, lot placement, flooring, and cabinetry. Design elements such as colors, appliances, and fixtures are not yet selected. Instead, the buyers estimate the cost of the house and provide a blueprint and elevation. These higher-risk items are more difficult and expensive to change later (the product backlog).

From that point, it's expected that the less-risky things will change later, so those decisions are deferred until the last responsible moment. However, potential risks are discussed, such as surprises that might be found at the groundbreaking.

With the blueprint comes a budget, which breaks out the details sufficiently for the builder to factor in profit and for the buyer to see each house feature (user stories).

LAST PLANNER

Last Planner is a planning system used in the construction industry that also takes advantage of scrum practices. Last Planner was partially inspired by experiments "on well-managed sites run by respected engineering and building companies" that found "only 54%, one in two, of tasks planned for delivery the following week were delivered in that week."

Decentralized decision-making, reduced specialty constructor costs, and early delivery of bad news are several aspects of many that make Last Planner so successful in delivering higher quality at lower costs and on tighter schedules.

Last Planner also challenges the traditional *push* systems, which typically result in dysfunctions like ceilings being installed before mechanical and electrical items are finished, eliminating rework (waste).

Five key conversations are at the heart of Last Planner:

- **Master Scheduling:** Roadmap planning
- **Phase "Pull" Planning:** Identifying dependencies and impediments, such as in daily scrums
- **Make Work Ready Planning:** Product backlog refinement
- **Weekly Work Planning:** Sprint planning
- **Learning:** Sprint reviews and sprint retrospectives

The budget for each feature (such as cabinets) is based on the description given to the builder by the buyer at the beginning of the project. Within that budget, the buyer gets to choose exactly what they want. Trade-offs can be made, or color coordination can occur when the buyer is looking at the actual home rather than pictures in a brochure. Although a certain quality of wood may have sounded great during planning, the buyer may change their mind and choose a less-expensive option, using the savings to add something else or financing less at closing.

Scrum in construction is real, it's becoming common, and its benefits are just as strong as in other industries, such as software. While this is one example, many more exist. Give it a try. Perhaps yours will be the next success story.

Manufacturing

Interestingly, the lines between software and hardware are blurring. Today, tangible products have a surprising amount of software within them. The car you drive, the refrigerator in which you cool your iced coffee, and the e-reader you're using to read this book are full of code.

TECHNICAL STUFF

Automobiles are now connected to the Internet of Things (IoT) technology, and they are becoming increasingly software-driven. A Tesla vehicle connects to your home Wi-Fi, and you download great new features periodically. After an error is found with its charger, Tesla can deploy a fix for thousands of vehicle owners with the click of a button. And we are now on the cusp of self-driven cars.

New demands are placed on manufacturing processes that aren't just connecting one widget to another. Complex systems — many of which are software-based — are interlacing and integrating. In fact, software is critical to the success of many manufactured products.

These trends are leading to larger, more complex development projects and teams with diverse arrays of talent. They also lead to increased complexity in incorporating product families (not just individual products), increased risk of defects as complexity rises, and a new array of compliance and required standards.

Survival of the fastest to market

Being the fastest to market is one key to winning the race to market share — which isn't a new concept. An equally important concept is keeping up with and even leading in innovation — specifically, innovation led by customer needs and desires.

KAIZEN AND SCRUM

Gabe Peterson shared his experience working in a manufacturing plant in Salt Lake City, Utah, where he successfully applied scrum in partnership with Kaizen to solve manufacturing problems. Kaizen, which is a Japanese term meaning "change for the better" or "continuous improvement," is found in most manufacturing environments.

How did he do it?

As the teams identified process improvement ideas, they added them to a "product backlog," which was shared by all cross-functional teams that were part of the production line. Beginning with sprint planning on Monday, each team added an improvement item to their sprint backlog. They held daily scrums to coordinate their improvement work, and then ended the week with a sprint review for stakeholder feedback and a team retrospective.

The scrum framework, in partnership with Kaizen, helped improve not only the manufacturing process but also their product and team.

You can be the fastest to market only if you're getting customer feedback upfront while addressing the highest-priority features and risks. Higher quality is built through early testing. Scrum enables an early, high-quality release to market. This sounds like a good fit for scrum. This reality is why Tesla and other manufacturers now employ scrum masters and agile coaches.

New technologies are astounding: robotics, artificial intelligence, 3D printing, and nanotechnology, to name but a few. Each of these technologies introduces new complexities to production. Scrum- and agile-based frameworks are ideal for problem-solving complexity.

Shareholder value

The bureaucracies that are traditional parts of the manufacturing industry emphasize efficiency, cost-cutting, and maximized shareholder value as opposed to added value for customers. This emphasis is their Achilles' heel. Companies that will excel in the future emphasize value to customers.

Scrum and its organic feedback cycle emphasize regular customer-value feedback. After each sprint, you have a working, shippable product to show to stakeholders and customers. Even if you can't get feedback during the sprint, scrum allows you to adapt as soon as you receive the feedback.

ROOFING MANUFACTURING AND SCRUM

Chances are, the shingles on your home were manufactured by GAF, a Standard Industries company and the leading roofing and waterproofing manufacturer in North America, with roots dating back to the 19th century. You may not know that starting in 2018, they aspired to accelerate the modernization of their offerings to better compete on speed-to-market and innovation. Using scrum as the foundation, they aspired to become more agile in delivering products and solutions.

How did they do it?

First, they had an important sponsor for the transformation in the newly named President & CEO, Jim Schnepper, who saw a need to accelerate innovation for the company and industry. Jim began by forming an agile transformation team led by Gerald Lackey and supported by high-performing internal talent and professional agile coaching support, which created a roadmap to improve business agility (both are discussed in Chapter 21). Cutting across marketing, R&D, manufacturing, and sales, they implemented cross-functional teams and agile project delivery capabilities that helped catalyze a change in mindsets and behaviors.

GAF put this change into practice with the launch of its new flagship product, Timberline HDZ® roofing shingles. This new product was not just a first for GAF but also an industry-first with innovative technology that enables speed and accuracy of installation. Applying an agile methodology, Timberline HDZ was launched in only nine months. *Popular Science* recognized it for product excellence on its "Best of What's New Awards" list as one of the "100 greatest innovations in 2020," and OpEx International recognized GAF for process excellence with an honorary mention in its annual awards for the "Best Enterprise-Wide Transformation Project."

As stated in the Agile Manifesto, the primary measure of success is a working product in the hands of a customer — the earlier, the better, and the more frequently, the better. Scrum does both.

Strategic capacity management

In building tangible products, you may not have a final piece of product to place in someone's hands at the end of a one-week sprint. This is fine. Just remember to keep the progression demonstrable and the feedback cycle as short as possible.

The idea is to have regular, frequent feedback from users. The specifics will vary with each product. Work to keep the feedback cycle as short as possible and decrease it when possible.

LEAN AND MEAN WITH TOYOTA

In the 1940s, a relatively unknown car company called Toyota devised a plan for producing cars while controlling costs. Rather than employing the standard assembly line procedure, which required huge overhead costs, the company created a just-in-time process.

Rather than producing everything at once, the company built only what it needed at the moment for a project. Just as a supermarket replaces only items that have sold out, Toyota built or procured only the needed parts. Because there was no huge inventory, costs were reduced.

As a result, one of scrum's roots is in manufacturing.

INTEL'S TRANSITION TO SCRUM

Intel has a long history of waterfall project management, given its manufacturing history. The company decided to test scrum for developing pre-silicon infrastructure and readiness. The idea was that if scrum worked for that project, Intel could implement it in other manufacturing processes.

How did they do it?

Intel hired a scrum coach to help it identify and break old habits, integrate new ones, and properly understand the scrum framework. Despite the coaching, however, transition issues arose. Not every senior manager attended the initial scrum meetings, buy-in by important people was slow, and real-world examples of why scrum works weren't being identified.

Eventually, Intel found that the best way to get its teams to implement and benefit from scrum was to follow scrum guidelines and avoid customizing scrum to fit their process.

Pat Elwer authored a case study entitled "Agile Project Development at Intel: A Scrum Odyssey" (www.collab.net/sites/all/themes/collabnet/_media/pdf/cs/CollabNet_casestudy_Intel.pdf).

(continued)

(continued)

In summary, the case study found that the teams discovered that scrum helped the project in four distinct ways:

- A reduced cycle time of 66 percent.

- Their performance remained on schedule with virtually no missed commitments.

- Increased employee morale. Ironically, their lowest-morale team turned into the best-performing team.

- Increased transparency, which has led to identifying impediments and unproductive habits.

After the teams and management bought into the process, the power of scrum soon became apparent.

Hardware Development

Many similarities exist between implementing scrum in software and hardware products. You may hear that the differences between the two products are so great that scrum can't work with both. That's not true. Anytime you can encapsulate the work to be done and prioritize it against other work, you can use scrum to your immense benefit.

A key element of hardware products done with scrum is to focus on feedback early and often. You may not have much to work with in the beginning, but keep producing workable increments during each sprint, and what you have to show customers and stakeholders will grow — with their feedback incorporated.

Early identification of high-risk requirements

You save time, money, and hassle if you discover defects and problems early. In waterfall, testing was left until the end. But why test only at the end when you can test all along the way and find (and resolve) defects early?

Scrum forces timely integration between firmware and software. Scrum breaks down functional silos and gets engineers working together to solve problems rather than coming together later to fix problems.

In the daily scrum (which is no more than 15 minutes), you can coordinate what's been done with what's going to be done and list what impediments are in the way.

TECHNICAL STUFF

Open-source hardware is a gift to scrum and engineering as a whole. As open-source submissions increase, organizations can quickly and creatively implement existing designs, frameworks, and architectures that get their products to market faster.

Live hardware development

In the following sections, we discuss four examples of the scrum framework successfully used for hardware development. Each situation is unique, but the essence of scrum is consistent. For the most part, whatever the product, you can use scrum to develop it faster and with higher quality and ease.

Johns Hopkins CubeSat

The Johns Hopkins University Applied Physics Lab used scrum in its Multi-Mission Bus Demonstrator (MMBD) product development effort for building two CubeSat satellites. NASA sponsored the program itself.

Three key elements were identified as being critical to the success of the product:

>> **Scrum teams:** These teams were made up of subsystem leads. All team members were co-located and given direct access to the NASA representative (the onsite product owner) for quick decision-making.

>> **Emphasis on a working system:** Only one design review was funded, and computer-aided design (CAD) models were used to simulate and manipulate designs. Informal peer reviews were conducted throughout the product, and documentation was minimal.

>> **Culture of innovation:** Change was welcomed and incorporated. Daily scrums were held to coordinate and identify the best ways of addressing the highest-priority requirements. Long-term planning was eschewed in favor of responding to reality.

REMEMBER

As in manufacturing, change is inevitable in hardware products. Fortunately, change in hardware product design and development is workable and practical.

Wikispeed modular car

Wikispeed is an all-volunteer, green prototype car designer. The company built a functional prototype car that gets 100 miles per gallon by forming self-organizing teams and using the scrum framework. The teams win races because their car is completely modular. They can swap out components based on how they're running that day, on that track, in that weather. Their competition doesn't have the same ability.

Wikispeed garnered four key takeaways from its scrum experience:

>> **Customer feedback:** Teams went to users for regular feedback and tested what they could every week.

>> **Sprints and reviews:** Regular sprint cycles were conducted, with meetings at the end of each stating what went right and wrong.

>> **Transparency:** All team members knew the goals, and anyone could make a suggestion.

>> **Peer-to-peer communication:** No one person was the boss; everyone was equal and contributed to achieving the sprint goal daily.

Telefonica Digital

Telefonica Digital began as a hardware manufacturing firm that used waterfall project management. As technology changed, it began to develop more software. As the focus shifted from hardware to software, the company adapted fully to agile and scrum.

When technology and the firm's direction changed, it returned to producing hardware. Because of its experience with scrum over the years, the company had no desire to go back to traditional project management, so it used the scrum framework for its hardware products.

The first issue was relocating the facility so employees could be co-located because the company understood the value of working in proximity. Telefonica also created a system in which it could easily procure equipment and materials on the day it needed them.

The company used scrum teams and fostered cross-functionality. It tested early and often, even using 3D printing and prototyping technologies to hasten the testing. It used lots of open hardware, which it could use for testing. At times, this process accelerated the hardware team's progress to the point of waiting on the software teams.

Saab jet fighter

Saab Defense uses scrum to develop the JAS 39E Saab Gripen jet fighter. Building this highly complex jet requires more than 1,000 engineers and more than

100 teams. Scrum provides team-level priorities and the transparency needed to expose, inspect, and adapt to changing variables regularly and quickly. Saab scaled scrum across multiple teams and departments. See Chapter 13 for more on scaling scrum.

Why building a complex fighter worked:

>> **Enhanced autonomy:** Teams are given degrees of freedom within a clearly defined framework. The focus on autonomous teams encourages decision-making at the lowest level and reduces bureaucracy (see Chapter 13).

>> **Modular architecture:** Saab used modular architecture to reduce monolithic dependencies and focus on flexibility for future changes.

>> **Continuous improvement:** Retrospectives after each sprint and short feedback loops from outside the team enable product and process improvements.

Chapter **10**

Services

There are more than 9,000 billing codes for individual procedures and units of care. But there is not a single billing code for patient adherence or improvement or for helping patients stay well.
— CLAYTON M. CHRISTENSEN, THE INNOVATOR'S PRESCRIPTION:
A DISRUPTIVE SOLUTION FOR HEALTH CARE

S crum within service industries has enormous potential. We rely on health care, education, and public utilities to maintain and enhance our civilized society. Still, there is room for creating lean systems of cost savings and quality improvement. And in many cases, scrum is already being used.

Each sector has specific challenges. Unique sets of circumstances exist that need to be dealt with in a tailored way. Many of the outdated systems of development and maintenance were developed in simpler times. But as the world grows more complex, so does the need for innovative and flexible frameworks. Scrum is ideal for dealing with new demands. We show you how and with what results.

Health Care and Scrum

For decades, health care has been at the forefront of news. Affordable and accessible health care is often considered to be a basic tenet of a civilized society. Yet, soaring costs, pressure to decrease development time without sacrificing quality, wasted spending, and increasing avoidable deaths have led to massive changes in how we pay for and receive medical attention.

In 1970, health care spending in the United States was estimated to be $75 billion. In 2020, spending was $4.1 trillion, or $12,530 per person, and accounted for 19.7 percent of the Gross Domestic Product.

Added to this situation is a health care culture in which insurance reimbursements are increasingly linked to customer satisfaction. Health care technology has an expanded and important influence on clinical outcomes and patient satisfaction. New paradigms exist, and new methods for meeting their needs are required. It should come as no surprise that scrum is being used more frequently to address health care issues than ever before.

Some of the highest-priority challenges facing the health care industry are

>> Procedural mistakes during health care delivery are now the third-highest killer in America, just behind heart disease and cancer. CNBC.com reported in 2018 that between 700 and 1200 people die each day from "errors, accidents, and infections" in hospitals.

>> Research and development on new treatments and medicines need continued funding and innovation.

>> Money is wasted on unnecessary medical tests and treatments. The Institute of Medicine Health claims a whopping one-third of the billions spent on health care each year is wasted. *The American Journal of Obstetrics and Gynecology* states that elective deliveries alone cost $1 billion annually.

>> New and increasing regulations require speedy and thorough adaptation.

>> The demand to convert to electronic health care records is monumental, yet the processes for achieving this conversion are sorely lacking.

>> There are concerns that new medical devices and systems have not been thoroughly reviewed for safety risks, and many of them are designed with traditional methods in which design comes first, and testing is left last.

In the following sections, we show you how scrum can help with the preceding issues. Scrum has been used within the health care environment with great success. It starts with administrative buy-in, followed by the implementation of scrum teams and their inherent roles. Then the process begins, following the roadmap to value like any other scrum product development effort. Follow the stages we outline throughout this book, and watch the positive changes unfold.

In general, scrum brings the following benefits to the table:

>> **Rapid and regular feedback:** Feedback is crucial for determining what's acceptable and what's not. Feedback is even more important when the development cycle involves adherence to a regulatory framework. To ensure better regulatory compliance, scrum accelerates the point at which internal auditing can happen.

>> **Accelerated time to implementation:** Health care is about saving lives, but competitive advantage can be an added benefit.

>> **Faster monetization:** Making quality health care profitable enables faster changes that are more likely to stick.

>> **Increased talent retention:** Focused workers are proven to receive more job satisfaction and remain engaged longer.

>> **Fewer product defects:** Higher visibility leads to higher quality and customer satisfaction.

Scrum is needed in the health care industry to help foster changes that support clinical decision-making within highly effective patient care and business administration. Health care struggles to evolve rapidly while also continuing to be compliant with the ever-changing demands of regulatory agencies.

Scrum has helped shorten development time for new administrative and clinical systems and increase quality and efficiency. The current health care environment is in flux between private and publicly funded care. Regulations and laws are being changed and refined. Therefore, a high degree of flexibility and transparency is necessary to survive in these turbulent waters.

Speed to market

Many of the diseases that our parents and grandparents suffered from as children are no longer daily concerns thanks to advances in sanitation and treatments, but new diseases are being discovered and exposed. Aggressive research and progress continue to find cures and prevent chronic and terminal illnesses. But health care professionals want to save more lives and save them faster.

Customer expectations regarding health care and the miracles of science are rising. Payers within the health care system are drilling down to find the best value in the medicines and treatments they're buying.

Pharmaceutical companies are under constant pressure to devise new medicines to keep up with the stiff competition, yet they must do this within a cost-cutting and economizing environment. To compete and succeed, companies in this industry (as in every other industry discussed in this book) must be the fastest, most nimble, and most cost-effective.

Yet, the pharmaceutical industry's output has, on the whole, stayed flat. Most pharmaceutical organizations are tackling new situations and technological advances with the same project management frameworks they used in the 1940s. They're surrounded by new ways of doing business, yet they've mostly stayed within traditional management mindsets.

Scrum can offer positive change in the following ways:

>> Every experiment begins with a hypothesis. In scrum, this hypothesis is the release goal.

>> In testing the hypothesis, premises are found to be true or false. Each premise is a sprint goal. The sprint backlog is broken into tasks and experiments needed to explore each premise fully. The definition of *done* for the sprint outlines the type of tasks and activities that must be conducted and accepted for a premise to be considered fully tested and explored.

>> At the end of each sprint, the team presents its findings to stakeholders, who ask questions and validate the team's sprint conclusions. Stakeholders should include representatives of regulatory teams. If something was missed, the scrum team knows early and can conduct follow-up activities to address the feedback in the next sprint if it's a priority.

>> After all premises have been validated, the hypothesis stands or is invalidated. Either way, the hypothesis reaches a releasable conclusion.

>> All the actions needed to test the hypothesis are the requirements of the product backlog and are prioritized accordingly.

>> For new products and improvements on old ones, scrum allows you to iterate quickly. The mantra "Fail fast, fail cheap" means that you can be as nimble as you like in trying new ideas and processes.

>> Self-organizing scrum teams allow developers to come up with the best research and solutions.

>> Customer, business, and regulatory involvement throughout the process means continual feedback and direction. For this reason, accountability is shared, and engagement rises.

Reduced mistakes, increased quality

Although current generations have the greatest technology and treatments ever known, we still have room to improve. Incredibly, mistakes during health care delivery in the United States are now the third-highest killer.

APPLYING SCRUM TO LABORATORY R&D

Kendra West, a scientist and agile coach from the Broad Institute of MIT and Harvard as well as The Gordon Institute at Tufts University, wanted to find ways to make her lab more effective. Her research led her to explore scrum and eventually become a scrum master.

In the Laboratory R&D environment each lab has multiple products and projects underway each with varying priorities and looming deadlines. The research itself also has challenging constraints such as the impossibility of controlling how fast cells will grow and the unpredictability of quantifying the results of or delays to experiments and lab procedures. Research often spans over long periods of time.

Application of scrum in an environment where scientists are rewarded for their individual discoveries, personal brilliance and self-led research seemed unlikely; however, Kendra and her mentor, Diolinda (Didi) Vaz, also an agile coach, found a way.

How did they do it?

As published in Kendra's www.theagilelaboratory.com, they began by helping the lab understand the greater "why" of their work and how it was in everyone's best interest to work together in pursuit of the greater lab mission. They organized into cross-functional teams. They helped people to see that "we" was more valuable than "me" and small, decomposed projects delivered results sooner. Their science itself benefitted from the transparency of failing projects fast.

The result was more focus as a lab organization on higher priority research. Instead of individuals working separately, they saw teams of people collaborating, increasing capability and knowledge throughout. Workboards and coordinated sprint reviews with lab advisors and the broader scientific community helped the entire lab stay connected and aligned. The focus on results furthered their research to practical, life-changing solutions benefitting the entire world.

The kind of health care mistakes that cause harm can be such things as complex surgical complications that go unrecognized to more minor errors regarding the doses or types of medications given to patients.

No one knows the exact costs of health care errors because the coding system used to record death data fails to record items such as communication breakdowns, diagnostic errors, and poor judgment, all of which can cost lives. But we know that there are both human and economic costs associated with errors in care. Human deaths in the U.S. are estimated to be more than 300,000 per year and serious harm to be ten times that high. The economic cost of medical errors can be estimated at $20.8 billion.

A report by the *Journal of Health Care Finance* estimates that these medical errors, if you include lost productivity in the workplace, may total up to $1 trillion annually. In many cases, these errors can result in a device or medicine getting banned forever on a very short notice, resulting in a complete loss to a company that has invested billions of dollars during the development cycle.

The causes of these errors may vary, but the quality assurance built into the scrum framework can ferret out problems and their solutions early. Scrum makes it easy to identify and deal with system inefficiencies, bottlenecks in workflow, communication breakdowns, and lack of timely feedback. Following are some ways scrum can help:

» As communication increases, inefficiencies become visible. Scrum exposes these inefficiencies through daily scrums and sprint reviews; real solutions can be tried, tested, and adapted.

» Although licensed physicians are the only people authorized to diagnose patients, self-organized teams (consisting of the entire staff) facilitate the necessary treatment rather than the command-and-control system of the highest-ranking physician.

» Feedback is rapid, and adjustments can be quickly implemented and retested.

» As quality goes up, unnecessary risks and wasted costs go down.

» As input from all members of staff and key groups is sought and used, buy-in increases, and morale improves. Buy-in or ownership is hugely valuable in health care, where many people are overworked, and burnout can be high.

Cost cutting

Those words alone are enough to pique the interest of any health care administrator. In a sense, every problem and solution we discuss in this chapter helps save costs. Avoidable illnesses and deaths, increased efficiency of care delivery and administrative flow, and ease in following regulations can all be improved to save costs.

REMEMBER

Cost savings are a hallmark of scrum. Scrum not only helps you increase speed to market, which accounts for a large part of the savings, but also streamlines processes, removes inefficiencies, and allows you to make better business decisions. The Center for American Progress stated in 2019, "Administrative costs in the U.S. health care system consume an estimated $248 billion annually — nearly double the amount per capita on health care compared with other high-income countries with similar utilization rates."

Consider savings in the context of unnecessary care costs. A 2020 National Academy of Medicine study estimates the United States wastes $765 billion annually on unnecessary health care. Causes include inefficient and unnecessary services, overpricing, excessive administration costs, and fraud.

Following are some ways scrum can help cut costs:

>> **Sprint retrospectives:** The sprint retrospectives in scrum routinely ask such questions as

- What about our claims process is unnecessary?

- How can we minimize repeat patient visits?

- What additional steps can we take to reduce patient risks even further?

- Where are the bottlenecks?

- What if form XYZ were electronic?

- What's stopping us from increasing our daily claims processing rate by 20 or 50 percent?

>> **Daily coordination of priorities:** During daily scrums, such questions as these can be asked:

- Is this necessary for this patient today?

- What's in the way of this patient's going home well today?

- How can we remove that obstacle?

>> **Transparency and simplicity:** With scrum, you want to maximize the amount of work not done, especially if it's harmful. Reducing the number of early elective deliveries (37 to 39 weeks as opposed to 40), for example, would eliminate up to 500,000 neonatal intensive-care unit days.

Adhering to regulations

With the changes brought by the Affordable Care Act in 2010 came a flurry of new regulations. These regulations are in place to protect patients and health care providers, and each health care organization needs to find ways to comply. Implementing solutions to address new regulations can be challenging and even tedious, and having fewer resources to work with makes the process more daunting.

Here are some of the ways that scrum helps health care providers understand and abide by new regulations:

>> Business value and risk mitigation can help create and prioritize a product backlog. Then the scrum teams and the organization as a whole have the rationale to make business and resource decisions during complex times of regulation changes.

>> Previously, the technical and business sides of health care solutions may not have seen eye to eye; after all, their mandates were probably different. However, their goals begin to align as a product owner covers the business side, and the technical side is covered by developers to design solutions. Scrum team roles are peer roles. Team members work together to facilitate the right environment for aligning goals and purpose, which is ideal for implementing changes to deal with regulations.

>> Self-organized teams define the best solutions. When new regulations are narrowed down and prioritized, it's easier to pinpoint solutions and implement them quickly.

>> The evolving regulatory requirements can be built into the scrum team's definition of *done*. This way, product owners and stakeholders can rest assured that they'll be in line when audits and inspections take place.

RISK AND ISSUE MANAGEMENT

Documentation is critical in risk and issue management for health care implementations for regulatory audit or legal action.

In traditional project management, documenting risks and tracking issues is typically achieved by creating and maintaining a risk and issue log that's based on initial requirements determined at the project kickoff.

As requirements change throughout the course of the implementation, they become hard to manage and often drive cumbersome change management processes.

In scrum, you can build risk management into your process by making it part of your definition of *done*. The product backlog can also be prioritized to address the most risky items first, increasing your runway for finding a viable solution. The requirement isn't complete until specifically stated risks are identified, mitigated or accepted, and documented.

Scrum's focus on continual review provides better outcomes than traditional project management methodology.

Scrum isn't an escape hatch for regulations. After all, regulations have the good of the patient in mind. Scrum is a tool for responding to changes by being tactically flexible while remaining strategically stable, thereby making sure that the goal — better health care — is achieved.

Medical device manufacturing and safety

Like the pharmaceutical industry, the medical device manufacturing industry operates within a highly competitive and cost-conscious environment. Many are beset by traditional project management mindsets. Upfront designing combined with late back-end testing means that defects are detected late and the costs of fixing them rise — assuming that the defects are detected before the product hits the market (see Chapter 4).

With scrum, you can

>> Build product testing into each iteration. Catch defects early, stamp them out, and implement better designs.

>> Co-locate designers with engineers so they're immediately accessible and can get real-time everyday feedback.

>> Add requirements as the development progresses. Many times, customers don't know exactly what they want at the beginning. After the initial high-priority requirements have been developed, scrum allows customers to see a fuller picture.

>> Inspect and adapt constantly. Only build what's most important and test and garner feedback regularly and frequently.

>> Get daily signoff with the product owner on work done.

>> Receive feedback from stakeholders at regular sprint reviews. This feedback gets them involved throughout the development process.

>> Coordinate early and often when syncing software and hardware development.

>> Share the definition of *done* for both teams and include integration and testing throughout each sprint rather than at the end.

GE IMAGING

General Electric's imaging unit found the following ailments in its traditional approach to developing medical devices before implementing scrum:

- **Predictability:** The company was running 12- to 24-month development cycles, usually with significant delays.

- **Scope creep:** Usually, business representatives pushed to add features beyond the original scope.

- **Phased approach:** Minimal customer interaction until the first round of testing was a major contributor to delays and soaring development costs.

- **Silo teams:** Artificial barriers existed among the organization's functional, technical, and business units.

Scrum healed these ailments in the following ways:

- Product owners were an integral part of the scrum teams, which significantly broke down silos and aligned priorities across the organization. The whole business began working in unison to release the right product to customers on time.

- Short sprints were held in which actual product increments were completed and demonstrated. The feedback received early steered the product to earlier completion than normal.

- Senior leadership was excited. By observing successes in a joint venture that used scrum, executive leadership saw what scrum could do, and their support accelerated adoption.

- Because of the industry's high regulation, G.E. built regulatory steps into the definition of *done* and acceptance criteria. Developers adjusted to this level of effort when estimating and executing.

By incorporating scrum into the medical-device manufacturing process, G.E. brought costs down and reduced time to market. Most important, the company reduced defects, which resulted in fewer reputational and regulatory risks. The chance that a product would harm a person went down because the product was tested and integrated so many times.

A Worldwide Pandemic

In 2019 the first known infections of SARS-CoV-2 were discovered in Wuhan, China. Soon to be known as COVID-19 it quickly covered the entire earth leaving destruction in its wake. When this book was written, Wikipedia estimated that 6.41 million people worldwide died, and many more were surviving victims of this terrible disease. For protection, people were mandated to stay home to avoid transmitting the virus to others. Schools were closed, and businesses shut down or transitioned employees to work from home. Societal debates waged between masks or no masks and vaccination or no vaccination. No one was left unscathed from the deadly virus.

While the virus attacked, many found ways to navigate the pandemic creatively using scrum. Let's discuss a few of the applications.

Patient care

The COVID-19 pandemic placed complex and heavy demands on health care systems worldwide. "Flatten the curve" of infections became the mantra as the world grappled with an unprecedented inflow of patients; ensuring hospital capacity was protected for those needing critical care was crucial. With cases increasing exponentially daily and casualties of the pandemic on the rise, hospitals turned to scrum to navigate their way through the pandemic, learning as they went.

Successful hospitals formed cross-functional teams bringing together clinical and nonclinical personnel across disciplines and departments. Together they streamlined a collaborative system that promoted efficient, effective, and high-quality patient care.

For example, the Royal Hospital in Oman found agile techniques such as scrum to be the only way to adapt to the little-known nature of the pandemic and the constant flow of new specialty-driven information, guideline modifications, and implementations. As a result, projects were defined and teams were formed to resume elective services such as surgeries or ambulatory care, while other teams enabled critical telemedicine services for their patients.

The hospital concluded that agile techniques such as scrum introduced structured methods to improve performance and processes in which teams worked together to eliminate unnecessary steps that were previously executed separately and were vulnerable to delays. They found their organization to be fast, resilient, adaptable, and suited to respond to shocks of the pandemic. They statistically improved the quality of care during the crisis months of the pandemic.

Ventilators

Because COVID-19 is a respiratory disease, ventilators were in short supply in hospitals around the world during the early days of the pandemic. Several manufacturing facilities, including automakers, changed their entire manufacturing lines to begin building life-saving respirators.

Science magazines noted that many manufacturers embraced agile values and principles to support their shift. In manufacturing, they shifted their development cycle to observing, analyzing, developing, testing, and demonstrating. Low-cost prototypes, some leveraging 3D printing, were created and rapidly tested by small, self-organizing teams who worked using the short feedback cycles of scrum.

By defining minimum viable products to meet regulations they created product goals and roadmaps highlighting MVP and future improvements (upscaled production). Figure 10-1 is an example of the roadmap for each of the ventilator's components. Table 10-1 focuses on the development of the facepiece respirator alone.

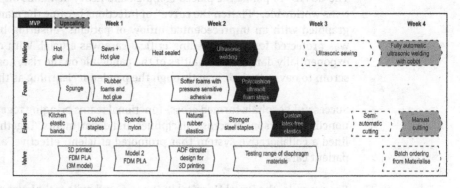

While the supply of ventilators struggled to keep up with demand overall, they became life-saving for those fortunate enough to have one.

Dutch government responds to COVID-19 pandemic using scrum

Around the world, each country responded to the COVID-19 pandemic uniquely with many similarities. For example, the Netherlands used an agile approach to navigate the pandemic for their citizens by forming a small team called the Outbreak Management Team or OMT. The OMT consisted of virologists, statisticians, pulmonologists, and intensive care specialists. They started by defining a goal with three objectives:

>> Flatten the curve; slow down the pace of the virus's spread

>> Increase intensive care capacity to be able to help more patients

>> Protect the Dutch economy from collapsing

TABLE 10-1

Summary of Typical Components in a Filtering Facepiece Respirator with Minimum Viable Product (MVP) and Upscaled Production (Upscaling)

Respirator Components	Considerations	MVP	Upscaling
Welded edges	The edges of the masks should be attached together without perforating them. Regular sewing is not an option.	Ultrasonic cutting and point welding by hand.	Ultrasonic sewing machine, Cobot point weld, ultrasonic cutting by hand
Head straps	The chosen head strap is a non-adjustable type made from elastic. Therefore the elastic band must have a good extension coefficient, to pull the mask firmly to the face. They should not lose their elasticity over time. Use non-latex materials or similar so the elastic bands do not slide off the back of the head.	Nonlatex straps of polyisoprene were selected for this application. The width was fixed at 6 mm wide for optimal balance between strength, comfort, and adaptability to various head sizes.	Same as Phase A
Strap attachment	The straps must be securely attached to the mask without perforating the mask. These attachments must be mechanically tested so they cannot come loose.	A Rapid 106E electric stapling machine was selected for this application. Type 66/6 staples were used, which created the necessary holding strength for the polyisoprene straps.	Same as Phase A
One-way valve (FFP3)	For most FFP3 masks, the filter material is difficult to breathe through. This could be dangerous for a multitude of reasons. Breathing out should then be facilitated with a one-way valve.	A new valve was designed and patented. It was designed specifically for 3D printing and rapid production.	Same as Phase A

With these goals clearly in mind, the team used data to inspect and adapt their way through the pandemic. For example, team decisions were directed by data about the number of people infected, hospitalized, and in intensive care. Other factors considered included the way the people respond to the advice of the OMT and the government or the duration of hospitalization or intensive care; lessons learned from other countries and new developments on treatments.

The OMT started by asking citizens to take increasingly strict measures starting with washing hands and avoiding handshakes. As more information came in, they asked people to socially distance and avoid contact with vulnerable people who were seriously ill or over 70. Other measures followed, including working from home, converting restaurants to food takeaways, and more.

For hospital capacity, they started by making 1,600 beds available and then increased to 2,400. When people didn't listen to the OMT's guidelines, they increased government communication by having the prime minister speak to the public (a rare event), and even the king himself spoke later.

Most impressively, the OMT held a sprint review each week using the parliament and the Dutch citizens as stakeholders. The sprint review was broadcast live throughout the country, giving insights into the spread of the virus and its impact on hospitals and society. As part of the review, the OMT communicated the goal for the next week ranging from increasing the number of intensive care beds to specific responses for changing the curve. Parliament members were given the opportunity to ask questions and make suggestions.

The results are still to be determined, but as of 2022, Bloomberg placed the Netherlands in the world's top 6, with a resilience score of 78.2 — 24 places above the U.S.

RAPID SARS-CoV-2 TESTING

Testing for SARS-CoV-2 became the largest global testing program in history, leading to the testing of hundreds of millions of individuals to date. The unprecedented scale of testing has driven innovation in the strategies, technologies, and concepts that govern testing in public health. Bain.com shared a story about a diagnostics company that successfully delivered a worldwide solution for SARS-CoV-2 testing in record time.

Before the pandemic, the diagnostic company managed innovation through a formal, multiyear stage-gate development process. Teams started with customer requirements gathering and product definition. Then, core teams worked in clearly defined swim lanes, with periodic executive input at major decision milestones. That linear and deliberate process was effective for products where the market evolution was gradual, and the regulatory guidance was fairly clear. But it was no match for the uncertainty and urgency of the pandemic. The diagnostic company inspected and adapted itself to a new learning cycle, with weekly sprints and daily scrums.

The rollout of COVID-19 tests was truly remarkable. The documented timeline shows the first cluster of cases in Wuhan, China, reported by December 31, 2019. Then, sharing the SARS-CoV-2 genome sequence on January 12, 2020, followed by the first PCR tests, granted an emergency use authorization to the U.S. Food & Drug Administration, leading to more than 10 million weekly tests run worldwide by June 2020. By the end of 2020, more than one billion tests were performed globally, and more than 200 new tests were granted authorization — a world-class time to market in diagnostics.

Education and Scrum

Throughout this book, we emphasize that scrum can be used in various industries — all of them, in fact. Products are vehicles to deliver value to defined customers and users. Scrum is a framework for developing products of all types, whether physical, virtual, services, or even something more abstract like a process improvement.

Education is another such example. Children are the future, as their children will be after them. Educating young people and ensuring that they have the ability to come up with creative, innovative solutions and decisions themselves should be the top priority of every culture.

Public education was created in a different landscape — that of basic education for workers. The need was simple because the work world was simple. Today, however, complexity has grown exponentially, as have students' choices of jobs and roles in the world.

Because of this change in the work landscape, education needs to prepare children to participate effectively in work. Many teachers are still trained to prepare and deliver material in the old way, but a better way exists.

Scrum in the classroom helps children adapt creatively and flexibly to change, prioritize their work and ideas, and develop new solutions. Technology and media are changing so rapidly that the information received by children is always in flux. With scrum, they learn how to turn change into an advantage.

Challenges in education

Education faces different challenges today than ever before. Students are the future, and preparing them for that future is complex. The curriculum is expanding in scope, underperforming students require more attention, and classroom sizes are increasing. Yet, despite this appearance of chaos, progress can be made with scrum.

In many respects, teachers inherently use scrum, but they use terms that may not be known to those outside the profession, such as *objectives*, *scaffolding*, *mini-lessons*, *modalities of learning*, and *reflection*.

Teachers already set goals for each lesson. They use the standards as the goal and set objectives for the lesson, as some standards require multiple steps. These multiple steps are called *scaffolding*. Teachers break the lesson into iterations so that students can be successful and accomplish each necessary aspect. Along the way, they use formative and summative assessments to gauge and modify learning. Students and teachers alike reflect at the end of each lesson, as in a retrospective.

Next, teachers are trained to use collaborative learning models and do assignments that engage students and get their buy-in.

Preparing students for the future

With scrum, students learn to manage themselves in what scrum educators refer to as the *self-managing classroom*. By practicing decision-making and collaboration skills, they become future-ready, which requires autonomous and adaptive problem-solving. These 21st-century life skills are not limited to the classroom and future work, but they're also useful at home:

>> Making better decisions at home and with friends

>> Supporting peers

>> Learning to collaborate and resolve sibling conflict

With student teams growing their capacity to manage themselves, the teacher can focus on better planning, foster deeper relationships with students, and provide more personalized feedback for each student.

Increasing curriculum scope

Curriculum requirements for teachers have been expanding for decades. More information must be covered, and teachers can be overwhelmed trying to keep up. These curriculum pressures come from four sources: school systems, governments, parents, and students.

Many topics and experiences used to be taught in the home by parents. School was for basics. Today, school systems cover subjects never imagined in the classroom. Following are a few newly introduced subjects:

>> Bullying prevention

>> Anti-harassment policies

>> Body-mass-index evaluation (obesity monitoring)

>> Financial literacy

>> Entrepreneurial skills development

>> Health and wellness programs

Nothing is wrong with these additional programs. In fact, they serve a great purpose. But teachers are being asked to include some of these topics — along with many other new ones — as well as the old standards of reading, writing, and arithmetic. However, they've been given no more hours in the day for teaching and often work with limited resources and funding.

Students themselves arrive with a host of experiences and knowledge that would have been science fiction a few decades ago. They're often computer-literate by their early years and have been exposed to adult themes and messages through television, films, and music. Although the teaching techniques we mentioned previously are inherently scrum, the spectrum of what's being taught has grown. But the overarching goal of education remains the same: well-educated students.

Effective prioritization and inspection-and-adaptation methods are essential for administering this growing curriculum effectively. Teachers reprioritize as they carefully plan each day and empower students to be self-organizing and self-managing. Rather than follow a rigid plan outlined at the beginning of the year, they regularly conduct assessments and adjust their schedules. Sometimes, they spend more time than planned on a subject to help a struggling class, and sometimes, they spend less time than planned when a class understands a concept faster than expected.

Teachers also recognize the value of refactoring. In the old days, you took a test, you got a grade, and that was it. As educators have learned from experience, adaptations have been made to allow students to learn from their mistakes and be rewarded for their learning. Continual-feedback loops allow for learning, followed by an assessment (pretest or quiz), with feedback and more learning followed by the final assessment. The grade isn't the only goal. Students are starting to understand and appreciate what they learn by using these same events used in scrum.

Moving low-performing students upward

Teachers are hugely instrumental in moving students through learning blocks. Sometimes, however, teachers work from a structured curriculum that requires them to move on with new topics and subjects even though not all their students may have full comprehension. Although they may want to spend more valuable one-on-one time with each student, they simply can't afford the time without preventing the overall curriculum from moving forward.

Therefore, the individual attention needed to help low- or moderate-scoring students is sometimes unavailable because of time constraints. Teachers need to keep progressing with their curriculums. Large class sizes can add to this conundrum.

As a result, low-performing students arrive in the next year's class without fully understanding the previous year's material or are held back and taught the same material again without new learning techniques. Evaluations are done, but teaching doesn't necessarily circle back to weaker areas of understanding.

Success in elevating individual students comes through collaboration among schools, teachers, parents, and students. If the scrum framework were applied for each student — and the team included a teacher, student, counselor, school administrator, and tutor — this team could set iterative goals leading to an end goal, with regular feedback loops, all the while inspecting and adapting progress and the process to fit the student's needs.

Increasing student-to-teacher ratios

Classes are getting bigger, and individual teacher-student attention is dropping. Managing an entire class (and the increasing curriculum) and providing student- and subject-specific teaching is a tall order.

REMEMBER

Teachers spend time building relationships, modifying lessons, executing lessons, and helping students one-on-one. Finding time is the most important challenge of education. As funding decreases but teaching methods and systems stay the same, education in the classroom will inevitably suffer. Scrum can help leverage teachers' time and increase adaptability.

An example approach using scrum

How does the scrum-in-the-classroom concept work? Kids love it. They become active participants with the whiteboards and sticky notes and are responsible for ensuring each bit is in its proper place.

SCRUM IN THE CLASSROOM

Scrum works in education like anywhere else. As scrum is based on goals, setting focused learning goals allows students to adapt their learning styles to their learning speed. Students can master each subject and level before moving on by focusing on one learning goal at a time. With scrum, teachers can emphasize high-priority learning items that students focus on.

Organizations like Agile Classrooms and EduScrum have transformed classrooms into student-centered, highly collaborative, and self-organizing environments to build technical, academic, and social skills that benefit all areas of life.

Scrum is also effective in large classes because smaller scrum teams can be formed for projects. Within limits based on the ages and natures of individual groups of students, these teams can be self-organizing and self-directed to reach educational goals.

Inspection and adaptation work remarkably well in learning environments. Studies have shown that students can improve their comprehension if they have lesson plans to adapt to and can work in specific areas in which they struggle. Iterative teaching models have been introduced to the classroom with remarkable results in the following ways:

- The teacher outlines the unit or project for all the students, and groups are formed (sprint planning).

- The teacher executes daily teaching, guides group work-learning tasks, and sets a time goal (sprint).

- The student and teacher assess student performance at the end of the timebox (sprint review).

- Students who perform above a preset cutoff level move to new material. If they perform below this level, a sprint retrospective is conducted.

REMEMBER

A sprint retrospective is not held only when a problem needs intervention — they're held each sprint. Just like with product development, students have an opportunity to inspect, adapt, and improve continuously. This is about how they grow as learners and grow their skills, learning processes, relationships with peers and teachers, and their learning environment.

- Using feedback received at the sprint review, problem topics for each student are identified.

- Students form teams to maximize the teacher's ability to help students by leveraging each student's challenges. These teams work together to increase their understanding of the topic.

(continued)

(continued)

- Material for these new groups is revised (product backlog refinement). Also, students come up with ideas about ways to better learn the subject material.

- Another sprint is run.

- Student performance is assessed.

This process is repeated, incrementally improving student performance.

In studies, student performance showed significant improvement. Also, students made fewer mistakes, had more confidence, and spent less time figuring out the problems.

Student scrum teams don't have to be shifted; they can be kept stable. That way, cross-functional teams can be created, made up of students who have higher skills in some areas than others. Subsequent sprints use the same techniques in pair programming and shadowing. By learning from other students, each student gains new skills, and advanced students expand their skill sets.

State and national standards dictate certain requirements for demonstrating mastery of subjects (which can serve as a basic definition of *done*), but each school or teacher can enhance the state or national definition of *done* to suit specific circumstances and work quality. What students learn and how they show that they've learned it are vital elements of the overall success of the sprint. Success will vary according to the situation, but the definition of *done* should be made clear to everyone, especially the students.

Following is how one teacher approaches scrum in the classroom:

1. **Set up an assignment with a duration of one to five class periods.**

   This is effectively a sprint. The teacher has the original plan but gets class buy-in through listing requirements. If the assignment is to understand the periodic table of the elements, for example, requirements could be sections of the table. Tasks might be the individual elements themselves.

2. **Scrum teams of students are formed, and team members decide who fills the scrum roles.**

   These teams have a high degree of autonomy. The goal is always to grow students' capacity to be more autonomous and make better choices.

3. **A product backlog is created, often using a task board.**

   The kids write down the requirements. The teacher serves as a scrum master and keeps everyone focused.

4. **Sticky notes on a whiteboard, wall, or blackboard are used to get children involved with ordering and prioritizing the requirements.**

   Children love the sense of accomplishment that comes from seeing things move from the to-do column to the doing column to the *done* column.

5. **Each day's session begins with a check-in (such as a daily scrum).**

   The students use scrum language, such as *daily scrums*, *scrum master*, and *sprint reviews*. (However, because class periods aren't always daily, they may not call it a daily scrum).

6. **At the end of each sprint, a review and retrospective are conducted.**

   Buy-in increases, and when appropriate, the students can contribute to goals for new assignments.

Children enjoy the hands-on process and progress. They quickly see progress and are amazingly flexible when it comes to adapting. In short, kids naturally iterate (see "The Marshmallow Challenge" in Chapter 1). Scrum is just a formalized way of dealing with natural brain wiring.

Blueprint & Hope High School

Blueprint Education in Chandler, Arizona, is a not-for-profit organization that creates and implements special-education options. School board members, led by Agile Classrooms founder John Miller, decided that having a high school diploma wasn't enough to prepare students for the 21st century. Students also needed collaboration, creativity, accountability, critical thinking, and teamwork skills. Interestingly, scrum naturally fosters all these qualities.

At one of Blueprint's schools, Hope High School, scrum has greatly impacted its students. Scrum roles were flexible based on the individual team context. Sometimes, the teacher was the product owner or scrum master; students took on these roles at other times. As team members matured and garnered more experience, they automatically took over the product owner role. The teachers simply identified the type of projects to be completed. Then, the students took over by developing their own goals, implementation, and reviews. Collaboration and teamwork skills took off.

The success of scrum in the high school led Blueprint to spread the idea into its elementary school with similar results. Blueprint experienced many positive anecdotal outcomes, including greater student engagement, more fun, greater empathy, independent thinking, and a more positive educational experience. One teacher said that her kids would even come in if they were ill because they didn't want to miss a single day of school, which is wholehearted buy-in from students.

EduScrum

In Alphen aan de Rijn in the Netherlands, scrum is being used in high school and in a secondary educational college. The program is called EduScrum, and educators who use it are experiencing amazing results.

Teachers and students use scrum in all subjects, forming scrum teams with all the roles intact. Three teacher scrum masters lead the charge, each facilitating the process in his or her class. The scrum masters also conduct daily scrums on the projects, sprint reviews, and retrospectives.

The school collected data on the results of this process with 230 students ages 12 to 17. The results were impressive. In the Netherlands, test scores range from 1 to 10. A score of 5.5 is fine, but students strive for 6.7 or better. The students who participated in scrum teams consistently outperformed those who didn't participate by 0.8 to 1.7 points — a significant increase in terms of percentages.

Half the students said they understood the subject material better, had more fun (hugely important for learning), could work harder and faster, and thought they were learning smarter.

Teachers also noticed greater engagement from their students and a more positive experience. Interestingly, corporations and organizations often report improved employee morale when they incorporate scrum. This model is now used widely in Europe.

EMPOWERED EDUSCRUM STUDENTS

In 2020, Scrum Inc. produced an EduScrum webinar by Jeff Sutherland, co-author of the Agile Manifesto for Software Development and Scrum, and Willy Winjnands, author of EduScrum. In the webinar, Willy told the story of how EduScrum was used in the Netherland classrooms.

First, the teacher enabled the formation of cross-functional teams by giving each student a survey of their assessment of their qualities and skills. Based on the student's answers, the teacher organized them into teams spanning the spectrum of qualities and skills.

Next, a project with a goal was defined for the students to decompose into a product backlog. The students organized and prioritized their backlog using planning poker and sticky notes. The backlog became a topic for the students to learn throughout the project.

On Mondays, the students held sprint planning as a team and set up their task board for the sprint. Each day, they held a brief daily scrum as they launched into their work; on Fridays, they shared their results with the rest of the class, followed by a brief retrospective. Jeff said when the bell rang, the students would rush into the classroom to quickly huddle at their boards and then raced to do their work without the teacher even saying a word. Jeff visited each team to check on their work and answer questions. The teacher became the classroom facilitator, turning the accountability for education and learning over to the students themselves.

The classroom became walls of learning dotted with team task boards, burnup charts, walls of both failures and successes, and even a definition of *fun* to ensure the students learned and found enjoyment. In addition, desks were moved together, simplifying team communication.

What were the results?

Jeff shared that high school students using EduScrum finished their semesters six weeks earlier with 20 percent higher grades. Students also reported that they had more fun. Even the demand for employing the students after high school was high. Some businesses learned that these students would choose not to work for them if they even hinted at having traditional or waterfall underpinnings. Local businesses even had to become more agile to employ EduScrum students.

TIP

An interesting side effect of scrum in schools was that the students reported simply having more fun with classes and learning. This made them more eager to go to school and participate. And those shy, quiet types? They flourished as their skills and contributions were noticed in the reviews and retrospectives. The team atmosphere also improved. Well over half the students learned to cooperate better and developed trust in their team members. They were open to giving and receiving feedback, and teachers noticed a more relaxed atmosphere.

Military and Law Enforcement

Many agile and scrum experts appreciate agile principles and the scrum framework because of their experience in the military. Military organizations are mistakenly perceived to value strong centralized decision-making, often called *command-and-control*. However, military strategists have long known that centralized decision-making leads to defeat on the battlefield. A commander can't possibly see all parts of the battlefield or communicate fast enough to understand a chaotic, rapidly changing situation or exploit fleeting opportunities. Wise commanders understand that they must empower those at all levels to make timely decisions.

TECHNICAL STUFF

Command-and-control actually refers to a *command* being given (a strategic vision or goal for an operation), but *control* and autonomy for completing the mission are delegated to those executing the plan.

In 1871, German military strategist Helmuth von Moltke (the Elder) sagely observed, "No battle plan survives contact with the enemy." Today, his approach to decentralized decision-making is known to the military as *mission command*.

The doctrine of mission command allows leaders to make agile decisions and adapt under conditions of uncertainty. The principles are practiced by most Western military organizations, including the U.S. Marine Corps and the U.S. Army. The U.S. Army operates the Mission Command Center of Excellence to train leaders in decentralized decision-making methods.

Turning the ship around

In 1999, U.S. Navy Captain David Marquet became commander of the USS Santa Fe, a submarine for which he had no training. The crew was trained to do what they were told. The submarine and crew were the lowest-performing in the fleet at the time. It was a deadly combination.

Captain Marquet's first orders to his new crew were to do something he didn't know the submarine was incapable of doing, yet the crew answered with "Yes, sir." But nothing happened. The crew had been immersed in a top-down culture of "Do what I say." It became clear to the new captain that the crew's culture would not work well with a captain trained on another type of ship.

Captain Marquet spent his time from that moment changing the culture of the USS Santa Fe from top-down to a "leader-leader" model. Instead of the crew coming to the captain and asking, "Requesting permission to submerge the ship," Marquet required the crew to come to him, saying, "Captain, *I intend to* submerge the ship. All men are below. Hatches are shut. Ship is rigged for dive. Bottom depth checked. We're in the water that's been assigned to us." The captain responded, "Very well."

With an assurance of technical competence of the crew and the clarity of purpose he gave them, Captain Marquet empowered his crew with psychological ownership to be effective, self-managing, and cross-functional to determine the right thing to do through continuous feedback. He turned the submarine from the worst to the most successful, and since his retirement, the submarine has continued to win awards for excellence.

Special forces

Special operations forces, also called *special forces*, are uniquely trained to be adaptable, self-reliant, and operate in uncertainty. In the U.S., special forces refer to notable teams like the Green Berets and Navy Seals.

In many ways, agile teams are analogous to special-forces teams. Both types of teams are small, highly trained, highly professional, cohesive, and cross-functional. Special-forces teams are small and cross-functional, so they can adapt to situations that arise. Cross-functionality means that every team member can do more than one thing; ideally, every team member can do every skill necessary.

Like agile teams, special-forces teams are stable and long-lived. Through hard-earned experience, their members know how to work together and trust one another, and they pitch in to do whatever is needed to accomplish the mission. That mission may require fluency in a foreign language, building relationships with local villagers, or even skilled use of deadly force if necessary. The mission may call for any combination of those things, yet carrying out the mission may involve something completely different. Special-forces teams know how to inspect and adapt.

Also, both agile and special-forces teams create a sense of mutual accountability. In high-stakes situations, whether in business or on the battlefield, the desire not to let a team member down is more important than any deadline.

Like scrum sprints, missions for military teams are normally broken down to be accomplished quickly, within weeks at the longest. Longer missions wear out soldiers, deplete supplies, and require significant ongoing support. You find an exponential correlation between the length of a mission and the cost and rate of failure. Short missions provide better focus, team morale, and success.

One of many examples in which a military commander succeeded by changing his command-and-control approach is Admiral Nelson at Trafalgar. Instead of requiring strict adherence to signal flags hoisted on his flagship, Nelson delegated substantial authority to ship captains, saying, "In case signals can neither be seen or perfectly understood, no captain can do very wrong if he places his ship alongside that of the enemy."

Scrum and the FBI

Cyberattacks of all sorts are increasing worldwide, from credit card hacking to government and military security threats. Military and cyberwarfare experts agree that controlling this expanding threat is a major concern. As a result, cyberthreat deterrence programs that can adapt to the ever-changing nature of these sophisticated challenges are needed — and needed fast. In many cases, it's an issue of national security.

The FBI has been increasingly active in finding response solutions to these cyberattacks on a national and criminal level. However, leadership knows it isn't enough to use old techniques for handling these uber-modern threats. New ways of applying technology, shaping their workforce, and collaborating with partners are required.

Not surprisingly, they're approaching this conundrum with scrum.

After the 9/11 terrorist attacks, the FBI began to work on streamlining its flow of information and coordination with all relevant entities. After a couple of false starts, it developed the Sentinel program: a comprehensive software case management system. The goal is to replace a current system consisting of a mixture of digital and paper information flow with a purely digital one.

For ten years, the project was conducted using the FBI's prescribed waterfall methods, including extensive upfront design and fixed requirements. A new CIO, Chad Fulgham, started requiring incremental delivery from the contracted developers. Here are some of the symptoms of the waterfall process used up to that point:

>> Only 4 of 18 workflows were live but with defects.

>> Less than 1 percent of the 14,000+ forms were created in the new system.

>> Cost to date was $405 million, with an estimated $350 million more to go over six years.

>> All delivered functionality was considered optional throughout the organization.

In three months of using scrum — with 5 percent of budget and 80 percent fewer staff — scrum did what waterfall couldn't do in ten years. Overall, excess staff was cut by more than 50 percent, user stories were created, and 21 two-week sprints were scheduled — an 85 percent decrease in the projected schedule.

Chapter **11**

Publishing: A Shifting Landscape

History will be kind to me, for I intend to write it.

— WINSTON CHURCHILL

I n any disruptive environment, quick and pivoting innovation tactics are needed. Publishing and the news media have gone through massive changes before our eyes. Traditional products and readers are changing, and no one knows where the change will end.

Publishing houses and news organizations need to continue monetizing current products and finding new sources of revenue. Trying a new form of native advertising, for example (such as ads intermingled in a feed of news articles or commercials with personalized QR codes), calls for quick turnaround time and quick response to customer feedback. Promoting a new book through an author's existing social media channels or developing new revenue-generating ideas for customer feedback requires a disciplined feedback cycle, focused development, and close customer interaction.

Scrum can handle this type of shifting landscape smoothly. When the goalposts keep moving, it doesn't make sense to aim for where they used to be. We don't know how publishing and news will continue to evolve, so we can inspect and adapt along the way. Those in publishing who are most successful are doing just that.

A Changing Landscape in Publishing

Enormous rates of change are occurring. Brick-and-mortar bookstores are suffering, and readers have shifted ways of finding books and authors. Even libraries are receiving less funding, and much of their shelf space has been converted to computers and other media.

On top of this, readers can now choose between reading or listening on desktops, mobile platforms, and, decreasingly, traditional hardback and paperback books. Now, different media forms compete against each other for the same content.

Traditional revenue models are changing for advertising and subscriptions in this new publishing environment, so new models are needed to take advantage of this new digital world. But publishers are still discovering those models.

The music industry experienced a similar seismic shift. Traditional album buying flew out the door when iTunes flew in. Free and often illegal music downloads stirred up a fresh debate on copyright law (enriching scores of lawyers along the way), and avenues for music today are dramatically different from those 20 years ago. But new songs and albums are created all the time, and musical life goes on. It just looks different.

The same can be said of publishing. For some organizations, massive industry changes are terrifying; for others, opportunity is recognized, flexibility is sought, and inspection and adaptation are seen as paramount. Some publishers say that because of the rapid change, they're not sure which data they should use to form their decisions. The sand is shifting under their feet.

Scrum can help the publishing industry flourish. The very qualities that so many people in the industry find unsettling — rapid change, shifting consumer needs and desires, and uncertain sources of revenue — are the ones in which scrum excels.

Inspecting, adapting, and refactoring

Inspection, adaptation, and refactoring are the heart of scrum, and they fit the world of publishing. Like each industry we cover in this book, publishing has its own set of challenges and scrum solutions.

Changing readers

What readers expect from a book, magazine article, or newspaper feed is changing. Immediate information and instant gratification are the norm. Unless the author is already a huge best seller with a wide following, most readers won't sit down to finish a 1,000-page tome.

A flood of data can be accessed by incorporating rapid feedback from readers via short articles, blogs, and analytical tracking tools for reader click-through rates and responses. The news media, publishers, and individual authors can quickly see what readers are responding to and adjust accordingly.

Not only does this rapid feedback cycle mean better content, but it also means faster monetization. As you inspect and adapt on the go, you can follow those paths that lead to more clicks and hits, incorporating more revenue streams through advertising and sales.

Changing writers

Brandon Sanderson, a sci-fi and fantasy author of the enormously popular books written in the Cosmere universe, broke records with his self-publishing Kickstarter campaign. The campaign was set up to raise $1 million within 30 days to fund four secret books written during the pandemic. It didn't take 30 days to blow past that goal, though. It took only 35 minutes! After three days, he earned more than $20 million, beating the previous record and landing nearly $42 million after 30 days. The author told *The New York Times* one of his objectives was to see what it would be like to challenge Amazon.

Similarly, but no less impressive, Hugh Howey broke more than one mold with his *New York Times* best-selling novel *Wool*. He published the original short story on Amazon for 99 cents a copy and received such an overwhelmingly positive response that he kept on writing.

Howey wrote and self-published five serial stories, getting feedback from readers with each one, and combined them to create the book *Wool Omnibus* (self-published by Broad Reach Publishing). It landed on the *Times* best-seller list and created a sweet seven-figure revenue stream for him.

After self-publishing and reaching the best-seller list, Howey signed a contract with a traditional publishing firm, Simon & Schuster. In yet another mold-shattering move, he sold only the print rights to the publisher, keeping all digital rights and proceeds for himself.

Serial stories are produced in sprints. Feedback comes from readers and potential book buyers. Some authors use self-publishing, where each detail can be inspected and adapted along the way. Both success stories were unintentional variations of scrum.

Changing products

What and how people read and listen are in flux. Graphic novels, manga, and interactive serials combine with novels, audible books, articles, and blogs to create a wide net within which authors place their work. Add e-readers, smartphone apps, and steadily decreasing hardcopy numbers, and you have a changing world.

No author or reader is untouched by this literary revolution. T.S. Eliot's classic epic poem "The Waste Land" has its own iPad app, but it isn't just a copied-and-pasted edition of the text. The app incorporates these features:

>> A filmed performance of the poem by Fiona Shaw

>> Audio readings by T.S. Eliot and actors such as Alec Guinness and Viggo Mortensen

>> Interactive notes to help the reader with cultural references and poetic nuances

>> Videos of literary experts providing insight on the masterpiece

>> Original manuscript pages that show the reader how the poem developed under the guidance of Ezra Pound

The publishers (Faber and Touch Press) aren't sitting on the sidelines lamenting the good old days. They're jumping right in and producing great art in new ways.

For publishers and authors alike, scrum's feedback cycle allows for fast input and an accelerated time to market, creating products that customers want and will pay for. Those who embrace this change and incorporate empirical frameworks (such as scrum) that allow for this feedback cycle are excelling in this new environment.

REMEMBER

"Survival of the fastest to change" is the mantra. See change as an opportunity, and you'll come out on top.

Applying scrum

As in other contexts, publishing content can be easily and frequently inspected, adapted, and refactored until it's ready for publication. For short works, the process is easier, but it can be adapted to all sizes and lengths.

For example, creating content for YouTube is a natural for inspection and adaptation. Post content, and with analytics, you can see an amazing array of data, such as how many people saw it, did they subscribe to your channel, how long they stayed, and what links they followed.

For longer pieces, the process works as well. For the first edition of Mark's first book, *Agile Project Management For Dummies* (published by John Wiley & Sons, Inc):

1. Mark established the product goal for the book (a field guide that can be used as a reference by people who were doing scrum).

2. He established a product roadmap: the book outline.

3. He broke the outline into book sections (releases). Each chapter became its own sprint.

4. He started with Chapter 1, writing it according to Wiley's *For Dummies* development standards.

   After he sent Chapter 1 to the Wiley editor, he was told that she hated it and why (feedback, feedback, feedback).

5. He implemented that feedback in Chapter 1, identified the lessons learned, and used those lessons to write Chapter 2.

   He sent Chapter 2 to the Wiley editor and was told that she didn't much like it and why (feedback, feedback, feedback).

6. He improved Chapter 2 and used what he learned to write Chapter 3. When he sent Chapter 3 to the Wiley editor, she told him, "It's okay, but it would be better if you . . . (feedback, feedback, feedback)."

   This cycle continued until Mark and the editor synced up with Chapter 5.

Had he written all 20 chapters and sent them all to Wiley at once, and the editor said she hated them, the book would not be in the marketplace today.

THE SCRUM IN *SCRUM FOR DUMMIES*

With the experience garnered from the first book tucked firmly under our belt, we applied what we learned in editions of both books since then. There's truly scrum in *Scrum For Dummies*.

We set up the work to be done for each book as a virtual task board. We use a virtual sticky note tool, and the columns from left to right are

- A product backlog listing all the chapters, front and back matter, and anything else relevant

- To do

(continued)

(continued)

- Doing

- Done

Each chapter included tasks such as research, write, edit (feedback!), revise, review, and approval. In some cases, multiple tasks were created (such as for multiple edits or images).

Requirements were chapters. Tasks were chapter activities. The publishing team members (developers) swarmed each section and chapter and then moved to the next. There were daily scrums in which each party outlined what he was doing and raised any impediments. Each weekly sprint was followed by a review and retrospective, in which team members worked out what could be done better.

The clarity is amazing. All authoring team members know what they are supposed to be doing and by when. It's no surprise our books become #1 best sellers on Amazon.

TIP

An incremental approach like this enables you to make a release decision at any point. Because each chapter was done to a printable (releasable) state, at any time, we could have said, "Enough, let's release. These chapters have enough value for the readers." Completing each chapter based on priority (value and risk) order allows us to make that call. AC + OC > V. (See Chapter 5 for more on making value-based decisions.)

News Media and Scrum

The news media has experienced a seismic shift all its own. Print has gone online, advertising changes with every new medium (such as print, audio, radio, TV, online, social, and mobile), and readers' news-gathering experience has metamorphosed. For example, many people no longer get a daily newspaper delivered to their homes.

But in scrum, change is good. At the least, scrum helps you harness change for improvement.

What the industry is experiencing is disruption. Harvard Business School's Clayton Christensen coined the concept of "disruptive innovation," which can be described as what happens when a new product or service enters an existing market and relentlessly gains share until it uproots well-established rivals.

The biggest challenges for traditional print media organizations are finding ways to monetize their current product offerings and going digital. Print and digital are different beasts. Smart media companies with both a print and digital presence have separated the two sides of their businesses to allow them to do what they do best. The digital side of these companies implement scrum. But what about the traditional sides?

Brady Mortensen, a newsroom veteran and Chief Technology Officer (product owner) at Deseret Digital Media, said

"In reality, news organizations have probably been practicing a lot of scrum techniques for many years without realizing it. Daily scrum meetings are not uncommon. With local TV stations or daily papers, the "sprint" length is one day, and the end product is a collection of newscasts and a paper. There is also a usable product created at the end of each cycle. Newsrooms live and die by these practices. What would help traditional news organizations is to recognize that what they already do is scrum-like, but to embrace the techniques even more."

The companies flourishing in this new environment have proved to be nimble — especially those that have adopted scrum to identify their highest-risk areas at regular intervals and pivot (inspection and adaptation).

Organizations such as *The Washington Post, The Chicago Tribune*, and National Public Radio use aspects of scrum in their newsrooms. Some specific techniques are as follows.

» ***Chicago Tribune:*** Teams begin by asking who the users are, what they need, and what features can be included to fulfill those needs. Teams then prioritize features in piles labeled Must, Want, Nice, and Meh. The teams toss out the bottom two piles and work from feature to feature. When the deadline arrives, iteration stops.

   The assigning editor is usually the product owner. The developers consist of journalists, designers, photographers, editors, and others related to developing content.

   Scrum reduces the number of meetings, which can be overwhelming, especially in digital media.

» **NPR:** NPR uses a two-week sprint cycle, with a two-hour-long sprint planning meeting at the start.

   Stand-up daily scrums last for 15 minutes. Teams coordinate who's working on what stories, and impediments are identified and removed.

>> *Washington Post*: The paper has a specific agile technique for developing content for its live-blogging platform.

The team begins with a product goal: What effect do they want it to have on the user?

In the daily scrum meetings, the team decides what they are working on that day. Journalists pair up for work, a process *The Post* has used long before scrum was implemented. Two journalists sit at the same desk and finish the article. This intensifies the work and limits distractions.

The goal is to go live with the news as soon as possible and then get feedback from the users and the group. Based on the feedback, the team adapts and adjusts for the next cycle.

Defining done for content

Using scrum to develop nonsoftware products and services, such as content for publication, is quite similar to using scrum for software. The definition of *done* for content developers should clearly outline what it means to consider content ready for prime time.

Going back to our roadmap to value, a publishing scrum team should have a product goal that states what readers' needs are, how the publication meets the needs of those readers and is differentiated in its market and industry, and how the goal ties into the corporate strategy. (For more on product goals, see Chapter 2.)

The roadmap reflects this goal by outlining the areas of editorial emphasis to be covered by the publication, including any seasonal considerations. The product backlog is a prioritized and ordered list of proposed features, series, and stories to be researched, developed, edited, and published.

The product goal is the framework for defining what it means to have done content, one story or article at a time. The definition of *done* might look something like this:

With each article, we have succeeded in fulfilling our product goal to [statement of how the need is met and differentiated] after we have

>> Addressed the who, what, when, where, and why in the lead. Those elements are not buried.

>> Ensured balance — both sides of an issue are represented.

>> Ensured search engine optimization standards and requirements were met in article elements such as the headline, tags, and body.

>> Cited at least one source for each side of the issue.

>> Checked twice for accuracy to avoid embellishing and bias.

>> Prepared accompanying content for social media posts.

>> Verified that line edits and copyedits are completed.

Consistency and clarity on what's expected and what success looks like are found in a newsroom where these criteria are front and center for content curators, editors, and producers to see at all times.

The news-media scrum team

A content team director for a major regional news site identified the following scrum implementation. This team's role was to curate, edit, and post daily content to the site. The site's adoption of scrum covered the following issues:

>> What is the product? (News content customers want to read)

>> What is the product backlog? (Potential news stories and associated media posts, which were constantly changing)

>> What is the release? (Continuous delivery; content is delivered as soon as it is edited and approved)

>> What is the sprint duration? (The 24-hour news cycle)

>> When is sprint planning? (First thing every morning; backlog stories that have received editing approval are discussed)

>> When is the sprint review? (End of each day or before sprint planning each morning, which includes a review of the articles published and resulting analytics for inspection and adaptation for the next sprint's articles)

>> Who are the developers? (Content curators, reporters, photographers, editors, graphic artists, and videographers)

>> Who is the product owner? (The managing editor)

>> Who is the scrum master? (A developer who understands and has experience with scrum and has the organizational clout to remove impediments for the team)

>> Who does backlog refinement, and when? (The developers and the product owner throughout each day, curating and evaluating proposed stories, including breaking news)

The broader picture comes to light when these basic questions are asked and answered. Each role, artifact, and event can be identified and assigned.

Sprint flexibility

Daily sprints in a news organization often provide the flexibility needed for daily news feeds. You can't plan the news five days from now, but you can plan a day of story time — most of the time. Breaking and unexpected news stories can be dealt with during the sprint by direct communication among team members.

Media with longer content cycles, such as magazines (online and/or in print form), can have longer sprint cycles for content. Each feature — a section, article, chapter, or other segment — can be broken into requirements and tasks when appropriate.

4

Scrum for Business Agility

IN THIS CHAPTER

» **Facilitating Big Data migration**

» **Enabling and securing IT tools**

» **Retaining and training talent**

» **Improving operational value**

» **Innovative maintenance and support**

Chapter **12**

IT Management and Operations

Any sufficiently advanced technology is indistinguishable from magic.
— SIR ARTHUR C. CLARKE

In Chapter 8, we discussed scrum in the software development industry, providing examples of scrum's power in this arena. Software development has to do with the creation of software applications that run on computer systems and electronic devices. Information technology is all about computer and telecommunications systems for storing, sending, and retrieving information.

Not every organization has a software development division, but it's rare indeed to find an organization that can survive without a staff of IT professionals devoted to the smooth flow and security of information.

IT operations can vary widely from one organization to another. Roles and responsibilities may differ, and even within an individual group, the type of work done may vary from day to day and quarter to quarter. Further, IT is experiencing rapid changes as technology continues to evolve and possibilities race ahead.

In any growing field, challenges abound. When the system gets overwhelmed and services get interrupted, mission-critical work may be delayed or even stopped, resulting in increased costs, wasted resources, loss of revenue, and even loss of customers. An IT team's backlog can fill up so fast that they can't keep up.

In this chapter, we look at IT management and operations and describe how scrum provides time- and cost-saving solutions for modern challenges.

Big Data and Large-Scale Migration

The sheer scale of data is astounding, and even as we write this chapter, it's getting bigger. Trying to get your head around the size of Big Data is much like trying to picture a huge mathematical phenomenon such as the speed of the expanding universe. Big Data is so big that it goes beyond what most people can imagine.

The following numbers are just a few examples of how big Big Data can be:

>> Walmart conducts 1 million transactions per hour, feeding databases of more than 2.5 petabytes (about 167 times the size of the data in all the books in the Library of Congress).

>> Instagram houses more than 40 billion photographs, and 95 million photos and videos are shared every day.

>> eBay adds 50 terabytes of information every day, processing 100 petabytes.

>> Decoding the human genome requires analyzing 3 billion base pairs. The first time, the process took ten years; now, it takes three-seven days.

>> Cisco estimated that in 2021, the annual run rate for global Internet traffic was 7.7 exabytes (EB) per day, a threefold increase from 2.4 exabytes per day in 2016.

The importance of Big Data can't be overstated. Much of this data is highly personal and sensitive, and it can affect lives as well as bottom lines. The challenge is to gather, manage, and interpret data quickly, effectively, and correctly. Also, possible future uses for this data must be considered in the design of storage and retrieval processes. This data needs to become useful intelligence, not just data.

A significant challenge is that 80 percent of this data is unstructured (such as emails, blogs, spreadsheets, text documents, images, video, voice, and search logs). This unstructured segment is growing faster than structured data. In other words, the majority of data is a huge mess.

HOW MUCH IS A YOTTABYTE?

A yottabyte is trillion gigabytes, or 10^{24} bytes of digital information. Here is the scale of data sizes:

- 1 byte is the equivalent of a single digital text character (such as the letter *a*).

- 1KB is a kilobyte, or roughly 1,000 bytes of digital information.

- 1MB is a megabyte, or 1 million (1000^2) bytes of digital information.

- 1GB is a gigabyte, or 1 billion (1000^3) bytes of digital information.

- 1TB is a terabyte, or 1 trillion (1000^4) bytes of digital information.

- 1PB is a petabyte, or 1 quadrillion (1000^5) bytes of digital information.

- 1EB is an exabyte, or 1 quintillion (1000^6) bytes of digital information.

- 1ZB is a zettabyte, or 1 sextillion (1000^7) bytes of digital information.

- 1YB is a yottabyte, or 1 septillion (1000^8) bytes of digital information.

ENTERPRISE DATA STRATEGY

Understanding and using data for making decisions is critical for businesses in today's competitive environment, but even more so for pharmaceutical companies. One of our multinational pharmaceutical clients saw building a data strategy as a scrum team pilot opportunity.

How'd they do it?

They began with an agile transformation team (ATT) made up of organizational leaders who hand-selected the team members with data architecture, database administration, information governance, data warehousing, data science, and communication skills. They saw their data strategy as an opportunity to explore using a team with a complicated problem to solve; the specific outcomes were unclear, but the returns could be significant.

As the new cross-functional team gathered and organized into roles, they started by creating a product goal with stakeholders from each business unit. First, they considered the enterprise data strategy as their product. Then they built a roadmap of everything needed to accomplish the product goal. Next, they pulled in the first backlog

(continued)

(continued)

items into a sprint and, you guessed it, started iterating to build their product increment. Not only did they hold daily scrums, but they also held sprint reviews and retrospectives every sprint. The product owner and scrum master came from the R&D organization that owned the strategic data warehousing capability and tool sets, while the team's developers were data architects, engineers, and former project managers.

The outcomes were quite remarkable! Not only did they engage every organization's business unit in the solution, building support along the way, but they also laid out all the steps necessary to build momentum for adopting and embedding the strategy into the culture. Another unexpected outcome was the agile transition team learned it would have been helpful to timebox the pilot team's focus because they learned that the deliverables created by the team at the beginning of their journey were the most valuable to the entire organization.

Data security and protecting privacy are more important than ever; at the same time, security is more difficult to ensure than ever. Traditional data management frameworks and processes aren't capable of processing this quantity. Speed, flexibility, and instant feedback are needed. Six months is too long to hope that a new, untested system works. And chances are that in six months, the requirements will have changed, or a new gap will be identified.

To deal with this tsunami of data, many firms and organizations are moving to the cloud. Many organizations have their own in-house clouds or virtualized environments. (See Chapter 8 for details on cloud computing.)

Data warehouse management

Data warehouses are traditionally thought to be difficult to manage. Although each segment or phase of the work may have a discernible beginning and end, the data warehouse itself is never finished; it's continually growing and changing.

REMEMBER

A data warehouse isn't some barbed-wire-fenced building on the outskirts of town. Rather, strategic and tactical decision-making is facilitated by a process or framework for handling data within a firm or organization or knowledge-based applications architecture.

Further complicating matters is that continuous merger and acquisition activity creates enterprise-wide data-integration issues. New assets and groups are acquired or spun off, and corresponding data and processes need to be managed. Maintaining diverse legacy applications that don't integrate well can be costlier than conversion projects.

LARGE DATA MIGRATION

An example of a successful scrum implementation is a multibillion-dollar energy company with operations in the United States and Brazil. Frequent mergers and acquisitions have created a need for timely, accurate data integration. Senior management needs reports created on the new entities, new products, and customers (specifically, management focused on energy-efficiency projects to keep a strong hold on that customer segment).

Data existed in multiple formats across multiple applications, including budget and financial data in spreadsheets, a customer relationship management (CRM) tool, and data from a variety of cloud-based customer surveys.

The scrum integration process went like this:

1. Roles were established.

   Stakeholders were identified as *end users*. The product owner represented the stakeholders and sponsors. The project manager left the decision-making to the product owner and, rather than directing the work, became the scrum master. The developers were represented by the data architect, system architect, and an ETL (extract, transform, load) architect.

2. The stakeholders and product owner determined the highest-priority starting point: budget data.

3. ETL was the scope of the initial chunk. As data became available, the product owner worked with stakeholders to identify reports that could be implemented incrementally and plugged them into the product backlog for prioritization in upcoming sprints.

4. In Sprint 1, budget data was loaded into the data warehouse. The data was verified with sample reports.

5. Sprint 2 involved loading CRM data into the data warehouse. Sample reports were used to validate the data.

6. After the second sprint, stakeholders identified new requirements in the budget data after comparing it with the loaded CRM data. These requirements were added to the product backlog and prioritized.

7. In Sprint 3, survey data was loaded and validated with sample reports.

8. During the third sprint, new data sources were discovered and loaded.

9. Sprint 4 verified the integration of all three data sources by running sample reports.

10. In the remaining sprints, reports were written according to priority.

(continued)

(continued)

In a matter of months, not years, the entire database migration was finished. The data warehouse was fully functional, and a process was in place for managing new data and changes along the way. Part of the success was because the business and developers worked together toward a common goal.

The process was quicker to market because it didn't entail the waterfall approach of loading all possible data from all possible sources and then testing. Rather, the highest-priority data was implemented first in phases and inspected and adapted along the way. New findings were incorporated in the next sprint, and the next-highest-priority data was implemented next.

Enterprise resource planning

Enterprise resource planning (ERP) is a suite of integrated and dynamic software applications that organizations and corporations use to gather, manage, interpret, and integrate business processes, including planning, purchasing, manufacturing, inventory, marketing, sales, distribution, finance, and human resources.

Implementing an ERP system usually means doing simultaneous development across various functional areas (such as marketing, sales, inventory, and purchasing) to conduct a specific business transaction. Implementation involves the design and configuration of many modules simultaneously. While being developed individually, these modules must also be designed for cross-functional application. For example, during the design of the sales module, careful consideration is given to both upstream and downstream processes.

Think about how sales fit in the overall end-to-end process. You start with inventory, and subsequently, you need to be able to bill your orders. Therefore, the sales module must seamlessly integrate with your inventory module and your finance module (and your inventory module must integrate with your manufacturing and purchasing modules, which must integrate with your finance modules, and so on).

Unfortunately, designing and building these individual modules traditionally takes years before the integrated testing phase begins. By this time, any gaps between modules require even more time to identify and fix. One small gap between sales and finance can result in months of extra work. Commonly, this fix may not integrate perfectly with another module somewhere else in the process. When everyone works in silos until the integrated testing phase, early detection of gaps and misfits is difficult.

Traditionally, ERP providers handled this interdependency by locking in a specific development sequence. In fact, even parameters that weren't going to be used needed to be configured in the order defined by the ERP provider.

Now, with scaled scrum teams (see Chapter 13), you can do that customization in parallel, with each scrum team focusing on a specific functional area and using automated integration testing to ensure that the business transaction works across the modules. Following agile techniques allows integration testing to occur every day (from the first day) as opposed to months or years into the product development.

Although these modular interdependencies may seem to be liabilities, they make it easier to divide the work into chunks that fit separate scrum teams running synchronized sprints. Product backlog prioritization is set at the program level, and incremental requirement changes are minimized. Sprint backlog prioritization also falls in line. You maintain the flexibility of scrum and dramatically accelerate the pace of implementation. (We dive into this vertical slicing model in Chapter 13.)

ERP systems architecture is increasingly becoming oriented toward Software as a Service (SaaS; see Chapter 8), which means that monolith components are more modular than they used to be for client installations.

Also, the tasks required to configure ERP systems are usually repetitive, so cadence and estimation can be established early and provide accurate sizing and timing predictions.

In Chapter 13, we talk about scaling scrum across multiple teams. To tackle more of an ERP implementation to speed delivery, multiple teams may work on each business-function component simultaneously. Effective use of scaled scrum enables multiple scrum teams to structure their definition of *done* to include integration, regression, performance, security, and regression testing at the sprint level rather than release. Alignment of the definition of *done* is required because ERP systems are difficult to correct when conflicts are introduced into production. Teams learn to be disciplined in their definition of *done*.

We've also found that scrum works well with this type of work when they focus on delivering business intelligence for the organization. Visual reports of data have a clear business-focused requirement for users. The work of preparing the data (such as aggregation and manipulation) makes up the tasks supporting the delivery of a report to the specified user (such as an executive or manager).

Multiyear ERP implementations used to be common, but organizations can't wait that long in today's fast-paced market. Organizations need solutions faster and cheaper. Customers want to see a return on their investment as quickly as possible, with improved customer satisfaction.

Iterating, inspecting, and adapting through scrum make shortened implementations possible.

Commercial-Off-the-Shelf (COTS) Implementations

Often we hear our clients say, "Scrum only works for software development." We emphatically tell them it is definitely not the case, as seen throughout this book. Prime examples of this are the work we do with clients to help them implement numerous enterprise commercial-off-the-shelf (COTS) platforms using scrum. Each client's results were remarkable. Here we highlight just three: Unifier, ServiceNow, and Clarity.

Oracle Primavera Unifier

Unifier is a product purchased by Oracle several years ago as it expanded into construction management. It's a configurable tool, but at the time of our engagement was built for only operating in one environment — production. The organization knew users would struggle with having the tool unavailable while updates were made, which could be daily. So, how did they address the product's shortcomings and use scrum to achieve their success?

1. First, they organized a team led by a product owner for the real estate leasing module. The developers included people with skills in configuring the tool, process designers, testers, translators, and training builders. (Translators were needed because this product was initially released in three languages: English, Spanish, and Portuguese.) The scrum master created and supported the environment for the team's success. Stakeholders from each regional area and headquarters group interested in the product's success participated.

2. The team began by defining a product goal and roadmap of the capability needed by the organization. They also established three different product environments: Development, Test, and Production.

   They established a definition of *done*, beginning with a definition of the workflow needed by the user, along with updating the security role matrix. Then they built the new workflow in Development and wrote manual test cases for the Development environment. Next, they manually built in the new workflow into the Test environment and executed their manual tests. The Documentation environment included everything needed to manually build the workflow in another environment. Table 12-1 shows an example of the definition of *done* used for this Unifier implementation team.

3. Once they had enough of a releasable product increment, they rebuilt the increment in Production and turned it over to the users according to their release definition of *done*. Feature by feature, they made more and more functionality available to their users.

TABLE 12-1 **Sample COTS Sprint & Release Definition of *Done***

Sprint	Release
Test environment	Help desk review
Configuration complete (workflow, roles, and so on)	RFC approval
Test cases updated	Validate Production
Security matrix updated	Remove test records in Production
ATF (automated testing framework) updated & passed	Refresh Test environment
Peer review	Refresh Dev environment
Security review	
Validate production ready	
Workflow documentation updated	
Data migration file updated	
RFC (request for change) submitted	
Update training materials	
Update Knowledge Base articles	
Release notes	

The approach worked quite well, and the team made good progress on their product development. During a retrospective, however, the team had an epiphany. They learned that a tool existed that captured key and mouse strokes. They realized they could use the tool to record every key and mouse stroke made to build the workflow in the Development environment. Then, they could test the recording as it ran in the Test environment to build and test automatically. Finally, after successful testing, they felt comfortable running the automation in the Production environment. Cycle time, or the time interval between identifying a requirement until it is available for users in the Production environment, reduced significantly — as did the product quality. This particular retrospective took the team into high gear.

ServiceNow

A popular IT Service Management platform based on the Information Technology Infrastructure Library (ITIL) is ServiceNow. The ServiceNow platform is highly configurable enabling many features from a service catalog, to help desk support of users, to incident, change, configuration, release, problem management and much more. Can scrum be used to implement this COTS product? Should it be? Absolutely!

Similar to all the other COTS products, our experience of success begins again with a product goal for the organization supported by a product roadmap of features and capabilities to enable it. The team works together, one sprint at a time, to design the desired workflow. The team writes test cases (which can now be automated with the latest ServiceNow toolset called the Automated Testing Framework or ATF). The minimum viable product can be defined, and then as more is learned about the users' needs, improvements can be made sprint after sprint.

This small cross-functional scrum team included developers who configured, tested and automated the product as it was developed. The product owner owned ServiceNow for the enterprise and was the single contact for both problems and requests. The scrum master created and supported the team's environment for success.

What was great about using scrum to implement ServiceNow was the richness of user data and traceability. The product owner was able to devour rich data sets of incidents and problems to identify tool improvement opportunities. As process improvements were identified, the product owner converted incidents or problems into user stories to be included in sprints or releases. Requests for Change or RFCs were traced to approved user stories and testing documentation, all in ServiceNow.

All this was done iteratively, rather than waiting until the entire system was configured, months or even years later. Value was actually delivered to the customer incrementally rather than all at once at the end.

Broadcom's Clarity

Clarity is used by many organizations for project and portfolio management (PPM). A few benefits of Clarity include enabling an organization to build an enterprise backlog of prioritized projects, including their financial investment proposals and actuals. While many out-of-the-box features support traditional project management, we not only helped the client implement Clarity using scrum, but we also used Clarity to support the scrum team as they implemented it. How'd we do it?

After building a solid product goal with a supporting roadmap, the team implemented features end to end, one at a time. As each feature was enabled in the Production environment, users were notified of its availability.

The cross-functional implementation scrum team included a product owner who owned Clarity for the client's enterprise and developers who were experienced in configuring Clarity. They partnered daily with their professional implementation partner (also a team developer), testers, and organizational training builders.

Scrum helped them to deliver the outcome of valuable functionality early and often.

DevOps and Beyond

In the past, development has been mistakenly kept separate from the rest of IT operations. DevOps and other agile practices are bringing those back together. This reunion ensures product development is aligned with all other aspects of delivering a quality product, including maintenance, security, architecture, and infrastructure. In this section, we'll discuss the various aspects of DevOps and agility.

Development and operations (DevOps) is a growing solution to a gap in developing software applications. Figure 12-1 shows how DevOps addresses coordination challenges.

Traditional IT tasks are being shifted to the scrum teams developing the product, which not only offloads tasks from IT but also enables developers to take their product development further to production with fewer IT dependencies. Virtualized datacenters make this practice increasingly possible because IT manages the platform, which makes creating new virtualized environments possible by people with DevOps access and capabilities on a scrum team.

IT dependencies can now be done within the scrum team. Higher quality and faster speed to finish are achieved within the sprints.

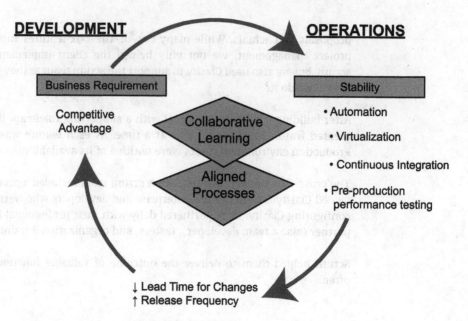

DEVELOPMENT

Business Requirement

Competitive
Advantage

Collaborative
Learning

Aligned
Processes

OPERATIONS

Stability

• Automation

• Virtualization

• Continuous Integration

• Pre-production
performance testing

↓ Lead Time for Changes
↑ Release Frequency

FIGURE 12-1:
DevOps balancing
a business
requirement
against stability.

Security challenges

You may have heard some of these terms: *bots, worms, malware, phishing,* and *security breach.* For some people, the Internet is fertile ground for malicious activities. Major data breaches are making the headlines far too regularly. Following are just a few examples of companies and organizations that recently experienced compromised customer information:

>> June 2021: LinkedIn (700 million people affected)

>> March 2020: CAM4 (10.8 billion people affected)

>> April 2019: Facebook (533 million people affected)

Too often, security is an afterthought. Managers sometimes consider it nice to have and say, "We'll deal with it when it becomes a problem." Security risks are increasing and need to be addressed earlier rather than later, which is a primary focus of DevSecOps. Following are some common ways that scrum can help expose security-related issues and facilitate improvements in the way they're handled:

>> Refine your definition of *done.* At both the release and sprint levels, the definition of *done* is critical. Decide on security requirements that should be met at each level. By adding a security task to each requirement to address your definition of *done,* costs of mitigating security risk can be spread out over the life of the product. Make security a high priority from the first appropriate spot.

GUILDS

Guilds are groups of people in an organization that share knowledge, tools, and practices. A guild is like a community of practice in which people regularly engage in collective learning and sharing knowledge of common interests or practices. Examples of guilds include security, system administration, database, quality, and agile practitioners.

Guilds should be open to anyone interested in mentoring others or learning more, including those who are new to the skill or practice.

The guilds should meet often enough to build knowledge and increase learning and skill levels across an organization.

Consider making sure that at least one person on every scrum team becomes a member of the security guild. This will go a long way toward ensuring that security practices are common and awareness is being built across and throughout teams.

>> As a scrum team member, if security isn't as high a priority as you feel it should be, address it at the next retrospective. The business stakeholders and/or product owner may need to be trained about the issues. Identify the issues and place them in the product backlog.

>> Have IT team members with security expertise attend sprint reviews and provide security feedback or someone with that experience on the team.

>> Automate security testing as much as possible. Consider automating penetration testing, cross-site scripting, and vulnerability scanning.

>> Consider establishing an organizational security guild that promotes awareness and skill development on security common practices and technologies throughout the organization.

Maintenance

After an application is deployed, maintenance teams provide support. This support can be in the form of responding to support inquiries, fixing defects, and implementing minor enhancements to address functionality gaps in production.

When scrum teams focus on product or broader project work, whether software or IT, triaging operational issues can be disruptive. Product development and maintenance work are quite different. They require different types of work and effort by developers, which also involves a different cadence. We like having scrum teams that create a product also be responsible for supporting it. Through that level of ownership, they create high quality and value for their customers. But if a scrum team is interrupted frequently enough to affect release schedules that are of business value and functionality to the customer, some adjustments should be made to how they operate as a scrum team. (See Chapter 13 for more about the cost of delays from thrashing developers.)

By separating maintenance from the scrum teams' new development efforts, maintenance can be streamlined, and new development can progress uninterrupted. We recommend a maintenance scrum team structure that separates these two functions so that interruptions are minimized without increasing overhead (see Figure 12-2 and Figure 12-3).

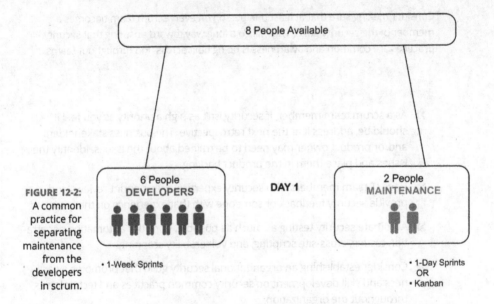

FIGURE 12-2:
A common practice for separating maintenance from the developers in scrum.

8 People Available

6 People
DEVELOPERS

DAY 1

2 People
MAINTENANCE

• 1-Week Sprints

• 1-Day Sprints
OR
• Kanban

Kanban within a scrum structure

We introduce the kanban concept in Chapter 6. Some scrum and agile teams use a kanban board to visualize their workflow. Here's how the process in Figures 12-2 and 12-3 works:

>> At the start of a new release cycle, split out a small subset of the developers with enough skill and knowledge to effectively maintain the product into a maintenance team.

As shown in Figure 12-2, if you have a eight developers, you can take two developers and form a separate maintenance scrum team, leaving six developers to do new product development work in the existing scrum team. Your team size may vary. Fewer or more than two maintenance team members may be needed. (Although the existing scrum team is now smaller, it will no longer be thrashing between new product development and maintenance work. Fewer people don't mean less output. Actually, because thrashing has been eliminated, the team should be able to become more effective.)

» The maintenance team runs one-day sprints or kanban to respond to rapidly changing requirements (often changing daily). Each morning, the team triages and plans the priorities for the day. It executes the work planned throughout the day. At the end of the day, the team reviews what it accomplished or its day's product increment and clears that work for release. (Release can happen anytime and doesn't need to happen daily.)

» Maintenance teams can be smaller than new product development scrum teams. The product owner and scrum master for the maintenance team are often the same as for the product development scrum team. Thrashing is minimal — if it occurs at all — because both are working on a single application.

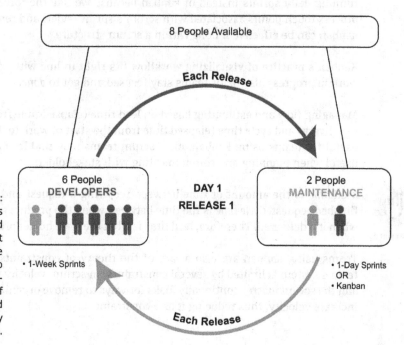

FIGURE 12-3:
Team members are rotated among teams at reasonable intervals to ensure cross-pollination of knowledge and cross-functionality of skills.

>> At each release, one developer transitions to the operations team to be a full-time dedicated member, providing the necessary knowledge transfer for supporting the release. Again, thrashing is minimized because it's done at the release level, and the team members continue to work on the same product. (See Chapter 13 for more about minimizing thrashing to maximize stability and profitability.)

>> At each release, a member of the operations maintenance team transitions to the developers' team to be a full-time, dedicated team member.

TIP

If a scrum team releases often (daily or even every sprint), then perhaps limiting the rotation to once every 90 days would be appropriate to maintain reasonable stability from sprint to sprint.

>> Eventually, everyone does both new development and operational maintenance work.

>> Cross-pollination of product and domain knowledge is a key benefit.

>> Cross-functionality builds through rotations as well.

Maintenance teams typically run daily sprints or kanban rather than one-week or longer sprints, as product development scrum teams do. We often recommend running daily sprints instead of kanban because we like the forced product and process touch points associated with scrum's sprint review and retrospective, but kanban can be effective if done within a scrum structure.

Kanban's practice of visualizing workflow fits right in line with scrum. Limiting work in progress also helps teams stay focused and get to *done*.

Managing flow and estimating based on lead time (elapsed time from the request to delivery) and cycle time (elapsed time from the start of work to delivery) is also useful for teams using kanban. Also, scrum teams may find lead and cycle time useful when planning and communicating with stakeholders.

REMEMBER

Lead time is the amount of time between receiving a request and delivering the finished request. *Cycle time* is the time between when the product gets started and when it's delivered. Therefore, lead time is what the stakeholder often cares about.

Teams using kanban are also aware of the theory of constraints, meaning the team's system is limited by several constraints. In scrum, velocity is a constraint, and the scrum master continually looks for ways to remove organizational drag to increase velocity, thus reducing it as a constraint.

Because kanban does not prescribe a regular feedback loop, teams using kanban often fall out of practice. Although they may perpetually communicate among themselves and with stakeholders, the report often sounds like, "Yeah, we have work in progress, and we're making progress." The kanban board is visible, but the efforts to inspect and adapt for both the product and the process may not be effective. On the other hand, scrum provides the structure for a regular improvement process.

In the context of one-day sprints, if you're concerned about the meeting overhead of daily sprints, don't be. A one-day sprint is one-fifth of a one-week sprint. The time cost works out to be incredibly efficient and minimal. Here's the breakdown in minutes, based on a one-month sprint as outlined in the Scrum Guide 2020:

>> **Sprint planning:** If you would spend up to one full day in sprint planning for a one-month sprint, daily sprint planning rounds to about 25 minutes or less.

>> **Sprint review:** If you would spend up to a half day in sprint planning for a one-month sprint, a daily sprint review becomes 15 minutes or less, where you do a brief review with whoever requested the work and make a go/no-go decision.

>> **Sprint retrospective:** If you would spend up to three hours in a sprint retrospective for a one-month sprint, a daily sprint retrospective is ten minutes or less. Be sure to inspect and adapt every single day, even if you have an emergency and everyone just wants to go home. Identify one small thing that could be improved the next day.

>> Also, sync retrospectives with the product development scrum team's sprint retrospective because this allows for larger-scale inspection.

>> Daily scrums won't be necessary because your morning sprint planning takes care of coordination and synchronizing priorities. Impediments need to be addressed as they arise throughout the day. However, the scrum master needs to be vigilant and proactively follow up on known or potential impediments throughout the day.

The key to one-day sprints is splitting the requests so that they fit in a day, which takes practice. In the beginning, our teams did one-week batch releases. When they first transitioned to their new one-day cadence, the number of fixes completed by week's end decreased. However, customer satisfaction increased because customers went from waiting a week to getting something every day. Waiting and satisfaction are opposing dynamics.

Profit-and-Loss Potential

The business value of IT is immense. Its value needs to be communicated and demonstrated regularly to the rest of the organization. However, this value is sometimes overlooked in the face of problems that piggyback on technology. A huge opportunity lies in communicating clearly the value that IT brings to everyone involved — even if these benefits are only in the form of risks mitigated.

REMEMBER

The key question is, "Does this task or activity improve our organization's core priorities?" If so, keep it in and prioritize. If not, figure out how to eliminate that function and focus on mission-critical tasks.

Increasing visibility to the organization (through artifacts like IT's prioritized product backlog and increments demonstrated at sprint reviews) helps the entire organization see how IT works to remove information and communication flow bottlenecks and provides the tools to enhance productivity. When the entire organization understands the value that IT brings, interactions between IT and other departments become more collaborative, and IT's solutions become clear enablers of corporate strategy.

Just like a scrum team that increases its velocity from 25 to 27, a small operational cost percentage savings is all it takes to make a big bottom-line improvement over time.

Energy efficiency is a hot button these days and is an example of how saving a little bit amounts to a lot over time. A wide array of tools is becoming available to help save costs on energy. Through better monitoring and application of energy-saving products, a few percentage points in cost can be saved, particularly if this improves the organization's core priorities; this allows IT to bring in more profits.

TECHNICAL STUFF

IBM estimates that IT and energy costs combined account for up to 75 percent of operational costs and up to 60 percent of capital expenditures in an organization.

It's estimated that a 25,000-square-foot datacenter uses more than $4 million in energy each year. While this number won't be eliminated at once, incremental steps to inspect and adapt can decrease costs gradually and appropriately. A small percentage savings out of $4 million isn't bad.

Innovation versus Stability

Organizations rely on IT operations for stability, performance, and uptime, yet IT must always be innovating, which implies the need to change quickly and often. Stability and change conflict. This conflict is solved by tightening collaboration between operations and developers. Rather than developing new technology and throwing it over the fence for operations to support and vice versa, the operations side of the business builds sandboxes, or sets of standards within which developers can build.

Every time developers make code changes in the innovation process, they can breathe easy, knowing those code changes are made within the set of standards agreed on between operations and development. Changes in database structures or designs within operational standards avert the risks inherent in the same changes made in development silos with little or no collaboration with operations.

These standards are incorporated into a team's definition of *done*. IT can rest assured that within each sprint, the teams are staying in the sandbox for each requirement. When changes in the sandbox need to be made, development and operations consult and establish the new boundaries.

The need for improved coordination is key, especially in software development, which is where DevOps comes in.

Chapter **13**

Portfolio Management

There is nothing so useless as doing efficiently that which should not be done at all.

— PETER DRUCKER

Portfolio management is the simultaneous coordination, integration, management, prioritization, and control of multiple projects and product development efforts across the organization.

The number-one issue in portfolio management is a failure of leadership to prioritize product development properly and allocate talent appropriately. This failure of leadership is masked by thrashing or moving people across several development efforts simultaneously. Communication fails, priorities get dropped, and the squeaky-wheel syndrome takes over. (The loudest stakeholder gets the most attention and resources.)

You have only one way to handle the situation of having more development efforts than you have talent: Prioritize effectiveness more than efficiency. If an organization is highly efficient but is working on the wrong features, how successful will that organization be? It's far more critical to be effective. Work on only the highest-prioritized products and the highest-prioritized features of those products. Profitability flows from this model.

In this chapter, we go through the main challenges in portfolio management and discuss the available scrum solutions. We look at how Lean Startup is a natural fit for scrum and how to scale large, multiteam product development efforts with scrum.

Portfolio Management Challenges

Four key challenges, when they're not handled effectively, prevent good portfolio management:

>> People allocation and prioritization

>> Dependencies and fragmentation

>> Disconnect between products and business objectives

>> Displaced accountability

People allocation and prioritization

Above all else, not having enough time, money, or people is the biggest constraint on portfolio management. Lack of resources forces leaders to prioritize effectively, reduce organizational drag (such as thrashing) on talent, or push the burden down to a level that doesn't have the clout to fight back. Unfortunately, many leaders choose the latter. Corporate strategy, not whims or the loudest voice, should drive prioritization.

Effective prioritizing means choosing only the highest-value and highest-risk product development efforts and feeding them to stable teams one a time. If you have only one scrum team, feed it one development effort at a time. If you have five teams, feed each team only one development effort at a time. If one product is too big for one team, have as many teams as needed swarm around the highest-priority development effort until it's done; then, feed the next product to the teams.

WARNING

Racing in reverse is a concept we teach regarding spending too much time on the wrong things. If you're not effective, you're racing in reverse. If you're pushing people to work more, put in overtime, and pump out beyond their means, you *increase* the number of defects, which increases future work and cost. You can see Mark's webinar on this topic at https://platinumedge.com/blog/video-mark-laytons-racing-reverse-presentation.

The prioritization conundrum can be addressed by asking one question: If this product isn't high-priority enough to have dedicated talent, is it necessary right now? If the answer is no, the best thing to do is finish the highest priority product development effort first and then ask this question again.

A HIERARCHY OF THRASHING

No matter what thrashing looks like in your organization, apply scrum to minimize its impact. Just remember — the more stable your team, the higher your profitability. Following are descriptions of the various faces of thrashing:

- **Entire product development stability — The team is stable for the entire product development duration:** Here, the development is stable with no thrashing because the team is focused until AC + OC > V. (See below and Chapter 5.) This is the most efficient structure. It will quickly produce the best quality possible and maximizes profitability.

- **Release stability — The team is stable for release duration:** The team is focused on project A until they have something releasable to customers. Then, they switch to project B until they have something releasable for customers. From here, they switch to project C and so on. Release stability is worse than entire product development stability.

- **Sprint stability — The team is stable for sprint duration:** The team is focused on project A for the entire sprint. Then, they switch to project B for a same-duration sprint, switch to project C, and so on. Sprint stability is worse than release stability.

- **Day stability — The team is stable for the day's duration:** The team spends Monday working on project A. Then, they switch to project B on Tuesday, project C on Wednesday, and so on. This is worse than sprint stability.

- **Hourly stability — The team is stable for blocks of hours:** The team spends every morning working on project A, the afternoon on project B, and so on. Hourly stability is worse than day stability.

- **Minute-by-minute team thrashing:** This is the most common portfolio management approach. Individual team members start working on project A, and 45 minutes later, an emergency occurs on project B, which takes them until lunch. After lunch, they attempt to restart project A, but something comes up on project C that takes the afternoon. The next day, they are back to square one with project A because of mental remobilization time. The process continues until a project close to an influential executive is so late that the team is forced to spend their evenings and weekends working on just that project. This is the worst-case scenario.

(continued)

(continued)

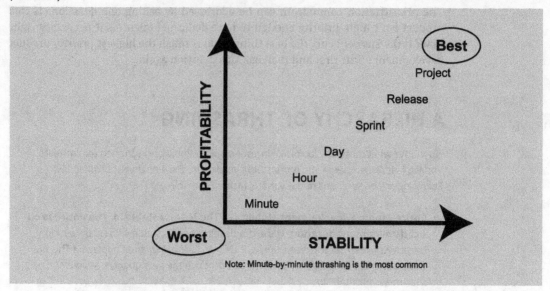

Note: Minute-by-minute thrashing is the most common

Dependencies and fragmentation

With product development efforts running simultaneously, bottlenecks from dependency issues arise, as do delays because of integration difficulties. In traditional project management, people, money, and equipment are shared. It's not uncommon for managers to allocate each person across multiple projects (50 percent here, 40 percent there, and the last 10 percent for some other project) just to feel as though they're using every ounce of power available and making the organization as efficient as possible.

REMEMBER

People lose a minimum of 30 percent of time in the cognitive mobilization–demobilization associated with task switching. Having employees divide their time among multiple product development efforts is detrimental to their productivity.

Historically, project managers end up trying to do everything at the same time because they're under pressure from business owners to deliver across several areas. They end up racing after different goals without separating and prioritizing what needs to be done first. Dependency issues tie the projects in knots because the core dependent project wasn't executed first.

Disconnect between projects and business objectives

Most projects begin in line with business objectives, but as time passes, managers continue to brainstorm product ideas and hypothesize all the directions the product could take. Unfortunately, the scope creeps in many directions without consistent feedback loops with customers and stakeholders or daily coordination with the developers. The more time that has passed since the initial planning, the more the common understanding of the objectives breaks down until the original objectives become unknown.

This scope creep reflects the lack-of-prioritization issue at the core of the problem. With scrum, prioritization and reprioritization happen continuously throughout product development at the roadmap, release, sprint, and daily-scrum levels. The product backlog always has the next-highest-priority items ready to go, and products are released in order of priority.

Displaced accountability

Being the bearer of bad news to management is no one's favorite task. Even when a team knows that its development is awry, members may hesitate to tell senior management because of the perceived negative effect on their careers. Unfortunately, the longer a team waits to deliver bad news, the worse the problems become.

Early and frequent communication of impediments and problems is the scrum style, whereas traditional project management supports a "tell me when it's done" mindset. Often, business owners don't know their project has gone astray until it's too late to correct it.

Accountability needs to be in the right place, not assigned to a middleman project manager who's not doing the work of product creation. Scrum's transparency removes this issue. The product owner has ownership of the business objectives and priorities, and the developers own how to implement those goals and how much they can commit to achieving. During each sprint, team members share their solutions with the product owner daily; at the end of each sprint, they share their solutions with the stakeholders.

The product owner doesn't answer for the developers, and the developers don't answer for the product owner. Each person answers for themselves. Scrum provides the opportunity for appropriately placed accountability, transparency, and ownership.

Scrum solutions

Scrum conserves resources for business owners by placing high-risk and high-priority items first. The approach is "if you fail, fail early, fail fast." If business owners don't think that a product development effort will come to fruition as they want it to, they have the opportunity to pull the plug early and save precious resources and time.

When the actual cost (AC) and opportunity cost (OC) outweigh the value of the product development effort (V), it's time to move on. Effective portfolio managers use the equation shown in Chapter 5 — AC + OC > V — as a termination trigger.

REMEMBER

With the scrum framework, a portfolio manager can determine whether a product is viable within a few sprints. The product feature moves forward speedily and efficiently, or it's removed from the backlog, and the talent is freed for higher-priority development efforts. Less stigma is involved in having a product fail because the costs of failure have been dramatically reduced.

REMEMBER

Chapter 5 discusses work in progress limits for developers. Those same limits apply to portfolio management. You can have as many projects open as you have scrum teams. A stable team can swarm on a requirement, a release, and a product until it's done and then take on the next-highest-priority project. If you have multiple teams, great. Align skills with projects. Because teams are dedicated and stable, they get projects done serially faster than if talent is thrashed among projects. *All* projects complete under a dedicated team model before *any* project completes under a thrashed model.

Figure 13-1 illustrates the difference between running serial projects (dedicated teams) and parallel projects (thrashing teams).

In this example, a portfolio has three projects, each running in succession (that is, serially). Assume that one unit of value can be produced in one unit of time and each project can produce one unit of value ($) when it's complete.

Many studies, including what Tom DeMarco references in his book *Slack*, reveal the cost of thrashing the team is at least 30 percent more time to finish each project. The American Psychological Association says it's 40 percent. For this example, let's say it's 33 percent. Over three projects (99 percent), that's roughly the equivalent of a whole project's length by thrashing the teams around.

Going only one unit of time past the deployment of the serial projects, the parallel projects return $$$ (3$ — one $ for each project deployed) at the end of that period. The serial projects return $$$$$$+$$$$ (10$, which is more than three times the return on investment [ROI]).

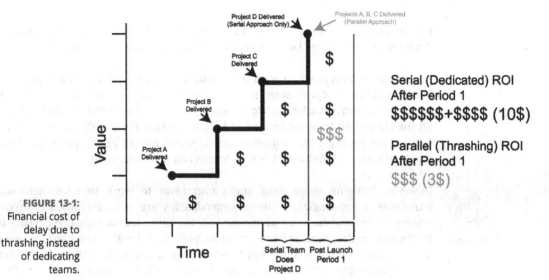

Project D Delivered
(Serial Approach Only)

Projects A, B, C Delivered
(Parallel Approach)

Project C
Delivered

Project B
Delivered

Project A
Delivered

Value

Time

Serial Team
Does
Project D

Post Launch
Period 1

Serial (Dedicated) ROI
After Period 1
$$$$$$+$$$$ (10$)

Parallel (Thrashing) ROI
After Period 1
$$$ (3$)

FIGURE 13-1:
Financial cost of
delay due to
thrashing instead
of dedicating
teams.

Stop thrashing. Run one project at a time through one team at a time. When you dedicate teams, everyone gets projects earlier and gets an earlier, higher ROI.

As executives start prioritizing to eliminate thrashing, the feedback loop of sprint reviews ensures that stakeholders (including executives) are brought into direct alignment with the scrum team's work. By communicating the highest-priority items, developers can ensure they get what they want and avoid squeaky-wheel syndrome.

Goals are kept in alignment, and strategies and tactics are prioritized. Constant communication means that problems and impediments are brought up early so that solutions can be applied or directions changed. Creative innovation and experimentation can be encouraged without fear of undue waste.

REMEMBER

Don't underestimate the cost of delaying delivered value. Delaying delivery is like paying a high interest rate over a long time because the organization cannot prioritize the portfolio. Have these mature and potentially difficult conversations up-front to avoid large debt payments in the future.

De-scaling Scrum for Large Portfolios

In essence, scrum was designed for decomposed products (products broken down to achievable goals) that could be started and finished quickly. If a scrum team consists of about four to five developers, a scrum master, and a product owner, a natural limit exists on what a team of this size can accomplish. Some product development efforts are large enough to require more than one scrum team.

Scaling scrum occurs when multiple scrum teams are working on a product or portfolio of products with some level of affinity. Microsoft Office is one example. One team may have worked on Word, another on Excel, and a third on PowerPoint. All the teams had to be integrated and work together effectively for Office to be sold as one package. Many product development efforts are so large that they require dozens or hundreds of teams. Scrum can meet this need.

REMEMBER

However, bringing more than one scrum team to work together naturally introduces dependencies. If those dependencies are not carefully addressed, scaling becomes even more unwieldy with the more teams added, especially if overhead is added. Scaling good scrum to begin with breaks down and removes those dependencies. Get scrum right first, so your scrum teams can work together with dependencies already broken down. That's what we mean by de-scaling. Stop adding the overhead that enables more dependencies. Organizations with highly aligned and highly autonomous or independent teams thrive.

Many models exist for scaling scrum. Following are different approaches you might consider, depending on your needs. We'll start with what we think are the more simple approaches.

A Vertical Slicing Overview

One of the simplest scaling approaches is known as *vertical slicing*, which provides a straightforward solution for dividing the work across teams so they can incrementally deliver and integrate functionality at every sprint. Vertical slicing is a solution if your scaling challenge is breaking down the work across teams.

Highly aligned and autonomous scrum teams do what needs to be done to meet customer needs. Developers working on the same product are each cross-functional enough to work on any item from the product backlog. Each team pulls items from the same product backlog and implements those requirements during sprints aligned on the same cadence. If one team lacks a skill required for any requirement, they work with teams who do to expand their capability, reducing constraining dependencies.

During each sprint, each team integrates its work with the work of other teams, ideally through automation, making integrations less costly and troublesome. At the end of each sprint, all product backlog items selected during the sprint are elaborated, designed, developed, tested, integrated, documented, and approved.

Figure 13-2 illustrates how a product can be vertically sliced to enable multiple teams to work on a single product.

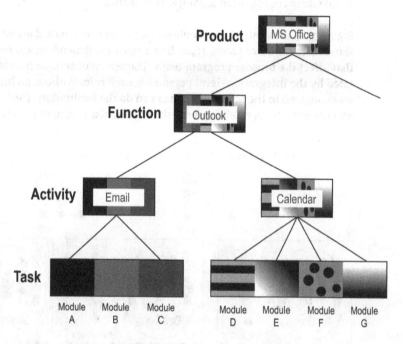

FIGURE 13-2:
Vertical slices of product features implemented by multiple scrum teams.

With a common baseline definition of *done* for all scrum teams, vertical slicing enables each team to be self-organizing in its development approach while being aligned with the overall release goal. The product vision and roadmap become the glue tying everyone together.

TECHNICAL STUFF

Technical practices that automate the integration of work between teams help flatten this model, so separate integration scrum team layers are needed less and less. Again, with scrum done correctly, additional scaling overhead isn't necessary.

A product has one product owner, one product backlog, and a common definition of *done* to ensure each scrum team's work can be integrated into a working, releasable increment every sprint.

Scrum of Scrums

The scrum of scrums model facilitates effective integration, coordination, and collaboration among scrum teams by means of vertical slicing. Almost all scaling frameworks we show you in this chapter use some form of scrum of scrums to enable daily coordination among scrum teams.

Figure 13-3 illustrates how people on one team coordinate daily with people in the same roles on other teams regarding priorities, dependencies, and impediments that affect the broader program team. The scrum of scrums for each role is facilitated by the integration-level person for each role. Without an integration scrum team, anyone in the scrum of scrums can do the facilitation. Thorough integration and release efforts establish a consistent, regular scrum of scrums model.

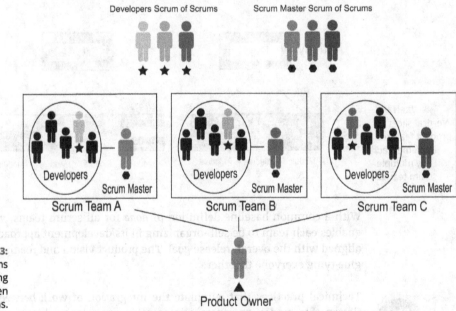

FIGURE 13-3:
Scrum of scrums
for coordinating
between
scrum teams.

Each day, scrum teams hold their own daily scrums at approximately the same time, in separate locations or web-conferencing rooms. Following these daily scrums, scrum of scrums meetings (described in the following sections) occur.

Developer scrum of scrums

Each day after the teams' daily scrums, one developer from each scrum team attends the integration team's daily scrum (which is the scrum of scrums for developers) and participates with the integration team developers in discussing the following:

>> Any integrations that need to be coordinated since the last scrum of scrums meeting

>> The integrations that will be needed between now and the next meeting

>> Technical concerns with which the team needs help

>> Technical decisions that the team has made

>> How to prevent potential issues

TIP

Consider rotating the developers who attend the scrum of scrums (the integration team's daily scrum) — daily or for each sprint — to ensure that everyone stays tuned in to the integration efforts of the portfolio.

REMEMBER

With continuous automated integration, the developer scrum of scrums may just be the representative developers from each scrum team without a separate integration scrum team.

Scrum master scrum of scrums

The scrum masters from each scrum team also meet with the integration scrum team's scrum master for no longer than 15 minutes to address any escalation needed to deal with each team's impediments. Typically, each scrum master addresses the following:

>> The individual team-level impediments resolved since the last time meeting with the integration team and how those impediments were resolved (if other scrum masters run into the issue and can implement the solution)

>> New impediments identified since the last meeting and which impediments the team needs help resolving

>> Potential impediments that everyone should be aware of

The integration team scrum master ensures escalated impediments are addressed after the daily scrum of scrums.

REMEMBER

With continuous automated integration, the scrum master scrum of scrums may just be the representative scrum masters from each scrum team without a separate integration scrum team.

WHO OWNS THE ARCHITECTURE?

Your organization should have existing architectural standards, other technical standards, and style guides. This way, each team doesn't have to reinvent the wheel. But a common question is, "Who is responsible for architecture in a vertically sliced program?" The answer is that it depends on which modules will be affected by the decision.

Consider an architectural decision that needs to be made and that will affect only module A. The developers of module A would make that decision. If it would affect multiple teams, the developers at the integration level shared by all affected teams would make that decision. That integration level might be one level up or four levels up.

Using Figure 13-3 as an example, the email integration team would make an architectural decision affecting two of the email module teams (A and B). The Outlook integration scrum team would make a decision affecting the email module teams and the calendar integration scrum team. Vertical slicing is a simple way to maintain the autonomy of each scrum team to deliver valuable functionality within a wider program context. It is also effective at helping teams have timely and relevant conversations about constraints and progress.

Vertical slicing is a simple, foundational approach to addressing the dependencies problem of scaling. Following are other frameworks many have found useful.

Large-Scale Scrum (LeSS)

Another method of incorporating the scrum framework into massive products is Large-Scale Scrum (LeSS).

Products have been successfully developed with LeSS with as few as four to five small teams to programs that encompass 1,500 people and span a half-dozen countries. In other words, how big would you like large to be? LeSS can scale scrum up or down to work in many environments.

At the foundation of LeSS is systems thinking, where a system is thought of as an organized entity (in this case, a product area) made up of interrelated and interdependent parts (teams). The creators of LeSS specifically see that optimizing the whole doesn't come from optimizing the parts of a whole. Optimizing parts only optimizes the parts, so LeSS optimizes collaborations between multiple teams, even across different locations.

LeSS has only a few rules and two frameworks: LeSS and LeSS Huge. The difference lies in the size of the total teams involved.

LeSS framework

Figure 13-4 illustrates the LeSS framework, which applies to products with up to about eight scrum teams.

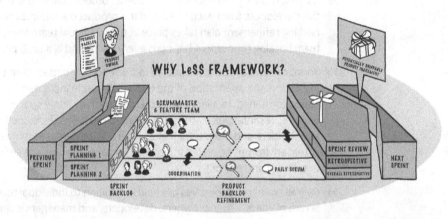

Courtesy of Craig Larman and Bas Vodde

FIGURE 13-4
LeSS framework.

In the LeSS framework, there is one product owner and one product backlog for the complete shippable product. The product owner shouldn't work alone on product backlog refinement; That person is supported by multiple teams of developers working directly with customers, users, and other stakeholders. All prioritization goes through the product owner, but clarification can happen directly between the teams, customers, and other stakeholders.

While much of LeSS remains true to the one-team scrum framework, the differences are important:

>> Sprint planning is split into two parts: Part 1 is common for all teams where the requirements for the sprint are selected, and Part 2 is for each team to plan the details of how they'll implement their part.

>> Sprint planning (Part 1) invites all developers from all teams, although not all developers are required to attend. At least two members per scrum team attend, along with the product owner. The representative team members then share their information with their respective teams for Part 2.

» Independent sprint planning (Part 2), involves retrospective and daily scrums, and members from different teams can attend each other's meetings to facilitate information sharing.

» Cross-team coordination is decided by the teams that prefer decentralized and informal coordination more than centralized coordination. The emphasis is on informal networks that involve cross-team talking, component mentors, travelers, scouts, and open spaces.

» Backlog refinement is done for the overall product backlog with representative developers from each team and the product owner. Individual team backlog refinement also takes place at the individual team level, but multi-team backlog refinement happens every sprint and is a LeSS practice.

» Sprint reviews are best conducted in a science fair pattern that enables the inspection and adaptation of the entire releasable increment from all scrum teams combined. In a large physical room with multiple spaces staffed by team representatives, each space is where the items developed are shown to stakeholders and discussed. Stakeholders visit the spaces of interest. (In a virtual environment, web-conferencing breakout rooms are set up for people to select in and out of.)

» Overall sprint retrospectives are held in addition to individual team retrospectives. Scrum masters, product owners, developers, and managers inspect and adapt the overall system of the product, such as processes, tools, and communication.

LeSS Huge framework

With LeSS Huge, the sky is the limit regarding overall product size. A few thousand people organized in teams could work on one product. Figure 13-5 illustrates the LeSS Huge framework.

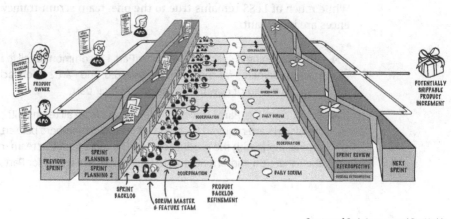

FIGURE 13-5
LeSS Huge framework.

Courtesy of Craig Larman and Bas Vodde

As in scrum and LeSS, you have one product, one definition of *done*, one product owner, and one sprint. LeSS Huge is a stack of LeSS for each "requirement area." Requirement areas provide structure for more than eight scrum teams to work together effectively without overburdening the product owner. An area product owner (APO) specializes in a customer-centric area and is given ownership to act as a product owner in that area. Each APO works collaboratively with the product owner and other APOs as a product owner team. Using the Microsoft Office example in the vertical slicing section above, requirement areas might be broken down to something like Microsoft Word, Excel, PowerPoint, and so on.

Each requirement area uses LeSS, and the set of all required areas is in LeSS Huge. Some of the differences are

>> A product owner team planning meeting happens before the sprint planning meeting.

>> Area-level meetings are added. Sprint planning, review, and retrospective meetings are done at the area level, and area-level product backlog refinement occurs.

>> Overall sprint reviews and retrospectives involving all teams are done. This review coordinates the overall work and process across the product program area.

LeSS is scrum-scaled and allows for the implementation of scrum and scaling in a way that holds true to Agile principles. Elements of the scrum framework are upheld with empirical learning, short feedback loops, self-management, effective collaboration, and coordination.

Leadership tools also exist in LeSS for good decisions that maximize ROI; deliver value to customers; and create happy, sustainable teams.

J.P. MORGAN AND LESS

Large in the context of J.P. Morgan means more than 3,000 employees working in multiple international locations. A group director decided to convert to LeSS. It began with a small pilot product. The results motivated the firm to get scrum rolled out on a grander scale.

The company began by choosing a single division to pilot — securities — and worked on solutions to create a customer-centric approach. Customers needed families of

(continued)

(continued)

components rather than individual ones, having a customer-centric approach, hugely simplified planning, and coordination because groups were planned rather than individual components.

One issue was choosing the new product owners because the business wasn't involved with development under the waterfall approach. The company solved this problem by choosing willing participants from both operations and research and development.

J.P. Morgan formed requirement areas. Each team was given a product, and a product owner was chosen. The teams were encouraged to develop cross-functionality to reduce bottlenecks and minimize the risk of losing the only person who can accomplish a task. Human resources eliminated job titles such as business analyst and tester. Even team leaders had the generic *developer* title.

At the end of the initial rollout of LeSS within the securities division, increased effectiveness, customer satisfaction, and employee morale were realized. LeSS helped scale scrum up to this operation size and continues to be used today.

You can learn more about LeSS at http://less.works.

Scrum@Scale

Scrum@Scale facilitates alignment through roles. The Scrum@Scale approach for scrum teams working together is a form of the scrum of scrums model for scrum masters and product owners, coordinating communication, impediment removal, priorities, requirement refinement, and planning. Using a scrum of scrums model for the scrum master and product owner enables daily synchronization among teams across programs.

Following the vertical slicing model of scrum of scrums, Scrum@Scale groups approximately five scrum teams into a scrum of scrums team (SoS), which limits the complexities for effective cross-team communication. The teams comprising the scrum of scrums team are responsible for a fully integrated increment of product at the end of every sprint. Figure 13-6 illustrates the Scrum@Scale scrum of scrums model.

In larger organizations, multiple scrum of scrums teams may be grouped into scrum of scrum of scrums (SoSoS) teams as needed to deliver larger and more complex solutions.

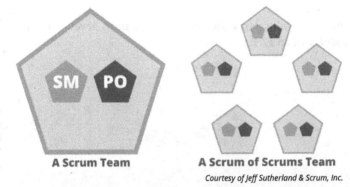

FIGURE 13-6
Scrum@Scale
scrum of scrums
model for
five teams.

A Scrum Team

A Scrum of Scrums Team

Courtesy of Jeff Sutherland & Scrum, Inc.

Figure 13-7 shows the scrum of scrums model for up to 25 teams.

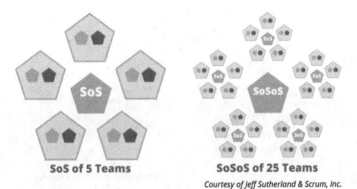

FIGURE 13-7:
Scrum@Scale
scrum of scrums
of scrums model
for 25 teams.

SoS of 5 Teams

SoSoS of 25 Teams

Courtesy of Jeff Sutherland & Scrum, Inc.

To coordinate *what* gets done in the sprint, Scrum@Scale scales sprint planning and sprint review. To coordinate *how* the work gets done across the program, Scrum@Scale scales the daily scrum and sprint retrospective.

The most notable activity in Scrum@Scale happens daily through the scaled daily scrum (SDS), which involves representatives from each of the scrum teams in the SoS inspecting their progress toward the sprint goal and making sure impediments raised are addressed quickly.

The scrum master cycle

A scrum master scrum of scrums coordinates release activities as the release team and continuous improvement and effectiveness of the SoS.

The scrum master accountabilities for an entire agile organization are fulfilled by an executive action team (EAT), removing the organizational impediments that the scrum of scrums groups can't remove.

Figure 13-8 illustrates the Scrum@Scale third-level scrum of scrums of scrums model with an EAT.

FIGURE 13-8
Scrum@Scale
third-level scrum
of scrums of
scrums model
with EAT.

The product owner cycle

For each SoS, a shared common backlog feeds the network of teams. Product direction is led by a product owner team (PO Team), including a chief product owner. The PO team's focus ensures priorities are aligned across all scrum teams. Essentially, they do what a single scrum team product owner does: coordinate individual teams' backlogs and create alignment with stakeholders and customers.

The product owners organize along the same lines as the SoS and SoSoS. An executive metascrum (EMS) fulfills the product owner role for the entire organization. The chief product owner meets with executives and key stakeholders as a forum for leadership to express their preferences to the PO Team, set strategic priorities, manage budgets, and align teams to maximize delivery of value. Figure 13-9 illustrates the Scrum@Scale metascrum for product owners.

FIGURE 13-9:
Scrum@Scale
metascrum for
product owners.

Courtesy of Jeff Sutherland & Scrum, Inc.

Synchronizing in one hour a day

In an hour or less per day, an organization can align priorities for the day and accomplish effective coordination of impediment removal. At 8:30 a.m., each scrum team holds its daily scrum. At 8:45 a.m., the scrum masters hold their scrum of scrums, and the product owners hold their level-one metascrum meetings. At 9:00 a.m., scrum masters meet in scrum of scrums of scrums, and the product owners meet in level-two metascrums. Finally, at 9:15 a.m., the scrum master scrum of scrums of scrums meets with the EAT, and the product owner metascrum representative meets with the EMS.

TIP

For a complete understanding and walk-through of Scrum@Scale, visit www.scrumatscale.com/scrum-at-scale-guide/.

The beauty of scrum is that it is designed to be flexible and to scale. Scrum@Scale is a simple way to maintain the autonomy of each scrum team within a wider program context.

Nexus

Dependencies between teams working on the same product impede the kind of productivity single scrum teams usually experience without those dependencies. *Nexus* is a scaling framework focused on treating multiple teams as a single unit. Reduction of inter-team dependencies is key to scaling success.

Inter-team dependencies usually revolve around how teams structure requirements and the product backlog, the domain knowledge differences between teams, and the software and test artifacts. Dependencies are reduced by mapping requirements, team members' knowledge, and test artifacts to the same scrum teams.

Nexus is a framework that describes how three to nine scrum teams — a *Nexus* — work together on the same product backlog under the guidance of a single product owner to deliver potentially shippable functionality to every sprint.

Figure 13-10 illustrates the Nexus framework.

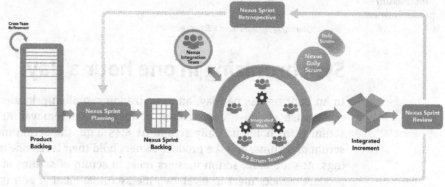

FIGURE 13-10: The Nexus framework.

In addition to scrum roles, artifacts, and events, Nexus introduces one new role, three new artifacts, and five new events to support the larger group of scrum teams operating together.

Nexus helps scrum teams working on the same product identify and resolve dependencies quickly and early, enabling each scrum team to move forward in their work unblocked and unimpeded. Inter-team dependencies are often created when product backlog items are not sufficiently refined or broken down into relatively independent items that a single scrum team can work on. Dependencies can also arise from differences in technical skills or domain knowledge between teams. Joint product backlog refinement helps teams identify dependencies and minimize them before they cause conflict.

Nexus integration team

Similar to the vertical slicing model's integration team concept, the Nexus integration team ensures that an integrated product increment is produced at least every sprint for the Nexus. The scrum teams do the work, but the Nexus integration team remains accountable for the integrated product as a whole.

The Nexus integration team consists of people from the member scrum teams of the Nexus. It is a scrum team that consists of the following:

>> **Product owner:** The product owner is accountable for ordering and refining the Nexus product backlog, so the maximum value is derived each sprint from work created by the Nexus.

>> **Developers:** Usually, developers are also members of scrum teams in the Nexus. The Nexus integration developers prioritize the Nexus integration team over the individual scrum teams, with the integrated product increment being the prime goal for each sprint.

REMEMBER

Dedicating scrum team members to one team eliminates the overhead of frequent cognitive demobilization and remobilization due to context switching. Always be aware of the risks of splitting team members' focus across multiple teams.

>> **Scrum master:** The scrum master is responsible for ensuring the Nexus framework is enacted and understood. This Nexus integration team scrum master may also be a scrum master in one or more of the other scrum teams in the Nexus.

Nexus artifacts

Three additional artifacts provide transparency at the Nexus level for inspection and adaptation:

>> **Nexus goal:** Having a clear, visible, common purpose for all scrum teams in the Nexus is key to keeping all teams in sync throughout the sprint, working toward the integrated product increment.

>> **Nexus sprint backlog:** Each scrum team has its own sprint backlog of implementation and integration tasks. The Nexus sprint backlog is not an aggregation of these sprint backlogs; it exists to expose and map inter-team dependencies and how work flows across all scrum teams in the Nexus.

>> **Integrated increment:** All integrated work completed by all the scrum teams in the Nexus during the sprint is the integrated increment.

Nexus events

Five additional events enhance inter-team coordination of dependencies at the Nexus level.

Nexus sprint planning

During Nexus sprint planning, the product owner from the Nexus integration team provides priority and business context for the sprint and sets the sprint goal. The individual scrum teams select work for the sprint while highlighting and minimizing dependencies. Each scrum team then holds its own sprint planning to plan the execution of the work it has pulled from the Nexus sprint backlog.

Nexus daily scrum

Nexus does not prescribe who should attend the daily scrum — the right people are members of individual scrum teams that understand how their work may affect, or be affected by, other scrum teams' work. The questions addressed are similar to a single scrum team's daily scrum but focus on cross-team integration, including the following:

>> Did yesterday's work get successfully integrated?

>> What new dependencies have been discovered?

>> What information needs to be shared across teams?

The Nexus daily scrum is held before each scrum team holds its own daily scrum to provide the scrum teams with input to better help them plan their day's work.

Nexus sprint review

Similar to other scaling frameworks, the Nexus sprint review can replace individual scrum team sprint reviews because the focus is the integrated increment. You can use various techniques to maximize stakeholder feedback to conduct the meeting, but none are prescribed.

Nexus sprint retrospective

The Nexus sprint retrospective is a formal opportunity to improve the way the Nexus works through inspection and adaption. The Nexus sprint retrospective includes three parts:

>> Representatives from Nexus scrum teams meet to identify cross-team issues and make them transparent across the Nexus.

>> Individual scrum teams hold their own sprint retrospectives.

>> Representatives from the scrum teams meet again to decide what to do to resolve Nexus-wide issues.

Scaled Agile Framework (SAFe)

Scaled Agile Framework (SAFe) provides enterprise solutions to scaling product development based on Lean and Agile principles. The SAFe Essential Big Picture is shown in Figure 13-11.

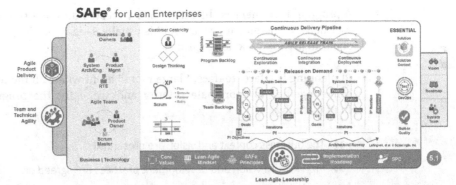

FIGURE 13-11: The SAFe Essential Big Picture.

In addition to SAFe Essential, other configuration options exist that build on the essential configuration:

>> **Large Solution SAFe:** For enterprises that are building large and complex solutions but do not require portfolio-level constructs.

>> **Portfolio SAFe:** Supports the development of multiple solutions across a portfolio.

>> **Full SAFe:** Represents the most comprehensive configuration, supporting large, integrated solutions that may require hundreds of people to develop.

Some aspects of SAFe that have made it useful to many organizations include agile release trains (ART) and program increment (PI) planning.

ARTs

The "agile release train" (ART) model is a team of agile teams delivering incremental releases of value. The train departs the station on a reliable schedule of release opportunities that each program can jump on if ready. If you miss one release, you can catch it when another one comes along. The ART provides a fixed cadence with which the program teams synchronize.

At this level of integration, the work of the individual teams comes together to form release packages continuous exploration (CE), continuous integration (CI), and continuous deployment (CD).

PI planning

A program increment is the functionality created during a timebox in which an ART delivers incremental value. A PI is usually 8–12 weeks long, most commonly about four two-week-long sprints.

PI planning is a face-to-face, "large room" event where all the teams of the ART come together to coordinate priority and scope for the program increment. In PI planning

>> The business context and vision are presented

>> Architecture vision and development practices are agreed on

>> Teams create their iteration plans and objectives

>> Management reviews the overall plan draft

>> ART teams make planning adjustments based on management's review

>> Program risks are identified and mitigated

>> Confidence vote across the ART to move forward or rework until confidence is achieved

PI planning enables fast decision-making through real-time, synchronous collaboration, builds the social network needed for the ART to work well together throughout the PI, and ensures development and business goals are aligned and dependencies are broken down in planning.

Portfolio managers like the SAFe model because of how visual it is. For larger organizations, it also provides the structure for middle management's involvement with scrum teams.

While many organizations have found success with scaling models, there are risks in implementing scaling overhead of any kind. Remember to get scrum right first before scaling. If you still think you need an additional scaling framework, we encourage you to consider the following.

Empowerment

Empowerment, or the authority or power given to someone to do something, is essential for true agility. Product owners, developers, and scrum masters are empowered to act in the best interests of the organization and team. Scrum encourages the people most familiar with the problem at hand to solve the problem.

A top-down approach to scaling can often lead to organizational leaders making decisions that should be made by the people closest to the problem or customer. Some leaders see themselves as the most knowledgeable about the customer's needs when, in fact, they may be somewhat distanced.

This lack of empowerment and centralized decision-making has the potential to convert teams from teams of thinkers and doers to simply doers, cutting off the legs of empowerment.

Complexity

If a scaling model requires hundreds of pages to describe the framework, flow, and roles, watch out for the excess structure it might introduce. The introduction of excessive additional roles, artifacts, and meetings can distract from good scrum and return you to high-compliance and oversight structures you're trying to get away from.

Organizational change

Scrum is a different way of approaching process and product development than what most organizations have been doing. Implementing scrum will require change, in many cases significant change. If a scaling model seems to be encouraging traditional, hierarchal, siloed, and specialist structures by simply renaming them, chances are the model will not lead your organization to increased agility. To avoid these pitfalls, return to the basics of scrum. Getting scrum right at the team level is the foundation for effective scaling.

Don't scale bad scrum.

Scrum is an exposure framework. It purposefully exposes everything so facts and ineffectiveness can be seen and addressed. Your scaling model should enhance and support this, not cover it up.

As mentioned at the beginning of this chapter, scaling is an antipattern. The best way to prevent the need for scaling is to enable your teams to become highly aligned and highly autonomous. Break down work and features into the smallest and most valuable increments.

IN THIS CHAPTER

» **Creating a culture to attract excellent scrum team candidates**

» **Developing talent for scrum**

» **Morphing into scrum with existing employees and new hires**

» **Identifying the benefits of incremental funding**

» **Improving the budgeting process**

Chapter **14**

Human Resources and Finance

When the winds of change blow, some people build walls, and others build windmills.

— CHINESE PROVERB

aby Boomers are retiring rapidly, new generations of employees are taking their places, and human resources (HR) has taken on high-level organizational value. Wasted funds from failed products indicate a smarter way to finance product development must exist. As in so many business functions, old methods of achieving goals are becoming outdated.

Companies that can recognize their core HR and finance issues and then apply the scrum framework to the solutions are staying ahead of the pack. Many opportunities exist to increase human potential and financial effectiveness through scrum.

In this chapter, we guide you through the challenges and solutions in these critical organizational areas.

Human Resources and Scrum

In a survey conducted by the Society for Human Resource Management (SHRM), two core challenges highlight the world of HR today: retaining and rewarding the best employees and developing future leaders. These two concerns are really the same thing. Your best employees often become your future leaders.

When the surveyors asked organizations about their largest investment challenge, the number-one response was "obtaining human capital and optimizing human capital investments."

TIP

We always encourage the organizations we work with to refer to people as *people* or *talent* rather than *capital* and *resources*. People aren't commodities. They have individual skills, experiences, and innovations. The term *resources*, used to refer to people, is a relic. Start seeing your people as people, and see their creativity and talents as the irreplaceable value they bring to your organization.

That said, the point made by the SHRM survey is still crucial. Different types of leaders are needed. We need leaders to make the hard product owner decisions discussed in portfolio management (see Chapter 13). We need servant leaders who work collaboratively to enable and empower teams, such as scrum masters (see Chapter 2). These people empower and enable self-organizing teams to come up with the best solutions. They value iterative approaches to building products based on rapid and regular customer feedback and know how to pivot and respond to that feedback quickly.

Historically, technology companies have rewarded leaders who managed crises well. In turn, these leaders promoted others who managed crises with a sense of urgency. Although these firefighters certainly saved the day more than once, we argue that this situation caused an unbalanced shift toward crisis resolution rather than crisis avoidance.

We need leaders in development who excel by learning new skills and mentoring others as they grow. We need collaborative leaders who can work in the dynamic environment of scrum. We need people who value complementary leadership styles. Egomaniacs need not apply. Companies need cross-functional swarming scrum teams to stay competitive. In other words, we need leaders who embrace the value of change.

Reducing risky single points of failure saves money for all the reasons we've discussed so far in the book. Teams that collaborate to solve a problem get quality products to market faster than teams that use traditional methods.

Creating the Right Culture

In Chapter 4, we discussed what motivates employees most: not money, but the autonomy and trust needed to do the job, opportunities to grow, and a sense of purpose. People want what they do to mean something and work with others who are growing and engaged in what they do.

The fruits of self-organization and self-management are created by an organizational culture that attracts and retains the best and the brightest. As we stated in Chapter 1, these are Agile principles 5, 8, 11, and 12.

REMEMBER

Creating the right culture has many facets. The number-one thing we look for in an effective scrum team member is versatility. Give us someone who is intellectually curious and has what we call a *contributor personality*, and we'll have success with that person. We can teach technical skills. Prima donnas, who think this thin slice of development is the only thing worthy of their time, will taint the entire team. The most important job on a scrum team is the job necessary to ship the product. Sometimes, that job is coding; sometimes, it's quality assurance; sometimes, it's documentation. Whatever that task is, it's the highest-status, most critical job of the entire project.

Crucial to the creation of an attractive organizational culture is the attitude of executives: what qualities they embrace and how they invest in their people. Like a magnet, leaders attract people who respond to the culture they provide.

Broad organizational culture is important, like an environment that embraces learning (even through failure), or encourages openness and transparency, and autonomy so team members don't hide problems, but rather expose them for the sake of being able to address them as a team.

Also important are tactical team skills. Cross-functionality within teams, fostering the ability to swarm, is critical. The keys are aptitude and skills, not titles. A cross-functional, self-managing team is the perfect environment for skill development. As employees grow, they can become more engaged in the organization's goal and purpose.

REMEMBER

Technology changes too fast to get stuck in the single-technology specialist mindset. The standard tech choice of today may be totally different from what's needed tomorrow. The specialty of tomorrow is the ability to learn and adapt quickly. You need team members who recognize this.

As skills are emphasized more than titles, a culture is created where you don't have to hire one person for each skill. Expertise (not specialization) is always needed. You don't need a specialist in every seat.

Situational leadership is important. If Jim has expertise in .NET, you'll probably defer to him when you're facing a .NET problem. Carol may have expertise in quality assurance. When discussing quality assurance, you may defer to Carol. Sam may have just come back from a .NET conference, and although Jim may be strong in .NET, Sam may have learned something that Jim doesn't know.

The following sections describe two ways to examine HR and scrum.

HR and existing organization structures

In this section, we look at ways to organize and manage employees within a scrum structure.

Incentivizing

Forced ranking and competitive incentive structures promote competition among employees. Scrum is team-centric. The team receives praise and suggestions for improvement. Incentives should be on the team level, too. If the team succeeds, the team gets the prize.

When a football team wins the Super Bowl, every person on the team gets a ring whether he played that day or not. If developers have a good year, everyone on the team might get a 15 percent bonus, not just a few select people. Depending on your seniority, 15 percent could be significant.

For large teams, this practice may not work. But with scrum teams being ten or fewer people, it's difficult for one or two team members to fly under the radar for very long. A self-managing team demands the contribution of every team member, so everyone earns the prize in the end.

Compensation

How do you stand out if a cross-functional team has no titles or specialists? You acquire knowledge and skill, sometimes being the go-to person on a subject. Someone who's a heavy lifter on the team has a lot of tasks in the task board's *Done* column, and other people want to pair with those people and shadow them on tasks.

Seniority and relative compensation are established by a combination of skill depth and breadth. Each developer has at least one skill. If you know how to do one skill, you're Band 1. You may be junior-level Band 1 or senior-level Band 1, but you're Band 1.

If you know how to do two skills, you're Band 2. You may be junior-level Band 2 or senior-level Band 2, but you're Band 2. If you have three skills, you're Band 3, and so on.

Each new skill gives the developer another band. As the team matures through shadowing, swarming, team pairing, and knowledge sharing, each team member should be adding skills (becoming more and more versatile). As team members achieve higher levels (such as Band 2 and Band 3), their pay scales rise accordingly.

This situation is a true win-win situation because an organization can pay team members more *and* save money by having teams of cross-functional employees rather than an army of sharpshooters who know how to do only one thing.

TIP

By incentivizing developers to learn more skills and therefore increase their value to the organization, you give them the opportunity to design their own education and career paths. Often, the skills they develop are those they're most interested in or have the greatest inclination to develop. They may be introduced to skills they would never have tried before but find they have an aptitude.

Team members have an incentive to gain more skills, and the company benefits by paying fewer people higher rates and developing scrum teams that are more effective and capable.

Underperforming team members

If anyone on a self-managing team isn't pulling their weight, scrum exposes this fact quickly so that the team can correct the problem. In Chapter 4, we discuss the Hawthorne effect, which shows that a worker's performance improves when someone is watching. Visibility and performance are directly proportional. Scrum also uses information radiators such as task boards and burndown charts, which raise visibility and performance.

TIP

One client had multiple flat-screen TVs in his building's lobby. The screens were split into quadrants and showed the day's burndown of four teams simultaneously, refreshing with new updates every 20 seconds. Everyone walking into that lobby (including suppliers and clients) could see every team's status of product development — a high-visibility situation for each scrum team and team member.

Lack of transparency in goals and expectations can also play a role in underperformance. If a person doesn't know exactly where she's headed, it's understandable that she can get off course.

Underperformance in scrum can easily be identified in burndown charts showing the status of the sprint backlog at any given time, where daily tasks are marked as accomplished or not accomplished. With this type of visibility, in which the team is accountable as a single unit, any lapses are easily found and solved.

In a traditional model, if a developer wants to hang out on Instagram or TikTok for three hours daily, they can easily do so. The developer can tell the project manager they need 4 hours to finish a 45-minute task. If the project manager says the developer could do the job in less time, the developer's response might be, "Really? Show me how." Because the project manager probably doesn't have the skills necessary to fully understand the task at hand, their only option is to let the developer get on with whatever they want to do. The rest of the team members figure as long as they're doing their jobs, the problem is between the developer and the project manager.

However, under scrum, teams are held accountable as single units. If a developer spends three hours on Instagram, this will become clear at the daily scrum or throughout the course of any given day, and their teammates will hold them accountable for not doing their share.

Here are some other ways that scrum can expose performance issues:

>> In the daily scrum, team members can suggest that a troubled developer join them in shadowing or pairing on a task before any escalation of an issue occurs. This suggestion is the team's idea and may be all it takes to solve the problem.

>> Sprint retrospectives are excellent times to identify gaps in skills and possible solutions. Causes of underperformance can be unearthed, such as team dynamics, the environment, and misunderstandings.

>> In sprint reviews, the team can encourage the struggling person to engage in the demo. In preparation for the demo, things may come to light that prompt ideas for the retrospective.

>> If all the developers know one person isn't carrying their weight, but they're uncomfortable bringing up the issue themselves, a good scrum master will facilitate the interactions needed to address the issue.

HR and scrum in hiring

When you make organizational changes and adopt scrum practices, you'll search for and hire new employees using different criteria than you did before. Following are some things you need to consider when you're hiring for each scrum role:

>> **Developers**

- Remove titles from the job descriptions and base your searches on skills. You'll not only filter your search results based on skill keywords that candidates include in their profiles but also filter out candidates who are more interested in touting their titles than their skills.

- Search for candidates who are curious and have a desire to cross-train — those who have demonstrated an ability to work outside their comfort zones.

- Search for generalists who have broad skill sets and experience in moving among skills.

- Find people who seek chances to work with a team. Even the most introverted soul enjoys working with respectful teammates.

>> **Product owners**

- Look for the key characteristic of decisiveness.

- Find people who have worked collaboratively with developers and stakeholders.

- Seek the soft skills of communication and proactivity. Providing effective, timely clarification is critical to a scrum team's success.

>> **Scrum masters**

- You want soft skills such as coaching and facilitation of conflicts and demonstrated effect on previous teams' performances.

- Look for someone who can protect the team, display empathy, and mentor as a servant leader.

- Don't advertise for a project manager hoping to convert that person to a scrum master. The project manager role doesn't exist in scrum, and it may not be the right fit.

Regardless of the position you're trying to fill, search for people who have positive scrum and/or agile experience. Regularly review job descriptions and update them with appropriate scrum role terminology and Agile principles to attract candidates who prefer working with scrum.

Performance reviews

After you have your new scrum-focused hires, performance reviews can be team-based. Reward people based on their contribution to the team, shifting the emphasis from the individual to the team.

HIRE AN AMAZING SCRUM MASTER

Finding a qualified scrum master for a team can be challenging. Unlike traditional interview approaches, where uncertainty is quite high about whether the candidate will fit and do the job well, consider using an agile approach like this.

Initial screening of the candidates was done per tradition by a Human Resources recruiter, followed by an initial screening by the talent development manager (both 15 minutes each). The candidate was then invited to come onsite for several different types of interactions.

This is how it went:

Step 1: Group discussion with agile coaches, talent manager, and product owner (30 minutes).

Purpose: To explore the candidate's understanding of agile values, principles and practices, evaluate their cultural and personal fit, understand their servant leadership strengths and weaknesses, techniques used in the past to facilitate team improvement, and to answer the candidate's questions about the organization and role.

Step 2: If Step 1 was interesting for the interviewing group, the developers were invited to join (30 minutes).

Purpose: To give the candidate an opportunity to demonstrate their facilitation skills with a timeboxed, 20-minute backlog refinement session followed by a 10-minute group retrospective.

The group observed the candidate's personality/servant leadership in action and how they adjust to mistakes, get comfortable with themselves and the team, and find a rhythm. It also helped the candidate gain insight into the nature of the scrum team with which they would work.

Step 3: Render a decision — fist of five or thumbs up or down vote (5 minutes).

Purpose: After thanking the candidate, giving them parking validation, and sending them on their way with what to expect for the next steps, decide as an interview group the candidate's destiny.

The approach created a safe environment to showcase the candidate's skills and overall fit with the team and organization. The interviewing group observed first-hand the most important things about their scrum master: facilitation skills, understanding of agility, organizational skills, prioritization approach, INVEST criteria with user stories, clearly defining *done*, choosing a sizing approach, and understanding of effective retrospectives.

Because the interviewing development team and product owner wanted a strong servant-leader scrum master to work with for a long time, they were committed to helping candidates succeed, increasing their confidence in the candidate's fit.

The transparency also benefited the candidate by allowing them to see the organization was dedicated to adopting agile values, principles, and practices. They met the people they would work with and evaluated the team's collective understanding of agile roles, user stories, sizing, and team personality. They gained more exposure to potential coaching opportunities needed by the team than they might in traditional interviews. The candidate left the interview much more informed about whether they wanted to work there.

This client hired an amazing scrum master, and both the team and the scrum master are happy with their decision.

Team-level performance reviews are a natural for scrum. Given the high visibility inherent to this framework, daily assessment is given through peers, and team output and outcomes are consistent and tangible.

Formal annual reviews of individual employees are, for the most part, artifacts of traditional project management frameworks. They've proved to be ineffective for several reasons:

>> People need and want regular feedback, not just a review at the end of each year. Regular coaching is the key.

>> It's difficult to assess an entire year's performance, with all its nuances and situational factors, in one review. By its nature, the review will be incomplete.

>> Poor performers should be coached and mentored early, not after a year has passed.

>> Positive, constructive feedback is much more effective than the appraisal format of an annual review.

The most logical, straightforward way to provide feedback that helps team members improve is to have each person's peers provide a 360-degree review (see Figure 14-1). On scrum teams, these peers are team members, stakeholders, and customers. Instead of being a formal performance review, a 360-degree review is a feedback tool. Each member of the team can understand the effect of her work on every other person involved. This holistic view shows how an employee is performing within the entire work environment.

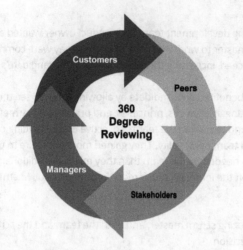

FIGURE 14-1:
The 360-degree performance review.

Use 360-degree performance reviews for determining compensation and (more important) for helping team members inspect, adapt, and improve. When you use them only to satisfy HR requirements or determine merit increases, you miss the full power of 360-degree reviews.

Some benefits of a 360-degree review are

>> Viewing an employee's performance from different angles allows for a greater understanding of which skills need improving and which are outstanding.

>> Growth depends on frequent, high-quality feedback.

>> Starting points for improving skills can be identified.

>> A baseline can be set for measuring improvement.

>> Personal blind spots in an employee's behavior can be identified.

In addition to helping clients use scrum to iteratively hire and onboard new employees, we've also helped clients organize around other human resources functions, like benefits administration, payroll management, and training development. Entire HR departments have significantly improved efficiencies by organizing small cross-functional teams around these functions rather than having HR specialists work them in silos. HR is all about people, and what better service to the people in an organization is there than having many people to go to for help with the people aspects of their jobs?

MANAGING HIRING WITH SCRUM

Scrum influences how you hire and develop talent to optimize the power of scrum. You can also use scrum for hiring and onboarding projects.

One global biopharmaceutical and medical device solution provider used scrum for a major hiring push that required 21 new hires, trained and ready to go. Developers, database administrators, business analysts, and technical writers were needed. From the start of the recruitment process to the project start date, the hiring team had only seven weeks to find, hire, and train these individuals.

Initial challenges were extensive:

- No onboarding process currently existed.

- No formal new-hire program existed.

- The current recruiting process was inefficient.

- No dedicated training department or content existed.

- New equipment was needed, such as workstations, phones, and computers.

The company incorporated the scrum framework for managing this project. To start, the product owner (the HR director) gathered all the hiring managers, the IT manager, and the HR staff for a one-day planning meeting. They identified everything they would need to do and who would do each part, such as

- Gather and create content for corporate, product, and industry overviews; agile development and software overviews; and IT and HR orientations.

- Create a weeklong, onsite training program utilizing the manual.

- Establish the new facilities.

- Purchase equipment and network and software tools.

- Recruit internal trainers (subject matter experts and managers).

- Gather and format current material that existed in various forms.

From this single day of planning, they were able to establish roadmap features and product backlog epics for

- The training program manual

- IT equipment procurement

(continued)

(continued)

- IT software, licenses, and credentials procurement
- Setup of the new facility
- Process for hiring new employees on time

For recruiting the new employees, they also identified the need for

- A portal and process for reviewing resumes
- An interview schedule
- Standard tests and interview questions

The managers used one-week sprints, and each week everyone demonstrated the progress on his portion of the manual and gathered feedback from each other. IT showed their progress in the facilities and equipment needs. They created the next week's sprint goal and went back to work.

The weekly touchpoints with IT were important. Several times, impediments were identified on the spot and could be resolved to keep IT in line with the deadlines.

Hiring managers gave each other feedback on the training material's content. This way, they didn't need an exhaustive edit at the very end. By the time the training came, they knew that even if they hadn't had time to review the entire manual, their content had been inspected and adapted along the way and was already quite refined.

Sprint retrospectives were held each week, and the outcome often involved plans for improving coordination and issues with the hiring portal vendor. Issues were fixed in a timely manner because attention was given weekly. Also, someone was tasked with addressing any issues as part of the follow-up action plan.

Within this organizational framework, the hiring process was incorporated. An onboarding company provided a portal for managing candidates through the pipeline. This portal provided visibility for each stage of the hiring process and helped with scheduling rooms and moving candidates from one interview stage to the next.

Results from the coordinated scrum framework included all new hires receiving the same training, and their big-picture understanding of their role was complete.

After this first wave of hires, inspection and adaptation were applied, and improvements were made to the system. Overall, the inspect-and-adapt cycle so inherent to scrum and the swarming of each feature meant remarkable success in a potentially nightmarish hiring project.

EXPERIMENTING TOWARD AGILITY

Zappos, a leading Amazon online shoe and clothes retailer based in Las Vegas, Nevada, has been through several iterations of reinvention through experimentation. Each iteration has led them to identify paths they want to keep and others they want to end, improving their business agility at every step.

Holocracy, a Zappos experiment started in 2014, is a method of decentralized management and organizational governance introduced by the late Tony Hsieh, former Zappos CEO. Holocracy distributes authority and decision-making through a holarchy of self-organizing, self-managing teams called "circles" rather than being vested in a management hierarchy.

Tony was inspired by the book *Scale* by Geoffrey West and argued that cities are resilient and flexible. Every time one doubled in size, productivity per resident rose by 15 percent. He believed the same benefits could be obtained if Zappos behaved more like West's city.

Zappos learned from the experiment that holacracy enabled many remarkable aspects, including self-organizing, self-managing teams, but fell short in several areas. Their findings led to the discovery of the Market-Based Dynamics (MBD) experiment in 2017, where the teams began to run like small, autonomous start-up businesses or microenterprises. Hierarchical budgeting challenges then led to the invention of Customer-Generated Budgeting (CGB) in 2018, where budgets were decided by their customers.

CGB's challenges of poor autonomy and accountability led to the creation of the Triangle of Accountability (TOA) in late 2019. TOA provided each microenterprise with three constraints to enable the maximum levels of autonomy and accountability (thus the triangle). This led to team-based compensation and many, many other experiments.

Zappos is an excellent example of a) experimenting with organizational structure to optimize the experience, creativity, and enjoyment of their people, and b) true business agility gained through iterative experimentation — the very essence of empiricism.

Finance

The goal of business is to make money to provide and improve products or services. Therefore, finance lies at the heart of any successful product development effort. Increasing competition and tightened budgets require making tough, wise funding decisions.

Billions of dollars are wasted yearly on products that failed or died somewhere along their protracted and painful development. Here are just a few examples:

>> Ford Motor Co. abandoned a purchasing system after deployment, resulting in a $400 million loss.

>> J Sainsbury PLC (UK) abandoned a supply chain management system after deployment, resulting in a $527 million loss.

>> Hewlett-Packard experienced a $160 million loss due to problems with an enterprise resource planning (ERP) system.

>> AT&T Wireless experienced problems with a customer management system upgrade, resulting in $100 million lost.

>> McDonald's canceled its innovative information-purchasing system after already spending $170 million.

These are only a few examples of preventable financial waste.

A survey conducted by KPMG on global IT project management unearthed some startling findings. When respondents were asked about their experiences in delivering value in projects after receiving funding, this is what they found:

>> 49 percent said they'd experienced at least one project failure in the previous 12 months.

>> 2 percent achieved their targeted benefits with every project in the same 12 months.

>> 86 percent said they'd lost up to 25 percent of targeted benefits across their entire project portfolio.

Most of this was likely preventable.

Incremental funding

Not surprisingly, companies want to fund an initial deliverable before they decide whether to keep funding a product. In scrum, product increments are produced every sprint and packaged for release every release cycle, so incremental funding is easily incorporated.

TECHNICAL STUFF

Incremental funding is a financially driven method of funding product development efforts. It focuses on maximizing returns by delivering sequenced, portioned customer-valued functionality to maximize a product's net present value — the present value of future incoming cash flows minus the purchase price and any future outgoing cash flows.

What used to happen in corporations is that the business team would go before a funding committee with a proposal and return on investment (ROI) numbers that team members believed were necessary to fund their product development effort. If they were successful, the team spent every nickel of that funding and then delivered results or asked for more funding. Few people looked at the ROI numbers from months or years earlier because the company wasn't going to get that money back anyway. Sunk costs meant that companies had to move forward at all costs.

In scrum, the product owner goes before a funding committee with his product goal and monetized product roadmap. He might say, "I need $3 million to implement all these features." The funding committee can respond, "Okay, we'll allocate $3 million for your project. But first, we'll give you $500,000. Show us that you can deliver the ROI promised for your initial release, and we'll give you more money. But if you can't deliver on a little bit, you can't deliver on a lot."

Many companies prefer to use incremental funding for their product development with or without the accompanying scrum practices. Incremental funding is used to do the following:

>> **Mitigate risk:** Stakeholders and product owners can test the projected ROI at minimal cost to see whether they hit it.

>> **Reduce costs:** A minimal investment is used at the start.

>> **Maximize returns:** Earlier monetization leads to higher revenue.

TECHNICAL
STUFF

Another way to look at team funding is in terms of MVP (minimum viable product), which we introduce in Chapter 5. You should be able to monetize the MVP (explicit ROI). If the MVP realizes the projected ROI, fund the next MVP.

Incremental funding creates an opportunity for product owners and stakeholders to examine their ROI at every release. At each release, if problems exist, depending on the size and complexity of those problems, stakeholders can invest in fixes or terminate the development before more money is wasted.

Revenue can be started earlier. The goal is not just less waste but earlier return — and earlier return means higher return. Value is delivered to the customer earlier, and his buy-in increases. Controlling risk and cost is important; so is providing value. If you can identify ways to deliver distinct features for generating revenue in earlier time frames, you should chunk them out and deliver them first, so the customer can realize revenue without having to wait until the lowest-priority item is deployed. As revenue comes in, the initial costs are offset earlier, and overall revenue and profit over the product's life are higher.

Figure 14-2 compares traditional waterfall project management financial implications against agile techniques such as scrum.

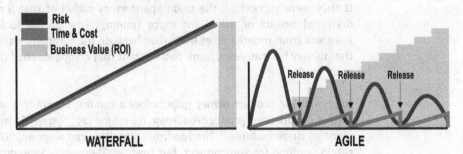

FIGURE 14-2:
Traditional
project
management
versus agile
risk — time and
cost and business
value comparison.

Historically, a product's ROI is projected, and funding is received based on that projection. Product development is rarely canceled because testing and customer feedback are left until the end of the development cycle. Even if problems are discovered, it's difficult to take money back after it's been allocated. Not surprisingly, ROI projections are sometimes inflated to get funding.

With incremental funding, the ROI is kept honest because it needs to be proven at each release. If the increment fails to deliver, no more money is invested.

This lower cost of failure allows developers to nurture their creativity and even form an intrapreneurial culture. Fresh ideas can be tested, and if the ROI is met, they can be continued. Company cultures change as trust is built through tangible delivery and the intrapreneurial spirit is nourished.

Failure no longer exists; it's replaced by consistent learning toward the next success when costs are low, and innovation is encouraged. Self-organizing teams have the freedom and motivation to come up with their own best designs and solutions.

The following sections discuss standard accounting practices that align with this incremental financing approach.

TIP

Intrapreneurship means behaving like an entrepreneur within a large organization. This type of thinking helps companies innovate and gain a competitive advantage. Organizations that encourage their employees to express new ideas and try things outside their assigned projects have created some of the most useful products, including Lockheed Martin's ADP, GORE-TEX fabric, Google Gmail, 3M's Post-its (a personal favorite of all the authors), Sony's PlayStation, and Facebook's "Like" button.

Scrum and budgets

Traditional budgeting methods, especially in private companies, entail creating a budget for the entire fiscal year. This budget is meant to capture all expenses and revenues for that year.

Management commits, tracks, and rewards based on this estimated budget projection. If a manager or product group exceeds revenue estimates or spends less than the estimated expenses, that person is group rewarded. If the manager or group falls short of revenue goals or exceeds estimated expenses, questions must be answered, but evaluating over- or underperformance is done by reflecting on what has happened in the past; it's a reactive process.

Organizations should accept a yearlong budget as what it is: an estimate. The next quarter's estimate should be the actual target and what teams measure their goals against. The team tries to meet or exceed the budget for this one quarter rather than the budget for the whole year.

Subsequent quarters are still considered to be estimates and treated as such. Teams can incorporate what they learn in the current quarter into the next quarter (inspection and adaptation in finance).

This is how Wall Street works with company estimates. Companies publish their current quarter's estimates and establish those further in the future. However, those estimates further out have less weight than the current estimate.

CapEx and OpEx

Capitalization is much higher with agile techniques. The United States Financial Accounting Standards Board (FASB) outlines three general categories for determining capitalization, each falling under either the "what" or the "how" of product development:

1. **Preliminary (the "what"):** The activities associated with determining the feasibility of a product. Feasibility is achieved when a project charter exists, which states the product is technically feasible, management has approved funding and committed resources to development, and there is confidence the product can be delivered successfully. Scrum teams use the Product goal and product roadmap to approve and fund development. These are often established in a very short time frame, usually one to two days, even on large projects. (OpEx)

2. **Application development (the "how"):** The creation of value-added functionality. Once a product is funded, this is the implementation work by

both direct and indirect laborers. Agile product development begins as early as day two or three, implementing one end-to-end shippable functionality requirement at a time in sprints. Each requirement delivers a new channel of value for the customer (external or internal) and is elaborated, designed, developed, tested, integrated, documented, and approved with product leadership before starting on the next requirement. This is repeated every iteration, incrementally releasing functionality to the customer for review and feedback as often as daily. (CapEx)

3. **Post-implementation (the "what")**: This stage begins once the last functionality requirement is released. Once the final product is released to the customer, it enters maintenance or operational mode. Throughout product development, whether there has been one release or 150 releases, the product is always being enhanced and exposed to the customer for gathering feedback and improving the product to meet customer needs. The Platinum Edge formula AC + OC > V is the trigger for ending product development — when the product is ready for its intended use. When the sum of actual cost and opportunity cost are greater than the value of remaining requirements, it is time to end current product development and redeploy capital on the next highest value product opportunity. (OpEx)

Each of the three FASB categories above is summarized in Figure 14-3.

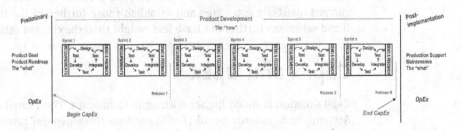

FIGURE 14-3: OpEx and CapEx mapped to product development releases.

Because agile development is driven by lightweight, high-level upfront planning (which establishes feasibility) and progressive elaboration of requirements throughout the development process, a much larger portion of costs can be capitalized. Formal phase gates as official starting points for capitalization begin much earlier (after the product goal and product roadmap).

REMEMBER

The United States Financial Accounting Standards Board (FASB) outlines what is appropriate for capitalizing and operationalizing expenses for internal software products in Accounting Standards Codification (ASC) Topic 350 and Statement of Position (SOP) 98-1 and for software products for sale under ASC 985 and Financial Account Standards (FAS) 86. You should seek financial and accounting advice from accounting professionals. This document is only a summary and commentary on how the standards have been or might be applied using agile product development approaches. Platinum Edge expressly disclaims any guarantee of accuracy.

Agile CapEx approaches

Scrum teams take a fundamentally different approach to product development than traditional product development. Scrum teams progressively elaborate and prioritize their requirements using a product backlog. In the product backlog, the product owner identifies and flags each product backlog item (PBI) that can be capitalized (which should be most PBIs). Organizations may choose to take one of the following CapEx approaches — all of which are defensible.

>> **Most common**

- **Preliminary:** The product goal and product roadmap creation are OpEx (expensed).

- **Application development:** All inspect and adapt activities (such as product backlog refinement, release planning, sprint planning, daily scrum, sprint review, and sprint retrospective) and artifact creation work (such as release plan, product backlog, sprint backlog, and product increment) to the last PBI are CapEx (capitalized).

- **Post-implementation:** Product maintenance after the last PBI is released is OpEx (expensed).

Product maintenance and defect fixes must be expensed. However, using good product development practices such as test-driven development and pair programming will significantly decrease the number of defects found in post-implementation production. Also, with scrum, up until the last PBI is implemented and released, product improvements based on customer feedback become new PBIs to deliver enhanced value to the customer. Although there are modifications throughout an agile development life cycle, they are implemented as new value PBIs and therefore, can be capitalized.

>> **Most conservative**

- This approach is similar to "most common," though some may argue the sprint retrospective is more process-related than product-related and therefore, choose to expense (OpEx) it. This is a very short timebox for each sprint (such as no more than 45 minutes per week of sprint), so this does not significantly impact the amount capitalized.

- In addition to expensing the sprint retrospective, some organizations may choose to expense instead of capitalizing all of the following: product goal, product roadmap, product backlog refinement, release planning and sprint planning. Each of these are timeboxed and collectively make up a small percentage of a scrum team's time. This approach still enables much higher CapEx than traditional approaches.

As you can see, organizations that can address their core HR and finance issues and then apply the scrum framework to the solutions thrive. Many opportunities truly do exist to increase human potential and financial effectiveness through scrum.

IN THIS CHAPTER

» **Improving marketing agility with scrum**

» **Increasing sales revenue**

Chapter **15**

Business Development

Success is not final; failure is not fatal: it is the courage to continue that counts.
— WINSTON CHURCHILL

The primary function of Business Development is to drive customer acquisition and retention. Marketing and sales are fundamental to the growth and health of almost every organization. After all, getting the word out about what you do, finding prospective clients, and converting them to paying clients keeps the motor of business running.

» **Marketing:** The strategic role is to understand the market, uncover what prospects and customers want, and bring that information to executives and product and service design and development. Tactically, marketing delivers information to engage prospective clients until they are "sales-ready." Marketing is highly measurable and pivots to new messaging and tactics to widen and deepen engagement with your company.

» **Sales:** At the point when an individual responds proactively to marketing, it's time for a handover to sales. Sales picks up the conversation, whether that would be an individual consumer (B2C) or an organization (B2B), guiding the prospect through the stages to purchase.

In this chapter, we cover how scrum can support the vital roles of marketing and sales and how valuable these functions are to product owners.

Marketing Evolution

Like most industries and business functions, marketing has evolved. As Anna Kennedy, author of *Business Development For Dummies* (John Wiley & Sons, Inc.), told us, recent changes in marketing include the following:

>> Marketing is the research engine behind understanding what target prospects want from our products/services and what the competition is up to. Keeping ahead of market trends is a crucial function of marketing.

>> Prospects can self-serve information to the extent that two-thirds or more of the buyer's journey happens before any formal engagement exists with the company. In some cases, direct purchase of a product online doesn't require the traditional sales function at all.

>> Marketing has embraced being responsible for generating leads.

>> Technology allows marketers to assess where prospects are on the buyer's journey and nurture them on a one-to-many basis.

>> The diversity of marketing channels, including social media, provides many opportunities for engagement between brands, prospects, customers, and influencers.

>> Marketing is an enabler between the market, product design, sale and their nurturing of individual prospects, and customer service and the satisfaction of your clients.

Firstly, given those trends, how can scrum help marketers embrace the changes and develop agility in responding to this shifting world?

Prospects are researching products and services autonomously before engaging with a salesperson. This might seem dangerous from the company's point of view if your marketing couldn't deliver the right information to those prospects precisely tailored to what they need in different stages of their research. A marketing scrum team can track the market's engagement with your company's marketing and can use analytics to inspect and pivot quickly.

Over the last decade or two, marketing has become a primary consumer of Big Data. Being able to consolidate, analyze, and react to market data and moving trends makes scrum an ideal framework to use for marketing.

Secondly, access to feedback from potential customer interactions with marketing channels enables a scrum team to process reactions more frequently and quickly. This feedback doesn't require waiting for a customer to attend a sprint review. Thanks to marketing analytics technologies, a product owner can access this data in real time. The relationship between the chief marketing officer (CMO) and the product owner is symbiotic.

Finally, marketing needs to be responsible for a key ratio that everyone in the business can understand. The ratio is:

>> Lifetime value of the customer expressed as net profit: (LTV)

>> Cost of acquisition of the customer: (CAC)

Initially, the first step is understanding the cost of marketing in producing a lead. In due course, marketing, sales, and other contributors to acquisition and retention can be rolled into the ratio to determine whether the cost justified the result. This ratio is key to arguing for a budget for a marketing team focused on driving results rather than doing tasks. What could be more fundamental to scrum than that? More on this in the section on scrum processes.

Scrum for Marketing

With traditional product management, it's difficult to know whether the correct product is being built. Without incremental user feedback, it's anybody's guess whether the product will be a success.

In some organizations, marketing suffers from the waterfall mindset in the same way that product development does. Marketing traditionally has a fixed annual plan (much like the yearly budgeting process discussed in Chapter 14). Firms come out with a product with no clear idea whether it'll be a success, and marketing tactics are often planned a year in advance.

Both product development and marketing need to respond to the twists and turns of the marketplace. Just as product development has adopted agile principles and practices, organizations should structure and resource marketing along the same lines. Just as a product owner sets the roadmap for the product based on MVP, a backlog of items, and customer feedback, marketing needs a team capable of pivoting quickly and a budget based on CAC and LTV measures, not on how much gets allocated to social media this year.

Customers have varied tastes and desires. Consider how many different styles and models of cars, clothes, and gadgets are sold in any given year, each seeking to satisfy individual preferences. Sometimes, customers don't know what they want until they get a product in their hands and use it. Despite the company's best intentions, a mystery remains about how and what to market.

THE AGILE ADVANTAGE

In one of its annual "Agile Advantage" surveys, CMG Partners, a strategic marketing consulting firm, interviewed chief marketing officers (CMOs), marketing leaders, and agile experts and found that they overwhelmingly agreed that long-term, highly crafted marketing plans are things of the past. Today, speed and agility are vital tools. Marketers need to be able to respond to changing economic landscapes and customers' shifting desires and needs.

The survey found three key benefits of using scrum within marketing campaigns and projects:

- **Increased business performance:** This performance increase took the form of faster speed to market and increased prioritization and productivity.

- **Increased employee satisfaction:** Self-organizing and self-managing teams, working with transparency and empowerment, lead to happier people.

- **Increased adaptability:** Adaptability is a hallmark of scrum that came to the forefront when marketing teams adopted agile frameworks. Adaptability is sorely lacking in waterfall.

Using scrum in marketing allowed greater collaboration between the end-user and the marketers. The product brand could then evolve with the customer in hand, rather than hoping that a fit would eventually exist.

Cost can be reduced because fewer plans fail with the new fine-tuned approach. With this increase in success rates, customer and employee satisfaction also rises.

The lessons from the report are clear:

- Understanding the evolution of customer needs using market research helps marketing keep pace. It needs to be ongoing.

- Marketing goals and tactics can be designed, deployed, and managed in increasingly responsive cycles.

- Marketing and product development should align around product design, development, and releases, with marketing both responding to product changes and providing input on the market's reaction to the overall aligned direction.

Starting in June 2012, a formal effort was launched to apply Agile Principles in marketing, and a set of recognized agile marketing principles called the Agile Marketing Manifesto was published at http://agilemarketingmanifesto.org.

Although the future is impossible to predict, prediction is precisely what traditional marketing asks people to do. What is predictable is that marketing departments will benefit from adopting scrum.

Determining the roadmap to value

As in product development, marketing needs to define:

>> The purpose and brief for marketing scrum teams. These will vary dependent on the nature of your company, products, and services but should include product development and marketing collaboration in mutually dependent cycles

>> The spring length and the planning and budgeting process for each team

>> The outcomes and value from sprint reviews and retrospectives.

By having self-directing teams in areas of marketing where learning, adaptivity, and iteration are critical (for example, social media or marketing analytics), the sprint cycle will support the backlog of requirements (scope) aligned with the scrum team's capacity to deliver. Plans should be adaptable — expect them to change as the year progresses.

Setting goals

In Chapter 2, we covered the importance of the Product Goal (see Figure 15-1.) In the same way, marketing (and sales) need clear goals to anchor their scrum efforts. As stated in Chapter 2, a goal is:

>> Internally focused, with no marketing fluff

>> Fine-tuned to the goals of the marketplace and customer needs

>> Strategic in nature, showing why and what rather than how

>> Reviewed annually (when part of a broader vision that looks out further)

>> Owned collaboratively by the product owner and the marketing leader (usually CMO or Director of Marketing)

At the senior management level, the strategy for the year and the key goals to be attained should form the foundation of marketing planning. Whether strategy exists or not, the alignment between product/service development and marketing should be established.

For marketing, the roadmap to value looks as follows:

1. Marketing goal:

Typically, this strategic goal will support the year's sales goal.

Example: Grow marketing engagement by 20 percent this fiscal year by expanding successful lead channels and finding at least one new channel for lead generation Increase LTV/CAC ratio by optimizing marketing cost of acquisition per lead.

REMEMBER

The goal model we presented in Chapter 2 is for product development. For marketing and other nonproduct development projects, it's appropriate to tweak that model based on practicalities.

2. Product roadmap (high-level) and product backlog (broken down):

A high-level roadmap definition details what's needed to achieve the goal.

Example: Adaptations need to meet the goal, such as

- Marketing strategy development
- Tool acquisition/ including analytics
- Research additional marketing channels
- Campaign development, deployment, and monitoring
- Budget proposals
- Lead monitoring and follow-up with sales

3. Release planning:

An intermediate-level plan for the next marketing cycle.

Example: Prioritize backlog items for the next quarter's marketing cycle.

4. Sprint planning:

The scrum team sets a sprint goal and creates tasks for the relevant backlog items.

Example: Research and analytics.

5. Daily during the sprint:

A daily scrum meeting to review progress toward the sprint goal and planned tasks and to identify impediments.

Example: Coordinate who needs help from whom on various research and analytics tasks.

6. **Sprint review:**

   Demonstrate the research results or product increment for the sprint

   Example: Recommend additional marketing channels with analytics and tie-in to sales goals.

7. **Sprint retrospective:**

   Review what worked well and not so well.

   Example: Facilitate learning to lead into the next sprint.

Marketing Tools

A handful of tools already in use in product development would be beneficial to marketing. In addition, marketing may be more expert with specific tools than product development is. Some key examples are below:

Product canvas

In *Inspired: How to Create Tech Products Customers Love* (Audible Studios), Marty Cagan wrote, "discover a product that is valuable, usable, and feasible." What he meant by this, as shown in Figure 15-1, is that successful product development hits the sweet spot at the cross-section of

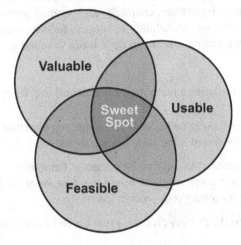

FIGURE 15-1:
The sweet spot where a product is valuable, feasible, and usable.

>> **Valuable:** Will customers buy it?

>> **Usable:** Do customers need it?

>> **Feasible:** Can we do it?

Many marketing teams use a visualization technique, such as a product canvas, to start to explore and understand the key factors, partners, unique value proposition, problems, and potential solutions that may contribute to finding the sweet spot, where value, usability, and feasibility meet.

The product canvas is a collaborative tool that enables teams to accomplish two tasks in a brief amount of time: One, start identifying desired goals or product outcomes. Two, start to validate assumptions about the problem to solve for the customer and ready the team for development. Product canvas exercises can inspire a clear product goal.

Teams use the product canvas as a visualization activity to create a shared understanding of the customer and their needs. The tool is a starting point for the team's assumptions and enables them to dive deep into gathering new product insights.

Many variations of canvases are available, such as a lean canvas or a business opportunity canvas. They all serve a similar purpose of organizing ideas, challenging assumptions, and collaborating to find a strategic direction. Figure 15-2 demonstrates the product canvas we often use with scrum teams. The left half addresses market and customer issues, while the right half addresses product and business issues. The left half defines the customer segment, customer problems with alternatives, value proposition, channels, and revenue projections. The right half defines the solution, key stakeholders, success factors, resources, partners, and costs. Both halves enable a team to do a more detailed market analysis of their product.

Following are some categories a team might use in building its product canvas:

>> **Customer segment:** Describe the target customer segment that needs the problem solved. For whom is the value being created?

>> **Early adopter:** Describe the initial target customer. Remember, your product can't be everything to everybody — at least not at first. What market segments are opportunities for testing your product idea first?

>> **Problem:** Describe the primary problem experienced by the target customer segment.

>> **Existing alternatives:** Describe available alternatives to your product.

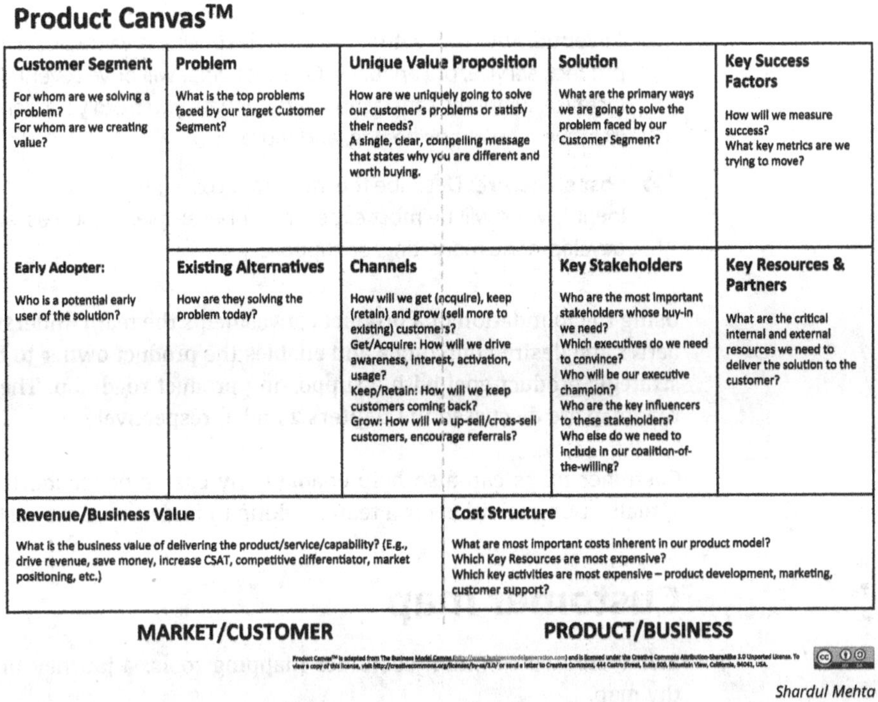

Product Canvas™

Customer Segment	Problem	Unique Value Proposition	Solution	Key Success Factors
For whom are we solving a problem? For whom are we creating value?	What is the top problems faced by our target Customer Segment?	How are we uniquely going to solve our customer's problems or satisfy their needs? A single, clear, compelling message that states why you are different and worth buying.	What are the primary ways we are going to solve the problem faced by our Customer Segment?	How will we measure success? What key metrics are we trying to move?
Early Adopter: Who is a potential early user of the solution?	**Existing Alternatives** How are they solving the problem today?	**Channels** How will we get (acquire), keep (retain) and grow (sell more to existing) customers? Get/Acquire: How will we drive awareness, interest, activation, usage? Keep/Retain: How will we keep customers coming back? Grow: How will we up-sell/cross-sell customers, encourage referrals?	**Key Stakeholders** Who are the most important stakeholders whose buy-in we need? Which executives do we need to convince? Who will be our executive champion? Who are the key influencers to these stakeholders? Who else do we need to include in our coalition-of-the-willing?	**Key Resources & Partners** What are the critical internal and external resources we need to deliver the solution to the customer?

Revenue/Business Value	Cost Structure
What is the business value of delivering the product/service/capability? (E.g., drive revenue, save money, increase CSAT, competitive differentiator, market positioning, etc.)	What are most important costs inherent in our product model? Which Key Resources are most expensive? Which key activities are most expensive – product development, marketing, customer support?

MARKET/CUSTOMER   **PRODUCT/BUSINESS**

Shardul Mehta

FIGURE 15-2: The product canvas.

>> **Unique value proposition:** Describe a single, clear, compelling message that states why or how your product is different and worth buying.

>> **Channels:** Describe the channels for acquiring, retaining, and increasing customers. List ideas for creating awareness, interest, activation, and usage. Describe what will entice customers to return and encourage referrals. List upselling opportunities.

>> **Solution:** Describe how the target customer segment's problems will be solved.

>> **Key stakeholders:** List the most important people to your product. This list may include people whose buy-in and support you need, executives, and influencers. Who are the people you can trust to criticize your product and tell you the truth?

>> **Key success factors:** Describe how success will be measured — measure outcomes, not outputs. Are there key metrics you can use to test your hypotheses?

>> **Key resources and partners:** Describe the critical internal and external people, equipment, or resources needed to deliver the solution to the customer.

>> **Revenue/business value:** Describe the business value of delivering the product, service, or capability. Consider what will drive revenue, save money, increase customer satisfaction, differentiate you from your competition, improve market positioning, and more.

>> **Cost structure:** Describe the important costs inherent in the product model. Identify what will be most expensive, for example, resources, activities, development, marketing, or support.

Using the foundation of a product canvas helps the team understand the customer better and desired outcomes and enables the product owner to build a concise yet strategic product goal with a supporting product roadmap. The product goal and roadmap are discussed in Chapters 2 and 3, respectively.

Customer maps can also help enable early customer feedback and are powerful visualization activities for a team seeking to understand its customers better.

Customer map

Below are two common customer mapping tools: a journey map and an empathy map.

A *journey map* helps the team visualize a customer's day-to-day experience when accomplishing a goal or addressing a specific problem. Actions follow goals in a timeline format by calling out the user's emotions or thoughts. The journey map creates a narrative. The insights gained inform product designs. Figure 15-3 outlines the flow of a journey map and the relationships between the customer's goals and their steps, insights, and emotions.

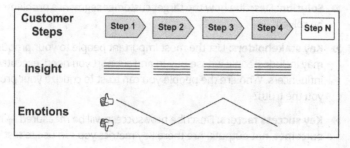

FIGURE 15-3:
A customer journey map.

An *empathy map* (see Figure 15-4) helps the team think through the user's emotions and senses. It explores what the customer sees, hears, thinks, feels, and does. It identifies the pain the customer experiences and how the product can give the customer the gains they seek.

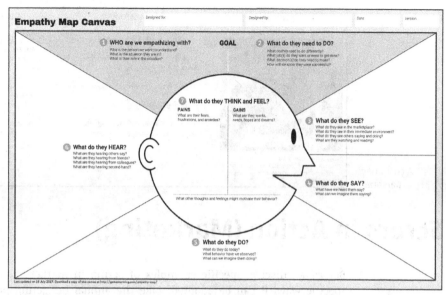

FIGURE 15-4:
A customer
empathy map.

Understanding team perceptions, observations, and insights validate their understanding of the customer and refine their marketing strategy.

Personas

Personas (also discussed in Chapter 3) are commonly used in marketing to take a customer grouping (for example, CEOs of construction companies looking for a project management tool that encompasses design and construction) and move from the generality to a specification of a fictitious individual. In the persona, the individual's lifestyle, preferences, pains, and needs are explicit, allowing both marketing and product development to imagine how a CEO user like Martin would respond to marketing messages or new features.

REMEMBER

You will most likely have more than one persona for your product. In addition to Martin (as shown in Figure 15-5), you may have one for Catherine, representing a construction foreman type of user, or another for Carl, representing a controller or bookkeeper type of user.

Developing a set of personas for a customer segment gives a 360-degree view of users, influencers, and decision-makers that marketing (and sales) have to interact with.

Martin	Characteristics	Challenges & Goals
	CEO of a local construction company.	Spreadsheets and other simple tools were enough when Marco's company was small, but growth over the past 6 months requires project data to be in one place.
	Has about 75 employees (double what it was 6 months ago).	
	Works with a dozen subcontractors.	Marco needs a tool that is easy for all his project managers and foreman to use, and integrates well with subcontractors' systems.
	In growth mode.	
	Good with spreadsheets and other simple data management tools.	

FIGURE 15-5:
A customer persona.

Photo by Sora Shimazaki.
https://www.pexels.com/photo/focused-ethnic-businessman-using-netbook-while-working-in-office-5668805/

Scrum in Action (Marketing)

Before we discuss specific examples of scrum in marketing, we look at some specific ways it can be adopted. Like the annual budgeting plan addressed in Chapter 14, the annual marketing plan is a guess that is refined throughout the year as the organization learns and adapts.

With scrum, marketing plans can be monthly, weekly, and even daily. After each iteration, inspection and adaptation are applied based on feedback from sprint reviews and retrospectives. Marketing plans can be adjusted, change can be thought of as progress, and customers can be marketed to in a way that speaks to their changing needs.

New marketing strategies can be tested with actual users before they're released to broader audiences. In the same vein, brands can be tested within sprints, saving enormous costs because branding is developed with customers rather than presented to them at the end.

How is scrum impacting the results that marketing departments can produce? See the case study below.

CA Technologies

Case study summary: The reasons behind CA's agile journey were familiar: be faster to market, iterate rapidly, prove their impact on the business, and improve team morale. It's taken two years and a lot of learning, but CA is now using agile marketing with over 100 team members across six delivery groups, each of which is aligned with a particular business unit. Sixty of those team members are full-time and part of the scrum teams. The rest are leaders, specialists, data scientists, and regional marketers who offer support as needed as subject-matter expert stakeholders.

Like many success stories, CA started with a small pilot team. Most members were co-located and worked on a single product: CA Agile Central. They also drew inspiration from the Rally Software marketing team, which they acquired in 2015. Once their pilot proved successful, they expanded steadily over the next 18 months or so.

While pipeline improved, delivery times shrunk, and win-rate tripled, the journey wasn't without its obstacles. A lack of co-location and marketing work that didn't lend itself to traditional two-week sprints kept them on their toes, but it was management that had the hardest time. The need to relinquish control and start coaching rather than directing was a tough hurdle in the early days.

Following are the most exciting takeaways:

>> Pipeline improved 20 percent with a flat budget

>> Campaigns can now be delivered in two weeks rather than one to two months

>> Win rate of marketing-sourced opportunities has tripled

TIP

To learn more about agile marketing examples with case studies visit `https://www.agilesherpas.com/blog/agile-marketing-examples-case-studies#CA-Technologies`.

The Gap Between Marketing and Sales

Historically, sales and marketing haven't worked well together. It all stems from a misunderstanding about what marketing can deliver; marketing efforts produce *marketing qualified leads (MQLs)* where an individual has taken action that indicates that they want to enter into a conversation with your company. Traditionally trained salespeople are looking for *sales qualified leads (SQLs)*, which assumes that the individual (or company) is ready to buy, meaning the timing is right, and budget is available.

Traditionally, there is a big gap between the two if only sales can deal with individuals (or in the case of online sales, customer service typically provides the personal touch.)

Sales practices should evolve to fill the gap with the help of marketing. What's missing is *nurturing* the individual until they are ready to buy, and who better than marketing to create the plan, messaging, and content to make the job easy for salespeople.

Although salespeople have taken on remote selling, interacting with people on social media, understanding their competition, and many more changes, the gap between MQLs and SQLs continues to be challenging.

Scrum for Sales

Sales isn't an island but part of a business development cycle that starts with defining what the market needs and the product and service that fulfills that need. Then the cycle goes through marketing, sales, delivery, and evaluation to leverage the customer for repeat sales and advocacy.

In traditional project management frameworks, sales is the classic, individualistic role. Individual quotas must be met (and ideally exceeded), and each individual's pay is based on sales-quota results. Salesperson of the week, month, and year are coveted accolades. Competition is fierce, and a few stars rise to the top in every organization.

In reality, modern sales departments have a variety of roles, from lead qualifiers, sales coordinators, salespeople, proposal/bid coordinators, and more. Sales teams are becoming more diverse in function and more collaborative in operation. Also, the salesperson might take all the glory; they know how much they depend on others for their success.

Scrum takes the traditional approach to sales and turns it on its head in several ways:

>> By its nature, scrum focuses on team success. Securing new customer loyalty requires skills and expertise from multiple team members from product development, account management, contracts, legal, finance, marketing, customer service, and more, all focused on the goal of making the sell. The entire sales team has goals. If the team fails to reach its goals, the members can work together to find solutions.

>> Rewards are team-based. A traditional sales team (all salespeople) is driven by competition, with everyone working in silos. A team structure means all team members swarm around a lead to get to *done* (close the sale).

>> Scrum is all about results over the process to achieve those results. It's focused on reality-based inspect and adapt. You have to inspect the process and adapt for each client.

>> **Results count.** Burndown and burnup charts (discussed in Chapter 5) can be used in sales. Rather than tracking how much has been done, sales tracks how much is left to do in that sprint (burndown). Tracking cumulative sales (burnup) shows real-time progress toward the sprint sales goal.

>> **Standing daily scrums work well because nobody wants long meetings.** If impediments are discovered outside the team, an outside person can be invited to the daily scrum and partake in an after-party removal of the impediment (see Chapter 6).

The scrum sales process

Successful salespeople are exceptional listeners and have keen observation skills. One goal is to discover prospects' problems and then show how the product or service solves those problems. To make this connection, a salesperson needs to establish a relationship based on trust. People buy things from people they know and trust.

Scrum selling is about gaining trust through teamwork. The supporting players may include presales, business development, account executives, field engineers, installers, inside sales and support, and service people. Any combination of these people can make up a scrum team and swarm to synchronize communication, supporting the effort to get the client to sign a deal. Swarming activities might revolve around the following:

>> Preparing for a trade show

>> Following up with trade-show leads

>> Developing time-bound proposals to potential solutions for a sales pitch to out-class the competition

>> Saving an at-risk sale by brainstorming and prioritizing action items

TECHNICAL STUFF

Sales cycles are more successful when a potential consumer or business is *pulled* toward a product or solution as opposed to responding to a pure outbound "cold call" approach. Pull strategies involve content marketing, webinars, trade shows, and social media marketing. Push versus pull models are discussed in Chapter 5.

Determining Roadmap to Value (Sales)

The scrum sales process is high-touch and common sense. It mirrors the roadmap to value as follows:

1. **Sales goal:**

   Like the marketing goal, this strategic goal will support the year's sales goal.

   Example: Grow gross sales in Dallas by 20 percent this fiscal year by increasing the company's social media presence and analytics. Follow up with a personal phone call or email to everyone who provides contact information.

   REMEMBER
   The goal model we presented in Chapter 2 is for product development. For sales and other nonproduct development projects, it's appropriate to tweak that model based on reality.

2. **Product roadmap (high-level) and product backlog (broken down):**

   A high-level roadmap definition details what's needed to achieve the goal.

   Example: High-level and low-level lists of changes are needed to make the goal a reality, such as

   - Sales strategy development
   - Acquisition of tools
   - Development of collateral
   - Sales process development and fine-tuning
   - Execution needed for specific deals in the process
   - Assigning key (detailed) social media sites to a team member
   - Finding a tool for tracking sales funnels that the team will use
   - Defining such reporting processes as analytics workflows

3. **Release planning:**

   An intermediate-level plan for the next sales cycle.

   Example: Prioritize backlog items for the next quarterly sales cycle.

4. **Sprint planning:**

   As a team, set a sprint goal and create tasks for the pulled backlog items.

   Example: Create sales collateral materials broken down into tasks.

5. **Daily throughout the sprint:**

Hold daily scrum meetings to review progress toward the sprint goal, coordinate warming tasks for the day, and identify impediments.

Example: Coordinate who will be reviewing social media copy and procuring artwork.

6. **Sprint review:**

Demonstrate the collateral materials developed in the sprint.

Example: Demonstrate to the stakeholders (such as the vice president of sales) that the Facebook page is operational or mailing lists of past customers are compiled.

7. **Sprint retrospective:**

Review what worked well and not so well.

Example: Facilitate knowledge transfer. If service/installation people are learning how new customers are being acquired, identify ways to help them continue the company messaging that leads to the sale.

Scrum in Action (Sales)

The sales process of converting leads to closed sales is also known as the sales pipeline or funnel. Figure 15-6 outlines a basic sales funnel.

Leads

Sales Call

Follow-Up

Conversion

Close

FIGURE 15-6:
A classic sales funnel depicting the sales process from beginning to end.

A sales manager at an agile-based organization implemented a backlog item task board. Columns included the sales funnel stages, such as Leads, Sales Calls, and Follow-Up. The sales team and management had an immediate picture of where the team was in the project. Sales estimates were inspected and adapted based on reality. Figure 15-7 shows an example of the sales funnel as a task board.

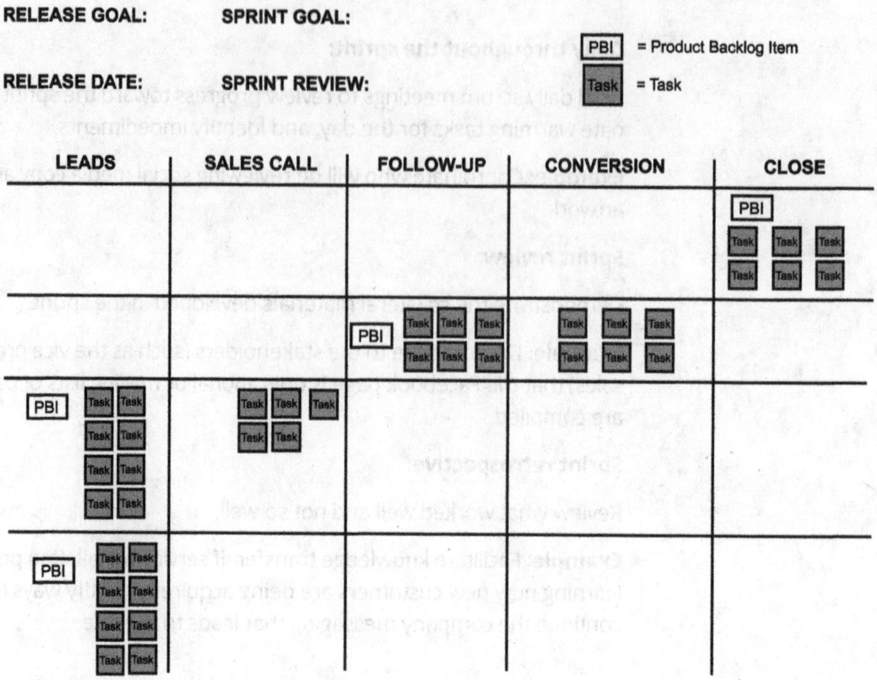

RELEASE GOAL: SPRINT GOAL:

RELEASE DATE: SPRINT REVIEW:

PBI = Product Backlog Item

Task = Task

LEADS	SALES CALL	FOLLOW-UP	CONVERSION	CLOSE

FIGURE 15-7:
A sales task board with columns representing the sales funnel stages.

A visible funnel in the form of a task board is quite valuable. The sales funnel in Figure 15-6 becomes the task board shown in Figure 15-7, as follows:

» **Leads:** Each row (swim lane) represents one lead. Leads arrive from various sources through a variety of methods, but they all land here and get discussed, vetted, and prioritized before the sales call is initiated. Although turning marketing qualified leads (MQLs) into sales qualified leads (SQLs) can be attempted by the marketing department, the trust that develops when a salesperson offers value to a not-quite-ready lead, is a big plus when it comes to closing. Scrum can help bridge the traditional divide between marketing and sales through visibility and coordination of the sales team.

» **Sales call:** An initial sales call is made to further qualify the lead (that is, define the prospect's need and position the offering as the solution). This involves various tasks outlined during sprint planning in the Leads column.

» **Follow-Up:** The lead has responded and expressed interest in the proposed solution to his need. The team coordinates, times, and executes a series of tasks.

» **Conversion:** Obstacles and impediments to closing the sales are identified, and the team swarms to overcome them.

» **Close:** The contract is won. The team documents how the contract was won.

All of this is done effectively as a team. Look at the skills required to make a sale, including marketing, sales enablement, sales engineering, subject-matter expertise, contracts, legal, and finance.

Ideally, you want cross-functional team members who can do everything, but having one person who can do everything well is unusual. Having a team of people who can do everything well is even less likely. Scrum provides a cross-functional team of people who collectively possess all the skills needed to self-organize, devise plans, and swarm around a prospect, event, or contract, producing better results than one person who tries to do everything alone.

Because scrum focuses on continuous communication among all parties, a scrum sales team clearly understands what prospective clients need and want. As a result, the team can present its sales ideas in a way that directly affects those prospects.

iSense PROWARENESS

iSense Prowareness is an information and computer technology consulting company (ICT) based in the Netherlands that adopted scrum throughout its sales processes. The problems that the company had been experiencing were diverse and based on a lack of transparency:

- The system tracked individual progress, but only the manager looked at this. The number and size of each deal were all the data that was shared, and each rep's progress was measured by these metrics alone. Every week, each individual estimated their numbers for that week and reported what they had achieved at the end of the week.

- The company had no way of knowing how individual efforts were impacting the sales of the overall team.

- No process indicators existed. The only measurement was the amount sold. The number of phone calls could be tracked, though the closing rate based on these was unknown. Management had limited ways to help its sales team because it didn't know what and where the individual impediments were. The only input was to work harder because there was no way to determine what "working smarter" meant.

- The sales reps worked hard to improve their numbers, but no structured time was spent reflecting or on the establishment of a system to improve.

(continued)

(continued)

Given this nonunusual sales situation, iSense began implementing scrum, beginning with

- Weekly sprints from Monday through Friday.
- Quarterly sales targets included 13 sprints to each "release."
- Each week, salespeople adapted what they learned from the daily scrums, sprint reviews, and retrospectives.
- A task board was created with a burndown chart and orders taken.
- Standing daily scrums were held in front of the task board.

After the completion of the scrum integration, revenue doubled, half of which sales managers attributed directly to scrum — an excellent return on investment for the transition to scrum.

Interestingly, important lessons learned included assessing which sales tactics were working and which weren't delivering total value. Scrum's transparency made abundantly clear that there is no value to an organization being unable to fulfill a closed sale. When the sales team increased their hit rate from this team-based approach, their pool of service providers had not increased to fill the demand. The sales managers recognized a way to help recruiters fill the demand through temporary contracts, which bought them more time to fill those positions permanently.

The team would cold-call to gather attendees for events highlighting the products. At the event, attendees would be turned from cold leads into warm ones, and then follow-up contact would result in some turning into hot leads and eventual sales. The team analyzed the process and results and found that they only converted 10 percent into actual sales. This allowed the team to discuss and identify gaps in the sales process, refine the sequence, and increase sales. Before long, they doubled that conversion rate.

Through the integration of scrum, the iSense sales team made another important discovery: Making the sale was just the beginning. The company had to deliver on the product to complete the cycle. Sounds simple, but through the process of sprint reviews and retrospectives, where employees from different parts of the company shared information, this gap, too, began to narrow, and the customer benefited.

The sales teams realized that instead of their primary focus being on creating new business, they had more to win with existing contacts and customers. The customers they had already done successful projects with could be used as a starting point for more business. They could become promoters of projects to other companies.

Chapter **16**

Customer Service

Get closer than ever to your customers. So close that you tell them what they need well before they realize it themselves.

— STEVE JOBS

C ustomer service is one of the most critical aspects of any organization. Agile values and principles almost all point directly to the customer, the benefit of the customer, the customer's competitive advantage, and so on. Positive experiences give us a reason to go back to a product or refer it to friends and family. Yet, customer service is the very area many customers and clients say is the most problematic part of the experience. They like the product, but its perceived value decreases with poor service.

Scrum teams always focus on the customer — before delivering value, while delivering value, and afterward. After release to the customer, their feedback and experience is the most important data a product owner can learn from. Product owners work directly with — and understand intimately — the customer's needs.

Product discovery is the continuous learning scrum teams go through to ensure they deliver the right things to the right people. Many of the things we do in product backlog refinement contribute to this (see Chapter 3). Throughout product development (creating and delivering value to the customer), we learn through the customer's feedback whether what we delivered helped them achieve their desired outcomes. We then adjust or pivot from that learning. Scrum teams are just as focused on product discovery as on product development.

Either way, it is all about the customer.

Customers are often external to your organization, but they can be internal, too. Inefficient internal support and incomplete communications lead to lost productivity and bad morale.

REMEMBER

Customer service equals sales (see Chapter 15). A happy customer tells friends and family members and goes back for more services and products.

Customer service is a huge opportunity to increase sales and, therefore, revenue. Close collaboration between the product development scrum team and customer service representatives can propel a firm to new heights. If customer service is neglected, it can affect a company's reputation and goodwill.

TIP

Knowledge of customers equals knowledge-based marketing. Finding new customers becomes more effective. Therefore, managing customer accounts can be considered an extension of sales and marketing and ultimately, product development.

In this chapter, we explore opportunities to use scrum to improve both your external and internal customer service.

Customers: The Most Crucial Stakeholders

Your customers are great sources of product innovation ideas and improvements. Knowing who they are is key for delivering what they need. Their feedback through release and sprint cycles will help you clarify what to do next and validate or invalidate your assumptions. The customer mapping and product canvasing you do gets refined and more accurate (see Chapter 15). A scrum team and their customer should form a strong partnership to ensure your collaboration leads to innovation and success.

On the other hand, alienating your customer creates ill will and cuts off a crucial feedback loop that can lead to innovation.

Internet service providers, phone companies, and local utilities consistently rank among the highest in customer service complaints. Where service providers are limited, customer service is commonly (although not always) weaker than in other industries. Customers frequently encounter long hold times, frustrating service, and labyrinthine automated service menus. Pressures on the bottom line have caused many companies to cut the budget for customer service, though customers are the most crucial stakeholders in any business and must be provided with good service. Without the customers, there's no business.

Although the need for service is enormous, quality is often lacking, and millions of people are willing to spend the time to make others aware of their experience. You want customers to make you aware of their experience. Customer service representatives need to have a clear path to providing feedback to the scrum team through the product owner.

The service conundrum

Perhaps the number-one failure in service is that customers often report that the agent doesn't even solve their issues. Customers need and expect service representatives to be able to answer questions and solve problems regarding their companies' products. Unfortunately, all too often, training in companies fails to provide the customer service representatives with the knowledge they need to meet this need of the customers.

The service representative may not understand the problem because the customer explains it poorly, or the representative simply doesn't understand the situation the customer is describing.

TIP

Seventy-eight percent of customers say their good customer service experience was because of the rep's knowledge, while only 38 percent said it was because of personalized service. Knowledge matters. Training development for representatives is a high priority. Preplanned answers don't carry the same weight as true depth of knowledge.

The cost of losing a customer is far more than the customer's annual subscription rate. Customer service divisions are often thought of as being cost centers, but in fact, they save and make their firms huge amounts of revenue. Following are some statistics that reflect how customer service can affect a business in ways that you may not have considered:

>> It's more than six times more expensive to gain a new client than to keep a current one.

>> 78 percent of customers have forgone a purchase or transaction due to poor service.

>> Loyal customers are worth up to ten times their initial purchases.

>> Twelve positive experiences are needed to make up for one negative one.

>> For every customer who takes the time to complain, 26 others tell their friends instead.

Information overload

In this day and age, too much data is quoted as a source of call center failures. Too much information can paralyze the effective functioning of a service representative. Service representatives can become overwhelmed with too much data that's hard to use, and many centers haven't managed this information so that it's useful to representatives.

Perhaps you've been on a call with one representative and been transferred to another, only to find that you had to explain the issue all over again. Often, a client's historical data doesn't get fed to the rep. It's frustrating for the customer to rehash his situation or to hear the ominous words, "I have no record of your claim here."

TECHNICAL STUFF

Getting the right information to the right people is part of the problem. Sixty percent of customer service centers say they can't even get certain pieces of customer information (for example, portions of customer history) to service representatives. On top of this, more than 30 percent of representatives don't gather and record customer satisfaction data.

Sometimes, data isn't consolidated between organizational divisions, or the data is hard to find. Firms are experts at gathering information, but timely and effective distribution of that knowledge is a problem.

COMMON CUSTOMER SERVICE METRICS

When service calls are assessed, management often measures efficiency over customer needs and satisfaction. Industry-standard metrics measured by percentage indicate:

- 79 percent gather average handle time.
- 75 percent measure abandonment rate.
- 71 percent measure the average time it takes to get an answer.
- Less than 50 percent actually measure customer satisfaction.

Scrum and Customer Service

Most of the high-level issues listed in the preceding section can be improved by scrum. These problems seem to be daunting, but they're not insolvable. Scrum offers solutions.

Inspect and adapt through feedback

One basic tenet of scrum is the feedback loop (see Chapter 7), which facilitates inspection and adaptation. In customer service, feedback is received from customers daily, hourly, and even by the minute. This feedback is on the product and the customer service department itself. This feedback structure is perfect for the per-call sprint cycle.

In each scrum event, customer service teams can ask themselves whether the data they have is what they need to provide the best customer service. Teams need to know whether the tools they have best serve the customer and whether their knowledge is enough to solve most problems. You can use the roadmap to value to address these issues for the customer service team:

>> **Customer Service Goal:** The goal of a service call is simple: to provide the customer with quality support that ends with the customer feeling good about their purchase.

>> **Sprint planning:** During each call, tangible steps toward solving a problem can be inspected and adapted. Each sprint might involve representatives asking customers a certain question during a call to test their progress toward solving the broader problem. If call data shows that the hold time is long, the representative might briefly ask the customer, "Do you feel that your hold time was reasonable today?" Collecting *yes* and *no* answers can validate whether progress is being made with existing processes or changes are required to solve the problem.

>> **Team daily scrums:** If service teams run daily sprints, the daily scrum naturally becomes sprint review and sprint planning. If sprints are longer than a shift or a day, individual issues and impediments can be raised for the broader customer service team to solve in a daily scrum. If a rep is having a hard time transitioning into asking the research question during the call, perhaps another service representative can offer to sit with the rep for a few calls a day.

>> **Sprint review:** A team of service representatives may not find it efficient to reconvene after every call for a review. However, inspecting and adapting at the end of each shift gives the team and the next-shift teams real-time feedback. Here, the team can assimilate the information gathered from the call to prepare for future calls. They reflect on what they learned from the previous shift and determine what questions they should ask in the next sprint.

>> **Sprint retrospective:** At the end of a shift, the team can ask whether a better way exists to gather customer information. For example, do the existing questions bait the customer to provide a certain answer, or are they truly objective? How well did they assess their findings? How well did they document them? What aspects of their process should they inspect for improvements?

Many service centers have enough representatives to require multiple teams, so vertical slicing or other scaled scrum techniques would be implemented (see Chapter 13) to enable coordination and integration of activities and shared knowledge. A scrum of scrums each day would be the natural place to share lessons learned and coordinate efforts across all the teams in a quick, focused manner.

TIP

At least one customer service team representative should participate as a key stakeholder on a product development scrum team that creates the supported product.

Customer service product backlog

Training knowledgeable customer service representatives is the most important factor in creating satisfied customers. Training isn't a one-time event. New products and services require updated training. Refreshers on how to handle complaints and miscommunication are also needed.

By making it incredibly easy for customers to provide feedback, companies can generate a product backlog containing issues that need to be resolved. These issues can be prioritized and addressed based on priority.

REMEMBER

For new-product-development teams, release planning (see Chapter 5) is when customer service can mobilize to prepare training for representatives about the new product as it's being developed (using the upcoming inspect-and-adapt changes to inform the training plan).

Also, if a consistent customer need arises, finding a solution to improve customer service processes can be placed in the backlog and given a high priority; doing so shortens the triage cycle as much as possible. For example, we have a major utility client in Nevada with several customer service scrum teams focused on improving their systems, environment, and procedures. Most scrum teams are made up of managers and supervisors focused on the work of running the department and empowering those on the front lines to make their customers happy. Every sprint goal is focused on making some type of improvement, continually adjusting the product backlog based on what their stakeholders (customer service representatives) are experiencing in reality.

Other customer needs that the product development scrum team can address can be submitted as product backlog items for enhancements or new features.

Customer needs can be discovered and addressed in real time. Prioritizing these needs and swarming on their solution helps customer service overcome product backlogs.

REMEMBER

Customer service is a crucial stakeholder for product development teams. Representatives' feedback should be considered as reliable as (if not more reliable than) market research. If customer service representatives aren't represented as integral stakeholders with product development scrum teams, product owners can't be sure that they know what customers want.

Customer service definition of done

The definition of *done* for customer service teams should clearly outline what it means for a customer to be satisfied with his level of service. The definition of *done* should include more than call length and abandonment statistics.

The customer service definition of *done* might look something like this:

With each customer, I succeed in fulfilling our vision to [statement of how the need is met and differentiated] when I

>> Fully solve the customer's problem

>> Add the problem and solution to product documentation

>> Thoroughly review customer history before offering a solution

>> Update customer history

>> Search the (ABC and XYZ) knowledge bases for answers

>> Seek subject-matter expertise from fellow representatives and/or my supervisor

>> Keep my cool

>> Help the customer keep his cool by [stated methods used by the organization]

>> Follow up on promises I made to the customer

Representatives need to understand what's expected of them to clarify what success looks like.

TIP Consider the definition of *done* for providing service representatives what they need to support a product or service. Regardless of whether this material is in the form of documentation, additional training, or some other metric, be sure to clarify it and then communicate it.

Look inward

Anyone who has worked in a large company likely has felt the level of customer service frustration described in this chapter. We've grouped external and internal customers here because many of the dynamics are the same. The following are some common complaints of both external and internal customers:

>> Companies grew too fast.

>> Budgets are cut.

>> Help desk staff has insufficient training.

>> Companies have a short-term vision.

>> The feedback loops operate poorly.

Inefficient support causes lost productivity and frustration, leading to high turnover, missed deadlines, lost sales, and frustrated external customers. It's no longer acceptable to use excuses such as "The system is down" or "I don't have a ticket." Scrum provides an ideal framework for handling these problems by making work visible and breaking down silos of knowledge through team cooperation and communication.

We've coached help-desk teams by using scrum and one-day sprints. The transformation of the team was amazing, and the team's perception within the company went from poor to excellent in a couple of months. One group described the change in these terms:

>> Better focus every day on priorities

>> Better overall picture of the workload

>> Clearer patterns (a few issues caused most of the workload)

>> Greater transparency with customers and management

By making the work visible and applying shared knowledge, the team was able to remove some of the underlying causes of problems and received management support for future initiatives.

REMEMBER

Information sharing is a critical component of growing proficiency. Make sure that the environment rewards knowledge sharing within the team as well as across departments. Be on the lookout for comments such as "She's the only one who can do that" and "That's not something I can do."

Scrum in Action in Customer Service

Many companies use scrum but haven't applied it to their customer service departments. These firms could greatly improve their customer service — and their bottom line — if they used scrum across the board. If an organization already uses scrum, it should have enough experience and knowledge to share with other departments.

So far in this chapter, we have discussed several ways of adapting scrum through events, the definition of *done*, and the product backlog. Integral to this transformation is ensuring that a customer service rep is present in every sprint review for product development scrum teams. Transparency and awareness stem from this integration between customer service and product development.

Service representative scrum teams can plan training and other process-improvement activities during sprints. Additionally, service representatives can learn from the product development sprint reviews and share this information with their teams.

L.A. WATER AND POWER

The Los Angeles Department of Water and Power implemented the scrum framework without calling it scrum. The goal was to enhance customer satisfaction in its net-meter Solar Incentive Program. The program offers incentives to offset the cost of installing a solar rooftop system at your home or business. The department wanted to reduce delays, streamline the overall customer experience, and increase transparency.

To increase transparency, the department implemented two dashboards, called Mayor's Dashboards, to help customers stay abreast of changes and improvements. One dashboard included weekly updates on metrics, including the status of rebate checks. The second dashboard displayed the Feed-in Tariff (FiT) 100-megawatt program, which the city used to purchase third-party solar power. The time and process involved in processing FiT contracts were displayed, and both dashboards displayed issues, solutions, and response times. A huge increase in transparency occurred.

These sprint backlogs were made available to all stakeholders and customers. The department also consistently inspected and adapted its process to streamline the process for reviewing applications. Results of this inspection and adaptation included increased staff to handle applications and hotline service, removed dependencies between rebate payment and turning on service, reduced review time of lease agreements through a lease compliance form, and the automation of routine email communications with customers and contractors.

The main improvements targeted root causes, streamlined existing systems, and increased clarity. By enhancing the customer experience, the department greatly increased customer service.

5

Scrum for Everyday Life

Chapter 17

Dating and Family Life

I don't want perfect. I want worth it.

— UNKNOWN

Scrum isn't just for business.

In the next few chapters, we discuss some areas of your life in which you may not have considered implementing scrum. Talking about your personal life in scrum terms may seem to lack emotion, but our personal lives involve prioritizing and making critical decisions with imperfect information and an unknown future, just like in business.

As you read this chapter and Chapter 18, keep the following in mind:

» In business, the product backlog applies to a product being developed — a vehicle for delivering value, which may be a software or hardware product, a service, or something more abstract. In family and personal endeavors, a product may be a vacation or wedding plan, a relationship, an education, or a retirement plan.

» When we speak of customers in business, we're talking about people who will use the product. In personal and family endeavors, a customer may be you, your family, your teacher, or your future self in retirement.

Don't let the terminology throw you off. It works.

In addition to benefiting you in the business world, scrum can help you develop personal relationships and make time to do the things you love. Most of us will say that our families or significant others are the most important thing in our lives, and scrum can help you prioritize those important people.

One of the main reasons we have found so much meaning in our careers teaching these principles and ideas to our clients is how much they resonate personally in addition to professionally. Each of us have applied scrum and other agile techniques in our own lives. We're excited to share several applications in these chapters.

Finding Love with Scrum

People have a very real drive to seek love and relationships. Even if each person has a different kind of ideal relationship, almost everyone seeks a loving, long-term relationship. But the truth is that although dating can be fun and adventurous, finding a lasting, loving, healthy relationship can be difficult.

Relationships have evolved. In modern relationships, people are seeking honest connections. Committed relationships are not only about being married because of societal expectations or ensuring that you don't grow old single. People seek fulfilling, satisfying relationships based on communication and compatibility.

Although technology has played a huge role in opening dialogue in dating and providing new ways to find potential matches, it hasn't eliminated all of the challenges. Despite these technological advances and conveniences, the challenge of leaping from connecting with someone on an app to connecting authentically with your heart when the next match is just a swipe away remains.

We want to show you how scrum can make dealing with dating challenges more comfortable and provide a framework for taking steps you may have never thought possible in your pursuit of happiness. Here are a few of these dating challenges:

>> **Time:** Life is about how you spend the finite amount of time you have each day. Everyone (single or in a relationship) has careers, ongoing education, side jobs, personal goals, hobbies, friends, and other nondating activities. There is often pressure to stay late at work or take on that extra side job or project, especially for those who may be single. Although many people *want* a relationship, they haven't structured their lives to have time for one. Making room for dating is about priorities.

- » **Communication:** In modern dating, communication has devolved to using dating apps. The technological advances that facilitate making connections can also hinder relationships because they replace the face-to-face interactions that are so crucial for minimizing misunderstandings and resolving conflict. No wonder a dating app makes it hard to get to know someone on a deep level.

- » **Meeting:** Finding the right person is difficult and feels like luck half the time, but it can be broken into something simple. Most relationships that don't work out fail for one or two simple reasons: attraction and chemistry or personality and values.

It can be difficult and tiresome to find someone you have genuine chemistry with and whose personality and values fit in with how you view life. These two categories oversimplify a variety of factors that affect compatibility, such as finances, selfishness, and intimacy. All these factors contribute to relationship success.

You might look at those problems and think they do not correlate with scrum because dating is complicated! But that's exactly why scrum works for finding love. Scrum is about simplifying and working toward a goal. Here are some ways you can apply the scrum framework to romantic relationships:

- » Responding to change (such as acceptance, rejection, love, heartbreak, connection, and embarrassment)

- » Failing early and fast (wasting as little time as possible on someone who isn't compatible)

- » Inspecting and adapting (becoming the right match for someone else and refining the right match for yourself)

Almost everyone has been through heartbreak (except for the lucky few who meet the love of their life the first time around). For some people, heartbreak leads to bitterness or introversion to protect against further heartbreak. Every layer of attempted protection, however, only prevents you from getting closer to the goal of love. Love is an offensive game, not a defensive one. To be clear, inspecting and adapting based on frequent empirical evidence are your keys to finding happiness.

The following sections look at how you can overcome complications of modern dating and focus on finding love with scrum.

Setting an end goal

The roadmap to value (or, in this case, the roadmap to love) begins with setting a goal (see Chapter 2).

Define what you're pursuing when you pursue a relationship. Clarity on your goal is key. Someone who defines their interactions by "I just want to have fun with someone I'm attracted to" will approach dating radically differently from someone who says, "I want to get married to someone with whom I can build a lifelong family."

Keep in mind that goals may change as your circumstances and stages in life change. This learning-as-you-go is the essence of empiricism. Keeping an agile mindset, adjust your goal.

REMEMBER

Personal goals, like product goals, are forward-looking internal statements. They describe how you see yourself or what you want to have in the future.

For example, dating to have fun isn't a bad goal, but it could be an inconsistent goal if your overall desire is to settle down and start a family sooner than later. Goals aren't met instantaneously, and simply having the goal of wanting a life partner doesn't mean that the next person you go on a date with will be that person. But knowing what you're pursuing, in the long run, should influence your interactions during dating.

Dating in layers

Relationships evolve. To know if you're accomplishing your dating goals, you should know and clearly define what each stage of a relationship means to you. If you have a goal of finding a life partner, you'll take a series of steps toward that goal. In scrum, these steps are your roadmap, and each major milestone is a release goal. Here are some examples of release goals on a roadmap working toward a goal of finding a life partner:

>> Get ready for the dating world (update your wardrobe, start a fitness routine, change your hairstyle, or buy wine glasses, for example).

>> Create a short list of must-haves versus want-to-haves in your ideal partner.

>> Start dating compatible people.

>> Get into a relationship (as defined by you).

>> Become committed long-term (dating exclusivity, polyamorous agreement, engagement, or personal equivalent).

>> Intertwine lives (cohabitate, make major joint purchases, marry, and/or have children).

Each release goal requires you to engage in tasks and activities that move you from stage to stage. The first release goal alone can take some time.

If you can define what each stage of dating looks like, you can determine what release goal you're working toward. Use a definition of *done*. For example, a definition of *done* for "getting ready for the dating world" might be accepting invitations to (and bravely showing up at) social opportunities where you can meet new people, along with setting up a dating profile on a reputable dating app. Each layer of a relationship should have a clear definition of *done* as set by you.

A clear definition of *done* could be helpful for boundary setting in your dating life. The transition from dating to relationship is complicated, but you can eliminate some of the confusion by clarifying for yourself the difference between dating and a relationship. For example, you may create a list of what you think describes a committed relationship (such as initial dating to find someone to move to the next level is done). Once you've dated someone to the point where the connection has evolved and has all the characteristics of your definition of *done* for a relationship, you can validate that you're in one. Using scrum to date means you're an active participant moving steadily toward your goal. This doesn't take the magic out of "falling" in love, nor does it mean love is no longer blind. But being deliberate with scrum gives you more visibility and control in the driver's seat.

REMEMBER

Just like with a business product, each person's definition of *done* for dating will be different and likely to evolve as one progresses towards their dating goals.

Discovering companionship and scrum

With your roadmap spelled out, you have the framework for your backlog of requirements: the activities you'll plan and take part in to accomplish your release goals, starting with your initial release goal.

Part of your product backlog in preparing yourself for the dating world may be exploring activities and hobbies that you enjoy. What kinds of people you connect with, the community you build around you, and the community you find while you're doing the things you enjoy build relationships that may connect you to people to date.

If you begin a relationship by spending time with someone as a friend, when the relationship evolves, you may forget to communicate about the shift in the relationship. Planning to have that discussion may be an example of a dating backlog item.

As you create your product backlog for dating, consider any areas of weakness you want to make stronger. For example, suppose you struggle with communication around the status of a relationship as it progresses. In that case, you can use dating retrospectives such as the following to ensure that you're moving toward your goal:

>> What do we like about where things are?

>> What do we want to change?

>> What should we do next to make that change?

Dating with scrum

The benefits of scrum include a structured approach to a goal, empirical evidence, the inspect-and-adapt factor, and saving time. Life is full. Most people have heard (or used) the excuse that they'd love to find a relationship but have no time for it. Scrum can help you focus on it when it otherwise feels like you don't have enough time.

Consider your life to be a product backlog. If your priority for your love-related roadmap and backlog items is always at the bottom, you'll always push it aside in favor of something else. On the other hand, if you decide that love is a high priority, you'll create space for it.

Continuing on the roadmap to value and using scrum in dating includes short sprint cycles, inspection and adaptation, and improvement for future sprints.

In scrum, each date is a sprint, so you're operating on a short sprint cycle meant to move you toward your release goal. Because you may not have a date every day of the week, this schedule gives you ample time between sprints to reflect (inspect) and plan changes and improvements for the next (adapt). The time between sprints (dates) is your opportunity for backlog refinement and process improvement.

The inspection part of inspection and adaptation may focus on how you see yourself and your date together. For example, you might examine things like the following:

- ➤ Am I attracted to this person?

- ➤ Do I have fun when we are together?

- ➤ Does this person meet my must-haves?

- ➤ How do I act when I'm around this person?

- ➤ What are my thoughts and feelings about this person when we're not together?

The adaptation portion is up to you. You may adapt what you're looking for (such as your goal), or you may adapt whom you're dating (such as by not running another sprint with the same person). You may need to adapt your interaction and try another sprint with the same person based on your review. If you want to try something more fun, try a date with more lighthearted activities or something you enjoy seeing how those adaptations affect how you feel about the other person.

The best part about using scrum for dating is the inspect-and-adapt process. You and your dating partner get to form your own version of *us* — or not. As in business, the ability to cut something short based on early empirical evidence that it doesn't fit your goal saves time, money, and disappointment on both sides.

Winning as a team

Unfortunately, modern dating is full of examples of game-playing, which typically pits people against one another. This mentality in dating overcomplicates interactions and closes communication. In scrum, you plan as a team, execute as a team, and are accountable based on the success or failure of the team. So, even if you feel that you're on a team of one when it comes to dating, remember that you're on a team of two. The best thing you can do for yourself is to embrace scrum's concept of being a team with your date and working for the team to succeed rather than engaging in a contest against your date. Then, with a scrum mindset, you can rise above the nonsense and avoid the games.

Honest communication is needed for any team and especially for any successful relationship. A common pitfall in contemporary dating is testing dates through loaded questions or actions. Because it is founded on transparency, scrum simplifies communication. Using scrum in dating means asking genuine questions and viewing the other person's answers as a chance to get to know them for the purpose of that sprint. Open communication means open dialogue by sharing your views and asking your date their thoughts. As you plan your date sprints, plan genuine questions and encourage honest answers to help determine whether this person is the right fit.

Focusing versus multitasking

Scrum is a focusing tool. Scrum is so successful because it edits out the noise of trying to do everything all at once by breaking up challenges into smaller and shorter goals. So, instead of doing all projects poorly, scrum helps you focus on doing one thing at a time with a higher level of quality than you'd achieve by thrashing around.

The following quote summarizes a recent study from Stanford: "Multitasking in meetings *and other social settings* indicates low self- and social-awareness, two emotional intelligence (EQ) skills critical to success at work." (Italic emphasis added.)

The study examined how multitasking lowered effectiveness in a work setting — but emotional intelligence is a life skill. It will be hard to find love if you diminish your self- and social-awareness skills.

Dating multiple people can be a good thing to increase your chances of finding what you're looking for in the early stages. If your goal is finding the person you want to settle down with, having many relationships at the same time later in your dating journey won't be a good fit for that goal (but it may be a good fit for a "having fun" goal).

Modern dating usually involves dating as many people as possible for as long as possible to keep all options open. The attempt to mitigate the risk that one relationship won't work out almost guarantees the risk that numerous or all relationships won't work out.

When you date two or more people simultaneously, your mind and emotions are more distracted by multitasking than focused on discovering whether someone is a good match. Multitasking in dating may also mean trying to rush through multiple phases of a relationship.

TIP

You can limit your pool of potential dates by using work-in-progress limits (see Chapters 5 and 6).

The roadmap to value takes you through the date (that is, the sprint) to the finish line (sprint review and retrospective). As you finish each date, take time to inspect the date itself (that is, your sprint review). Ask whether you liked the person and whether you liked yourself with that person. Then move to a retrospective for possible process changes, such as the way you went about planning the date, the questions you asked during the date, and the tactics or tools you used to evaluate whether your date was a good match. Your definition of *done* should be specific and clear enough to make it easy to inspect whether your sprints were successful and adapt your backlog for the next sprint.

When a potential relationship ends or doesn't move forward to the next release, another product backlog item (potential mate) can take its place. As in business, pivoting isn't bad as long as you pivot early to minimize investment (time, emotional drag, and money) and as long as doing so moves you closer to your goal.

All of this is really to say that scrum can help you be more intentional about your dating in many practical ways.

Planning your wedding with scrum

Congratulations if you've already found love and are in the middle of an engagement! Weddings are some of life's biggest celebrations, meant to weave together families and friends and to acknowledge the beginning of a lifetime as a couple. Wedding days are full of many positive experiences, but the time leading up to the big day can strain the couple trying to plan it.

Use scrum for what it's built for: delivering a valuable product, and a wedding is the ultimate product. In wedding planning, you have a set date and (ideally) a set budget. Setting priorities and making decisions accordingly are necessary for having the kind of wedding you want. Planning a wedding successfully with scrum involves the following components:

>> Setting a goal. Talk about the ideal must-haves as part of your wedding and the experience you want to take away.

>> Setting a schedule (wedding day) and budgetary constraints.

>> Establishing and prioritizing wedding requirements (such as the venue, invitations, and cake) into a roadmap.

>> Establishing release goals (such as venue acquired, officiator scheduled, friends and family notified, decorations and place settings lined up, and photo shoots established).

>> Organizing your first sprint to address the highest-priority backlog items, breaking them into tasks, and swarming those tasks to completion.

>> Executing sprints and reprioritizing any new requirements discovered in each sprint.

>> Using sprint review to inspect and adapt (not only priorities but also product backlog items such as remaining budget) and making new decisions moving forward.

When examining a wedding backlog, you may immediately see what needs prioritization. Some locations allow outside caterers, for example, whereas others require you to use a specific one. Also, locations frequently have strict time rules. Because location can affect other backlog items, consider it a high-risk item (if not the highest-risk item) to address in an early sprint. After that item is set, it may change your existing backlog. For example, you may decide on big-budget items that you have prioritized early on to know the remaining budget for other items.

Toward the end of wedding planning, most couples still have long lists of small items to do. Try using a task or kanban board to move small items forward and visualize what still needs to be addressed.

Weddings are expensive. As we discuss in Chapters 5, 13, and 14, using incremental funding and doing the highest-priority requirements first ensures you finance the most critical features, even if the money runs out before you complete the entire backlog. If the venue and food are already taken care of, it may not be a big deal if a few party favors have to be left off the list.

REMEMBER

See Chapter 5 for more on release planning, Chapter 13 for more on portfolio management, and Chapter 14 for more on financing product development.

Families and Scrum

Busy is the defining word of families everywhere. With multiple levels of work and school commitments, it's difficult to find time to genuinely connect as a family. If you don't relax by connecting with your family, your stress levels remain high, lowering your effectiveness in many areas of life, including work. Connection and recreation with the family are vital parts of mental and emotional well-being.

Families can get caught up in a cycle of short-term communication via texting and long "to-do" lists. Each family member tends to work on their own list. As a result, family members miss out on maximizing the amount of support they could give one another because of a lack of communication and coordination.

The challenges facing families are as diverse as families themselves, but the following issues can apply to most families and can be addressed with scrum:

>> **Conflicting family priorities:** One family member wants a vacation; another wants to buy a car or go to college; yet another wants a home renovation. As in business, not all goals can be met simultaneously. As in successful businesses, planning and coordinated decision-making are vital for achieving a goal.

- **Communication:** Short text messages. Conversation cut short by a call from work. Faces buried in mobile devices sharing photos on social media. Communication is more vital to families than even work relationships, but exhaustion and busyness deplete real conversation.

- **Conflicting schedules:** It's become a luxury for family members to be in the same place at the same time. Scrum can help you track who is involved in what activity and create a schedule to connect.

- **Personal responsibility and accountability:** Every family copes with the pressures of daily life, such as chores, cleaning, errands, and paying bills. Often, one parent feels unsupported or overburdened, or one child feels too much or too little responsibility. For single parents, this problem is compounded. Scrum can help you balance responsibilities across family members.

With the challenges of modern life tugging at the bonds among family members, it's important to find innovative ways to stay connected and grounded. Stability and healthy relationships within the family affect what you do outside it, from school to career to friendships.

In the following sections, we show concrete examples of scrum being implemented into daily life by simplifying communication, using a family product goal statement, prioritizing a family backlog, making decisions as a team, and increasing responsibility through visibility and ownership.

Setting family strategy and goals

The biggest challenge in making family decisions is conflicting priorities. In ancient times, families frequently had mottos or sayings that defined their character, and we suggest that it's time to bring this tradition back with a modern twist. Wouldn't it be nice to be able to address conflicts inside and outside the home by recognizing that the behavior doesn't fit the family strategy?

A clearly defined family strategy or mission can provide behavior, values, and structure to guide a family in all its decisions. Family strategies work especially well when all family members own the strategy statement rather than having it dictated by a parent.

As we say in Chapter 2, the product goal is where the roadmap to value begins. A product goal statement for a project must support the overall strategy or mission, or a disconnect occurs between product direction and overall business strategy. The situation is no different for families. As families plan projects, they start with a goal of the result of the project, and that goal ties directly into the family's strategy.

One of our favorite authors is Patrick Lencioni, known for his best-seller, *The Five Dysfunctions of a Team*. In one of his other books, *The 3 Big Questions for a Frantic Family*, he tells a fable illustrating how his advice for business leaders is applied to families navigating life's complexities. As families answer three simple but powerful questions, they find clarity in defining their family strategy. The three questions are:

1. What makes your family unique? What makes your family different from every other family in your community? To answer this question:

   - Identify core values — positive qualities that are undeniable about your family — to help you clarify who you are as a family. These core values just are. They're not aspirational, just two or three things that describe your uniqueness.

   - Choose a strategy — two or three purposeful decisions your family makes — that drive how you live. Couples can brainstorm all the true things about their family and then look for themes. Two or three themes make up the strategy statement. This guides a family, keeps them centered on what's important, and lets go of things outside that focus (product goal).

2. What is your family's top priority — a rallying cry — right now? Based on your family's strategy, it's where focus begins. "If we accomplish just one thing as a family before the end of the year, what would that be?" To make it stick,

   - Limit yourself to one primary answer. Any more than that will likely result in the most important one being procrastinated or avoided.

   - Identify an appropriate time frame, usually between two to six months. Less than two months isn't much time to accomplish something. On the other hand, anything beyond six months invites procrastination. In other words, be reasonable and realistic.

   - Break this rallying cry down into defining objectives — the categories of things to do to achieve your rallying cry (product backlog).

3. How do you talk about and use the answers to these questions? Meet regularly and make it visible.

   - Meet regularly about it. It doesn't have to be formal. Imagine how your family might benefit from reviewing your progress each Sunday afternoon and identifying what needs to be done in the coming week to accomplish your defined objectives.

   - Make it visible. Write it down, and make it seen by all. Hang it in the same place as the family calendar in the kitchen or other high-traffic areas.

Planning and setting priorities

Most families take life a day at a time or even hourly. But realizing goals takes planning and priority management. Scrum provides a framework for progressing toward goals.

As a family defines its strategy and decides on projects and activities that carry out the strategy, the projects and activities become clearer and easier to prioritize and plan. Scrum's iterative approach to planning, executing, inspecting, and adapting leads families to success.

Project planning

Families establish a strategy (if they haven't already done so) and then define the project's goal (see Chapter 2). Each family member gets to brainstorm the ideas to achieve the goal, which becomes the roadmap for that family project. The family estimates the effort and complexity of each idea and prioritizes and orders the ideas based on their effort, complexity, value to the project, and risks involved. The family team owns the roadmap.

TIP

Chapter 4 describes methods for creating estimates. Family estimations may not need to use the Fibonacci sequence. Estimating is simply a way for the family to get an idea of the relative effort to complete things so they can plan accordingly. Using affinity estimating with the more familiar concept of T-shirt sizes may be all you need. Or maybe use different sized animals if you have small children.

Release planning

Families can identify minimum viable product (MVP) releases (see Chapter 5) leading up to completing a project and plan each in detail one at a time as each one is completed. When you're planning a birthday party, for example, the first release may be selecting and reserving a location. When you don't know the location, you don't know all the details of what you'll be able to do for the birthday party. When you know the location, you can send out invitations, choose a caterer, and select decorations.

Always use a definition of *done* when tackling each sprint and release. If a family-product backlog item is so vague that no one knows how it can be considered *done*, it shouldn't be considered to be ready to execute in a sprint. Vague or open-ended backlog items that make it into a sprint tend to sit in the Doing column for a long time. If your family backlog has items such as the following, you know that you need to break them down and quantify how they can be done:

>> Clean the house. (This item could take days, depending on the type of cleaning and the portions of the house that need cleaning.) Cleaning the

house can be broken down into each room that needs to be cleaned starting with the bathrooms. They could be broken down even further by types of work, like tidying up, dusting, or vacuuming.

>> Save money for a trip to Yellowstone. (This item says nothing about how much money is needed or what means will be used to earn or save the money.) Saving money could be broken down into researching options, applying for jobs, organizing a yard sale, or listing old toys to sell online.

Sprint planning

When you know the long-term goal, how to get there (roadmap of how to get there), and the big steps needed to get there (releases), breaking the work into sprints is easy. Weeklong sprints are a natural cadence for families as well as businesses. For most people, work and school schedules are predictable; one day of the week usually serves as a start or end point with a logical place to reset, plan, and review. Even if you don't have a consistent break in routine, the family can establish one.

Sprint planning for a family doesn't need to take long. With a task board, a family can quickly identify the items from the backlog that can be accomplished during the week. Each family member can identify how to help with each backlog item. Members move the items from the backlog to the To Do column and discuss the tasks required for each item in the sprint backlog. Then they identify when they'll be able to accomplish those tasks during the week. (See Chapter 5 for more on sprint planning.)

Then you'll have hugs, kisses, and all-around high-fives as family members agree on the plan and go to work throughout the week. Later in this chapter, we describe how to implement this type of planning into existing or natural family interactions.

REMEMBER

Visibility and transparency are every bit as important for families as for businesses. Create a family task board just as you would in a business. A tangible task board is best. Children love the satisfaction of moving a sticker, magnet, sticky note, or index card from one column to another as much as adults do. Families can use virtual task boards as well. Find what makes the most sense for your family, but make sure your board is easily accessible and visible because family members will refer to and update it daily.

Daily scrums

Giving family members an opportunity each morning or evening to say what they did, what they'll be working on next, and what help they'll need from other family members to accomplish those tasks can happen quickly and greatly improve the chances of success that day.

TIP

Use swarming techniques to move sprint backlog items to the *Done* column. A good way for older children to learn leadership and service is to allow a younger sibling to shadow them to learn a new skill. A good way to increase unity and teach cooperation and collaboration is to encourage family members to work together on backlog items.

Scrum teams are cross-functional. Embrace the concept of shadowing and pair programming in your home by having family members teach new skills when appropriate so that responsibilities can be shared. If one person is responsible for all the cooking, cook together. For the cooking project, one of the children may be able to take on the product-owner role by prioritizing and ordering the tasks for the other family members to carry out and then practicing her decision-making skills by accepting or rejecting the work along the way. Parents can guide children throughout the process.

These projects are not only opportunities to bond but also to pass along vital life skills that enable each family member to take on certain tasks.

WARNING

Thrashing occurs to families as well as businesses. Families are like large organizations in that they frequently have many projects going simultaneously. (Read Chapter 13 for information about the effects of trying to do too much at once and a discussion about the hierarchy of thrashing.) Planning a family vacation, a family reunion, and a home renovation project while preparing a child to leave for college are too many projects for a family to plan simultaneously. As in business, family leaders must decide which projects are the highest-priority to ensure their success. You may have pressure to do all projects at the same time, but you don't have to. As a family uses scrum's planning structure to determine what projects to take on, they assess the effort and complexity of each project. Then they can determine what bandwidth they have to prioritize and order, and the big-picture view enables them to make better-informed decisions.

Thrashing on multiple projects means that completing these projects takes at least 30 percent more time. Working on one project at a time is faster than multitasking. See Chapter 13 for details.

Communicating with scrum

Scrum provides ways to increase critical communications, even when time is short. Scrum uses a variety of tools for communications, one of which is prioritizing face-to-face communication whenever possible. On a scrum team, major decisions are never enacted via text or email. This one simple change can dramatically revitalize the dynamics in a family. Parents know that when the tone and body language are present, understanding can dramatically improve!

LETTING GO AT HOLIDAY TIME

Family holiday celebrations can be a joy. They can also be a burden, especially on the host. Steve's wife, Gwen, prepares an amazing Thanksgiving spread all by herself. At least she used to do it all by herself until the time she decided she had enough. She was tired of it being all on her, dreading the month of November. Although she liked keeping control of the kitchen and had difficulty letting people share her space to help prepare, she knew she needed to let go. But how?

Inspired by someone (we can't remember who), she started writing down each task needed to prepare the meal, from mashing potatoes to brining the turkey — one task per sticky note. She didn't place them on a whiteboard or wall, though. She placed them in a bowl on the kitchen counter, where everyone walked by over and over. Each task she wrote down was a task she was willing to let someone else do.

Fortunately, the rest of us knew she was burnt out, and we'd been offering for days leading up to Thanksgiving to know how we could help. In response to our invitation, she instructed us to look at the bowl, and every time we walked by, we should pick up a task and do what it says. We could work the tasks in whatever order we chose, but they all needed to be done.

Finally! We knew exactly how we could help. And we did. The kitchen was busy but not stressful. Gwen let go. We pulled a task as soon as we were freed up from the last thing we were doing. That year was the first time we ate Thanksgiving dinner on time. And Gwen enjoyed her Thanksgiving for the first time in a long time.

Put down the mobile devices in your home and talk to other family members face to face. Or make it a house rule that if a conversation is taking place, no participant should be watching television, playing a video game, working on a computer, or using a mobile device. A family's mantra might be, "Look up when we're talking."

Face-to-face communication works only if both people are participating in a focused conversation. Reduce miscommunication and length of conversations by quitting the habit of conversational multitasking.

To put face-to-face communication to good use, some existing family activities can provide a natural forum for sprint planning, daily scrums, sprint reviews, and retrospectives. One such activity is family mealtime.

Author and speaker Bruce Feiler presented a TED talk on "Agile programming — for your family" (www.ted.com/talks/bruce_feiler_agile_programming_for_your_family/transcript), where he discusses the dramatic change that his family achieved in minutes a day using a daily scrum model.

Think about the value that a daily scrum could add to your family in a simple 15-minute timebox! The following are some examples of benefits your family might reap from taking the time to communicate without distractions:

» Hearing updates from every member of the family about what happened during their day

» Sharing plans or goals for each person's upcoming day

» Listening to current challenges for each member of the family

» Providing an opportunity to problem-solve as a team or support one another through challenges

» Celebrating accomplishments daily

Though family dinnertime is a good time slot for a family meeting, those crucial 15 minutes can happen anytime during the day. A daily scrum over breakfast, dinner, or even before a certain television show will work as long as the time slot is consistent and limited to 15 minutes. Daily scrums aren't long enough to resolve all the daily life issues, but they accomplish the task of opening lines of communication and establishing trust and support. That way, if greater challenges arise, the family support foundation is already in place.

Inspecting and adapting for families

Sprint reviews and retrospectives are as important for families as businesses. For busy families, it may make sense to review accomplishments (sprint review) and then review processes and tools used as well as communication, relationships, and discipline techniques (sprint retrospective) during the same meeting time just before planning a new week (sprint planning).

Sprint reviews may include results from the school week, progress made toward planning the next family vacation, and successes in sports, music, and other activities. Sprint reviews are also times to review events scheduled for the future to identify items for the backlog to help prepare for them, like a birthday party or getting the house ready for extended-family guests who will be visiting.

For weekly family meetings, the following questions follow scrum's sprint retrospective model:

>> What worked well this week?

>> What didn't work well?

>> What can we agree to work on next week?

You may be surprised by the feedback coming from family members. During the family meeting, everyone should choose at least one improvement they agree to work on for the following week.

SCRUM FUNERAL

One of the most emotional and difficult events we all face (or will face) is the funeral of a loved one. Dean, one of our authors, recently experienced the loss of his mother and found help in using several scrum techniques for navigating the aftermath. As emotions climbed, his family gathered to discuss their grief and concerns about moving forward. During the conversation, his father set a vision for the type of experience he wanted for the family, which became their aligned goal. A pad of sticky notes came out as the ideas were captured for making this goal a reality, including the funeral, burial, family gatherings, final affairs, and more.

The sticky notes enabled the family to discuss each topic allowing everyone to participate. They discussed the outcomes they wanted and aligned on the approach. They debated the priority of the cards and sized them using Fibonacci so that no one person or family was overloaded with work. The stickies allowed the entire family to self-organize in pulling from the backlog by priority.

With the sprint planning done, they watched as the events unfolded, each family member bringing their all over the next days. Quick huddles, or daily scrums, were done at key events to check if anyone needed help. The sprint review was transparent for all to see as the family events and proceedings were conducted and held.

When the crowds left and quietness ensued, Dean's family reflected on the experience. They found comfort in the events and experiences they created, as well as with the process. Sitting together and planning and collaborating, made them value each other even more and, in the end, strengthened their entire family.

As an aside, the family also asked if they could use the same approach to plan and carry out the next family reunion.

The family may also choose what consequences should occur if rules are broken or if one family member doesn't meet their commitments. In a scrum model, rather than the traditional model in which consequences follow actions, the team (the family) agrees on lessons learned and how to improve them before taking on the new sprint goal. The team also agrees about the benefits or rewards of meeting new goals. The reward for achieving the family goal is a wonderful motivator.

Making chores fun and easy

It would be wonderful if chores could simply be handled without difficulty instead of escalating into arguments. Many parents are discovering how to empower their children to motivate themselves to do chores by using personal a task or kanban boards.

Human beings have an innate need to feel accomplished. Most adults make to-do lists, but we like the items that are easy to accomplish quickly, so we can cross them off the list. Children crave the same sense of accomplishment. They need to know that their contributions are important. Participating in the household is essential for helping children know they're valued. Choosing age-appropriate ways for children to participate in running the household molds the family together as a unit. Task boards make it easy for everyone to see what it means to be successful.

TIP

If kids struggle with larger chores, treat the larger chore as the user story and help them by breaking down important tasks. If they struggle to accomplish the "clean your bedroom" task, have "clean your bedroom" be the user story, with smaller tasks such as "organize books," "put dirty laundry away," "make bed," "wash bedroom window," "put away toys," and "dust bookshelves." That way, children can have the user story "Clean your bedroom" in the Doing column along with other smaller tasks until all tasks are complete. They can ask for assistance with larger, more difficult tasks until they learn how to accomplish them.

REMEMBER

As in business, family task-board requirements (user stories) should be ones that can be accomplished within a sprint, and tasks should be ones that can be completed in a day or less. For younger children, tasks should probably be much shorter to set them up for success.

TASK BOARD FOR BEDTIME

Blogger Chris Scott of the Agile School (http://theagileschool.blogspot.co.uk) posted a brief video of his 5-year-old daughter using a simple task board to get herself ready for bed. Each task is represented on a piece of paper with a picture that helps her remember what the task is. Prompted by her father, she looks at the To Do column and chooses the next task, which is indicated by a photo of a puppy (representing "wash feet"), and moves it to the Doing column. Then she turns to her dad and tells him it's time to wash her feet. This video is a great example of how even the youngest children can understand the basics of scrum and have fun moving themselves through their responsibilities. We know many families that struggle with putting young children to bed, but the task board helps young children practically parent themselves to bed.

Chapter **18**

Scrum for Life Goals

If you have built castles in the air, your work need not be lost; that is where they should be. Now put the foundations under them.

— HENRY DAVID THOREAU, WALDEN

The universal applicability of scrum is more than likely starting to become clear by now. Scrum is simple enough to be applied to any business or personal goal and adaptable enough to work for any important project you want to address.

Everyone has goals in life that end up feeling too big and too distant to approach. The best part of scrum is taking the overwhelming and breaking it into manageable pieces.

Getting to Retirement

The reality of life is that a time will come when you'll no longer be able to work full-time. But retirement can be defined as any time you reach enough financial freedom that your passive income — the income you don't actively work for — is enough to cover your expenses. If you define retirement this way, it becomes a goal to work toward at any age, and your product backlog of items and release goals supports reaching the goal of financial freedom. The farther in the future retirement is, the harder it can be to focus on the things you can do today to reach those important financial goals, as in-the-moment financial needs crop up.

A big challenge for younger generations is how to cope with rising costs of living while salaries aren't rising at the same rate. You can use scrum to address this challenge and progress toward financial independence each year.

The best way to bring a long-term future goal into the present is to use the roadmap to value in developing your retirement goal, create your backlog, define your release goals, and use sprints to work toward each goal.

Saving for emergencies

If your end goal is financial independence, an initial release goal might be saving for financial emergencies. Emergencies are bound to happen and may come at a significant financial cost. Medical bills, a job loss, repairs to your home or car, and divorce or family issues that result in unpaid time off work can cause financial strain. The only way to protect your future financial safety is to plan for emergencies now by developing a savings fund that covers emergencies, bears interest, and isn't locked into penalties if you must make a withdrawal for an emergency.

An emergency fund is one release goal in your product goal of financial independence. Sprints should include ways to adapt your budget, focusing on setting money aside.

The most common financial goal for emergency savings is to have the equivalent of six months of expenses in savings. To support this release, you decide sprint lengths (no more than a month) and work each sprint on backlog items that support building a savings plan.

REMEMBER

Your income less expenses equals surplus. Surplus generating interest over time equals wealth. The equation is

$$\text{Surplus} \times \text{Interest} \times \text{Time} = \text{Wealth}$$

If you have little or no surplus at the end of each pay cycle, you need to examine your budget and reorganize your backlog of priorities to increase your income, decrease your expenses, or both. Keep in mind this motto: Live free before living well. It might be nice to have expensive things, but not if it costs you your financial freedom.

WARNING

When building your savings, resist the urge to use emergency funding for non-emergency reasons. It's the surest way to backpedal your progress toward your goal. Create a separate savings account for discretionary-purchase goals (such as travel, a new pair of skis, or a new car) to avoid dipping into emergency savings. Acknowledging the need for pleasure purchases is an important step in having a sustainable plan for savings. The key is to balance short-term fun purchases against long-term financial goals.

Your sprints should consistently focus on ways to open your ability to create surplus toward savings. Review the outcome of each sprint to inspect, adapt, and make changes earlier than later. Don't let yourself get stuck sprint after sprint in a passive-income endeavor that isn't achieving your goal, for example. Sprint and release goals, and your definition of *done*, should help you define backlog items that are specific and clear about what success is. Don't be afraid to move on with increased knowledge from your mistakes. Lean Startup (see Chapter 5) may be helpful to you if you decide to take the entrepreneurial approach to increase your income.

Building retirement

After you have a safety net, you can shift your savings to building for retirement. This portion of your goal progression remains in progress even as you move on to other release goals. Your sprint cycle includes examining your options to get the greatest return on investment. At the end of the first sprint, if your benefits package from work includes some matching funds, for example, your product backlog should be updated with items that get you the maximum possible matching point.

When running sprints to save for retirement, focus on how to safely achieve the maximum return on investment. If you're farther from retirement, don't be shy about being more aggressive with your investments in the beginning years of your saving. You can look online for retirement resources to help you determine how much you should be saving to balance your future goal and your current budget.

TIP

Most people consider themselves retired once they're actually 50 percent retired — able to spend six months out of the year traveling or dialing back on work hours to 20 hours a week and surfing/cycling/gardening most of their time. Using information radiators to show progress towards retirement can help with motivation, such as showing a dial from 0 to 100 or a histogram showing cumulative progress over time. Seeing progress hit 50 percent — and every bit of progress after that — is an opportunity to celebrate and renew motivation. It's not all or nothing.

When using these tools, we define retirement as the point at which you can stop actively working because your passive income is enough to support your expenses. Although most online tools and retirement advice calculate based on retirement at age 65, your retirement age is actually defined by you and your goal.

WARNING

Section 72(t) of the United States tax code allows investors to take money out of most retirement plans penalty-free before age 59½ for income, but you'll have to take substantially equal periodic payments over time. Withdrawals can be spread over your life expectancy but must be for at least five years. This is one example of the inputs you'll use to determine the age and account balance target for your personal retirement goals. Different countries may have similar options and constraints to consider.

Securing financial freedom

After you reach both release goals of emergency savings and actively saving for retirement, your next release goal is building assets. We use simple definitions for assets and liabilities. An *asset* is anything that brings money to you, and a *liability* is anything that costs you money. Building assets is a personal decision and may require several sprints to research and increase your knowledge to support your high-level product goal of where you want to be. You can use a spike (the agile term for *research* or *risk assessment*) as a product backlog item to research and dissect an issue to answer a question.

Examples of early sprint goals to consider include

>> Structure your budget to allow and automate a set amount of monthly index fund purchases.

>> Find ways to decrease monthly expenses by 10 percent to divert to savings.

>> Identify ways to increase income by 5 percent by monetizing doing something you enjoy.

TIP

Don't assume the only way to find more money for savings is to reduce expenses. Sometimes, it can be easier to increase income.

Your sprint goals would continue to be broken down to the requirement level, such as

>> Create a budget.

>> Set up an index-fund automatic purchase.

>> Establish a website for your online business.

Another example of a sprint goal is determining whether purchasing a home would create an asset or a liability. Product backlog items involve steps and activities for discovering whether the purchase of a home is the best use of your money, such as the following:

>> Analyze whether the home will bring a sufficient return on investment.

>> Determine whether another place or investment would bring a higher rate of return.

By this same measure, a large, expansive house might be nice, but it brings greater liability if it can't be easily sold at a profit. Research carefully and use early sprints to inspect and adapt toward the release goal of building assets. Building assets is about building passive income to support your retirement goal.

REMEMBER

Houses are liabilities (they cost you money) until they generate income through a rental or are sold at a profit. Your primary residence is likely not an asset; you need to live somewhere. But you may consider it an asset if your mortgage payment is less than your rent would be. Or, if you can leverage your equity to reduce debt interest, your house might be considered an asset.

In using scrum for building financial freedom, you use empirical evidence and the inspect-and-adapt process in the same way a software product would. You can see if you're tangibly moving toward the goal and determine how you can achieve the goal faster. You can see what roadblocks are in your way and come up with a plan for removing them.

A perfect example of asset building and addressing roadblocks is considering academic education. If your educational status prevents you from moving forward financially, examine the potential asset outcome against the liability. Some questions to consider are

>> How much will the education I'm considering cost (actual cost plus opportunity cost)?

>> How much income will it generate when I'm finished?

>> Does the income it will generate greatly outweigh the education cost?

DIGGING A HOLE

In 2022, Americans continue to be burdened by student loan debt. According to the federal reserve, among the class of 2020, 55 percent of bachelor's degree students took out student loans graduating with an average of $28,400 in debt. While 14 percent of parents with students in the class of 2019 (latest data) took out an average of $37,200 in federal parent PLUS loans.

Americans owe nearly $1.75 trillion in student loan debt among 46 million borrowers.

As with purchasing a home, you should have a clear financial asset outcome for getting additional education before you embark on it.

Reducing debt

Another part of financial independence for you may be some form of being debt-free. Scrum can be an effective strategy to pay off debts by breaking the achievements into small, measurable increments such as the following:

>> Treat paying off a loan or credit card like a release goal.

>> Pay more than minimum balances so that the overall principal goes down.

>> Retrospectively look at progress and celebrate when you achieve your goal.

A holistic approach to your financial goal

What if you need to address many or all of these areas of your personal finance, in addition to budgeting for things like vacations, paying for children's college, or home improvements? (We've been there.) How would you attempt to climb that mountain?

Using the roadmap to value (Chapter 2), start to define your overall goal (product goal), possibly starting with the questions shared in Chapter 17 from Patrick Lencioni's *The 3 Big Questions for a Frantic Family*. If you arrive at something to the tune of sustainable financial security as your goal, this may help you decide which of these (reduce debt, save for emergencies, apply for home equity loan, and so on) are actually important (your roadmap).

Your first release goal should probably be the one that gives you the quickest win (value) and addresses your highest risk (such as, "We have nothing to fall back on if I lose my job, so maybe we should start by saving for an emergency."). See Chapter 3 for more about prioritization.

Each sprint, you can work on the things you need to progress toward that goal (such as decreasing expenses, increasing income, setting up a savings schedule, and so on). Once you achieve your emergency savings goal, you can assess which of the remaining release goals is the highest priority (according to value and risk), and break it down into action items for each sprint. So on and so forth.

Figure 18-1 is what a product roadmap, broken into prioritized release goals and the work to accomplish those goals might look like.

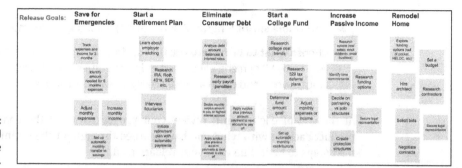

FIGURE 18-1:
FIGURE 18-1:
Sample financial
independence
roadmap.

Achieving Fitness and Weight Goals

If fitness is a goal, using scrum to achieve that goal is one of the best ways to succeed. When it comes to weight loss and fitness, many people struggle with the so-called yo-yo effect. Many people can start a fitness-and-diet regimen, but often after achieving the result, they slowly but surely slide back to where they began.

One reason why this happens is focus. The drawback is that in weight loss, this focus is often on an extreme, regimented situation. After you fall off the wagon, so to speak, you immediately begin unraveling your hard-earned work. Scrum allows for focus, but that focus is in small, measurable, and achievable segments. In other words, scrum is about taking steps toward your goal and achieving it sustainably, not just jumping on an extreme roller coaster and then burning out.

Work through the roadmap to value, just as you would with any other major product development effort. Following are some examples of applying the roadmap to value to weight loss and fitness, which you can tailor to your own goals:

>> **Set a product goal.** You want to be back to your physical shape in college, which was 185 pounds, 32-inch waist, running a mile in seven minutes, and bench-pressing 200 pounds.

>> **Create a product roadmap.** Initial roadmap items may include things such as losing ten pounds (you may have this item several times because incremental improvement is the goal), running three miles without stopping, or lowering your blood pressure.

>> **Create a product backlog.** This backlog might include making new recipes to cook, joining a gym, and having diet and exercise plans.

>> **Set your first release goal.** In two months, you may want to have lost three pounds and be able to run a mile.

» **Determine sprint lengths.** A sprint may last a week, for example.

» **Choose what to bring into the first sprint.** You may decide to cut soda volume by 50 percent, eat dessert only three times a week, walk a mile three times a week, and do an aerobic activity at least once a week.

At the end of each sprint, review your progress toward the goals, update your product backlog with what you have learned throughout the sprint, and adapt the next steps to be in line with your release goal.

You should use the sprint retrospective to inspect and adapt even after one sprint. Ask yourself the three sprint retrospective questions:

» **What went well?** You might say, "The cooking website I used has good recipes. I should keep using it. The mobile calorie tracking app is easy to use. My family is being really supportive."

» **What do I want to change?** You might say, "I don't like to do cardio on days I eat sweets. Nighttime workouts are hard to stick to. My lunch group gives me a hard time about my new health goals, which is discouraging."

» **How can I achieve that change?** You might say, "I'll establish set days of the week for sweets, which won't be cardio days." You might try morning workouts the next sprint to see whether it's easier to be consistent at that time of day, cut lunch groups to once per week (or not at all), or find a new lunch group.

Run your next sprint incorporating both what you want to improve and the new items from your backlog. At the two-month mark, review the whole release to examine whether you've achieved your goal and to determine your next release goal.

The key in using scrum to move forward on your weight-loss goal is recognizing that each step is a small but truly incremental step. At any time, not meeting your goal isn't a failure, but an opportunity to find a new way to move forward. Even if you fall back on bad habits, getting back on track isn't a massive commitment because the sprint cycles are so short.

Consider a high-visibility task board for transparently moving your exercise items to *Done*. To continue the preceding example, you could have three workout tasks, each of which gets moved over each time you complete your exercise. Giving yourself a visual depiction of completing also helps you identify opportunities (exercises that you enjoy) and bottlenecks (exercises that you avoid), and it helps you create ideas for your next sprint.

MICRO GOALS

Mark had a friend who was struggling with her weight, which was impacting her self-esteem. She had heard all the advice around fitness, but it just seemed overwhelming given the amount of weight gained over the years. So, Mark devised a plan based on scrum.

Like most people, Mark is busy, and when his friend would call, he would tell her so but would always try to get back. Sometimes, he was good about this; sometimes, he was bad. But one day, he told her, "I want you to walk one block after work today. When you start, call me, and I'll make myself available." Mark's friend thought walking one block was silly but agreed. When she called, Mark stopped what he was working on and answered. He told her, "I'm not going to have a lot of time today, but I'll talk during your walk." When she completed her one block out and back, he said, "I have to go tonight, but tomorrow, do two blocks, and let's pick up the conversation then." Honestly, she wasn't happy about the very short call but agreed to pick it up the next day.

Again she called, and again, he dropped what he was doing and chatted during her walk. It's not hard to see how this progressed — two blocks became three, four, ten, and twenty. And guess what? Twenty blocks out (one mile) means twenty blocks back (one mile). In about a month, this person, who would passionately complain about having to park too far from a store door, was walking two miles *per day*.

By the way, do you want to know what happens when a person is walking two miles a day while chatting with her friend? (Friends. I was quickly relegated to a roster of many.) They start looking at what they are eating and drinking. Then, they start seeing results and get even more motivated. Then, they up their goal to a 5k, a 10k, and by February 2022, a 70-pound weight loss and a half-marathon completion medal. Do not underestimate the power of incremental progress!

TIP

An example of a visible and achievable plan which has brought success to many is a novice plan to participate in a half-marathon (www.halhigdon.com/training/51131/Half-Marathon-Novice-1-Training-Program). Every week, the Sunday goal is clear and incremental.

Keeping Life Balance

One big challenge in life is managing emotional and mental well-being. Life can be a roller coaster, and it's your responsibility to find a way to minimize volatility and maximize enjoyment and fulfillment.

Mental and emotional health is a wide category, covering everything from a temporary increase in life stress to diagnosable mental health issues. Scrum is a framework for addressing goals and prioritizing issues, not a substitution for mental or emotional health services. You'll probably want to team up with someone you trust to provide ongoing support and accountability as you build your product goal, roadmap, and backlog and work through the scrum events. Don't go it alone.

If life becomes overwhelming, the source can be from a variety of places (some of which are addressed in Chapter 17, as well as those in the previous examples in this chapter). The building blocks of our lives get moved and shifted over time. With stress, everyone has a breaking point. For one person, a bad breakup might be the building block that makes the other stressors in life seem like too much. For another person, financial hardship or the loss of a job is the building block that, along with other life factors, ends up feeling like too much.

When stressors are becoming burdensome, use scrum to find solutions. Here are some questions to ask yourself as you start defining your product goal, roadmap, and backlog:

>> What are my stressors?

>> Why are they causing such high stress right now?

>> What stressor makes me feel overwhelmed?

Asking yourself these questions allows you to identify the source of the issues and the factor that currently creates the most stress. From this identification, you begin to move through the roadmap to value.

Using the current highest stressor as the priority, you build a product goal of what you'd like to see in your life. From this point, you break down your first release and then identify sprint goals and tasks that you can take toward achieving that release.

As in sprints in any other life goal endeavor, you consistently return to inspection and adaptation. You may ask, "Is this still the highest stressor and the one that I need to focus on solving to feel more balanced?" If so, keep working until you achieve the release goal. If not (AC + OC > V; see Chapter 5), finish that release, and set a new release goal.

As you move through sprints, addressing one issue at a time, you may find to your surprise that you feel less stress, but another item has taken priority, and it's time to focus on that item to feel more mentally and emotionally stable.

REMEMBER

Thrashing among multiple top priorities not only increases the time by at least 40 percent (according to the American Psychological Association), but it's also overwhelming. With your mental and emotional well-being, focusing on one thing at a time is your best bet.

As you progress through the roadmap to value, use the following questions to define your product goal, release goals, and sprint goals:

>> **Product Goal:** What do I ultimately want my situation to look like?

>> **Release goal:** What smaller milestone would progress me toward that product goal?

>> **Sprint goals:** What items can I bring in from the product backlog to work on first that would mean I am taking steps toward achieving that release goal *right now?*

REDUCING LIFE STRESS

John is in his early 30s; he's struggling with feeling overwhelmed and doesn't know how to address the many frustrations in his life. First, he examines his stressors and discovers the following:

● Work is very stressful and a negative environment; additionally, it doesn't pay well, causing financial stress.

● His current apartment is a stressful, unsafe place to live, but he feels he can't move because he doesn't earn enough from work.

● He frequently feels alone, and although he wants a relationship, he hasn't found the right person to be with and doesn't feel ready to be in a relationship. His friends and family members feel distant because he is stressed at work and home.

John decides that his bad work situation is the worst of these factors (priority decision). He writes a product goal that reflects what he wants: "I want a job that pays at least $80,000 a year, with full benefits and a steady work schedule, not the long and unpredictable hours that I currently work." (This goal is clear and specific.)

His first release goal may be to begin searching for new jobs. His first sprint may include dedicating one hour per night to updating his résumé and applying to five new jobs during the sprint. He may also include tasks such as reconnecting with acquaintances, looking for job leads, or searching for positions starting at $80,000 with specific working hours.

(continued)

(continued)

After several sprints of focusing on applying to new jobs, John moves to the interviewing phase. After each sprint (that is, each interview), he holds a review and uses inspection and adaptation to adjust his job search or reexamine what stressor needs focus.

At any point during any given sprint review, John could decide that he's reduced his stress enough to release that goal and focus on a new stressor. The point of using scrum to keep mental and emotional balance is that it combines the concept of taking measurable steps to address a need with the sprint review to inspect and adapt those steps or, if necessary, address another issue from the product backlog of stressors.

Planning Travel

Vacations are amazing opportunities for relaxation, exploration, and connection as a team. Even travel for business can accomplish similar objectives. Teams, families, and friends often struggle with frustrations about financing and finding time for travel, as well as differing opinions on what to do and how to relax. Also, circumstances can change at any time when traveling — both before and during the trip. Scrum is perfect for this kind of project. Think about it: You have an exact date and often a fixed budget; everything else is prioritization of the scope of the trip. Instead of one person calling all the shots and hoping that everyone likes the decisions made, working together as a team brings about engagement and satisfaction from everyone. For example, everyone would work together to come to a consensus on the following things:

>> Create a product goal for the trip or vacation.

>> Set calendar dates.

>> Know your budget.

>> Create a vacation backlog of items from the stakeholders (such as family members and travel companions).

>> Prioritize the backlog to achieve the best result possible.

With family travel, every member of the family can and should participate in what an ideal vacation looks like to them. Keep in mind that if taking a trip becomes a family habit, this year's vacation product goal may not have the same ideal qualities as last year or next year, and that is the point. Reviewing the plan as a family provides insight on how to focus the budget.

As in any scrum endeavor, if you travel on a fixed budget, the budget is the factor you want to decide first. If family members are focused on activities that cost a higher value, the family can examine more budget-friendly places to do them. Likewise, if a specific location is the highest family priority, the vacation can be planned around more budget-friendly options in an ideal location.

Don't be afraid to include children in discussing priorities according to budgeting. Although they may or may not have the responsibility of saving the money in the bank or setting the total budget, they should be involved in a trade-off decision as a team. You might say, "We can snorkel in Hawaii or go ziplining, but not both. Which would you like to do? It's important to teach kids that setting financial priorities and sticking to a budget are major family life skills. Scrum thrives when everyone involved has ownership of decisions.

TIP

Rather than a simple vote structure, in which each member only says yes or no, try fist of five (see Chapter 4), followed by dot voting. In fist of five, you show your support for an idea. Putting up one finger means total resistance to the idea, whereas displaying five fingers means it's a great idea. For a decision to pass, everyone in the family should at least have three fingers up, meaning that even though they may not love it, they don't hate it and are willing to support the decision. Using fist of five voting first allows narrowing a pool of options that no one in the family hates. You follow with dot voting for a final decision. In dot voting, all family members have five votes each. Using sticky notes for the ideas, they put dots on the choice(s) they want to vote for. Also, they can put all dots on the same option, vote on each of the five different options, or allocate votes in another way to indicate a preference for certain decisions.

Items from the product backlog need to be executed by each family member. Reservations need to be set, but changes based on the reality of availability or price, or perhaps changes in expected weather, need to be addressed on an ongoing basis. This approach allows the major items with higher risk to be done early, with risk declining as the date gets closer.

As dates for vacation grow closer, fewer large decisions will be in progress, and vacation planning will evolve into tasks that need to be accomplished before departure. Keep an eye on the calendar and establish short sprints to accomplish any remaining items. Break the product backlog items down so that items are easily moved to the *Done* column. Shopping for the appropriate clothing and also packing for the trip can't be done in the same week without causing stress and chaos, for example. Place shopping in a sprint that's long enough before the trip that items are available when it's time to pack. In fact, in an earlier sprint, do a mock packing activity to help you identify things that you'll need to shop for so that no surprises occur during the real packing the night before you leave.

VACATION PLANNING WITH SCRUM

Travel — both business and pleasure — can be unpredictable. Steve planned an anniversary vacation to Hawaii a few years ago with scrum. He scored some last-minute (less than two weeks in advance) travel deals and didn't have much time to plan the trip in detail. He and his wife had never been to Hawaii, so he asked friends and family for ideas about what to do and where to eat. With luggage, plane tickets, hotel and car reservation, and a list of potential things to do (roadmap) in hand with a general budget amount in mind, they boarded the plane. The goal was simple: Relax with no pressure to see or do everything.

On the plane ride, finally catching their breath, they took out their trip backlog of activities and places to eat. They planned the first day and estimated about how much of the budget it would take. Then they enjoyed the rest of the flight.

At the start of the next day, they crossed off the things they did on the list and identified a few other things that sounded interesting. One of those things involved making a tour reservation, so they scheduled it for three days out.

Each day, they did the same thing, adding to the list, crossing off completed items, and adjusting the priority based on their interests. Some items never reached the top of the list or got thrown out as their interest in the item decreased. The process hardly felt like planning.

They were fortunate to have had an open-ended return date (not a prerequisite for using scrum). They found that after eight days instead of their projected ten days, they had had enough, accomplished their goal for the trip, did the things they wanted to do, and ate where they wanted to eat. They returned home fully satisfied (AC + OC > V).

Studying

Learning is a necessary part of life from birth until death. Theoretical physicist Albert Einstein is quoted as saying, "Once you stop learning, you start dying." Human curiosity propels us toward the life we want to lead. Primary school is a structured format of learning from the age of 5 (or less for some learners) until the 12th grade, but formal learning often goes beyond primary school through trade certifications, undergraduate or graduate studies, and professional education.

In the United States, the school system is meant to unify basic competency skills for children and help them identify potential areas of interest for further exploration. As we examine in Chapter 10, scrum can help schools at administrative levels and teachers at classroom levels. Although schools and teachers work to improve things at those levels, students themselves can use scrum to enhance their experiences with their own education.

Students can use the roadmap to value to work toward their goals. They develop a goal, generate a backlog of items from an overall roadmap, identify a first release, run short sprints against that release, and use a sprint review to inspect and adapt their product (such as homework) for the next sprint. They run a sprint retrospective to inspect and adapt their processes and tools to help them optimize progress with their education. This process allows students at every step to refine their product backlog or adapt their study sessions as needed.

Learning early

If you're a parent or a teacher, you see kids struggle with learning in some form or another. Depending on their ages, it can be hard for kids to feel like they need to learn something difficult because they don't always have the sense of how it applies to their future. If they don't see a connection between their learning and what they want, it's hard for them to want to fight through the difficulty. Even young children can use scrum. Scrum is simply three roles, three artifacts, and five events. It empowers children and makes it fun to get through their own backlog of items. In this section, we address early learners as students in grades kindergarten through grade 8.

Helping young learners identify a goal and correlating that goal to their own lives are keys to getting them to engage. Help them correlate things they're interested in and like to do with what they're studying.

Early learners can also benefit from using task boards to work through their homework on many levels, because task boards are easily adaptable as the homework changes and the student grows.

We talk about thrashing in just about every chapter, especially in Chapters 6, 13, and 15. Multitasking reduces quality and effectiveness, and scrum reduces that error margin by focusing on one project at a time. Students of all ages are thrashed across many subjects at the same time. The key to using scrum for students is running short sprints against certain topics or projects. Perhaps sprints last several days or even a single day to enable students to focus on one item at a time.

Regardless of sprint length, students can use the Pomodoro technique (see Chapter 2) to shift tasks more easily. The Pomodoro technique creates a natural resting point and provides an easy opportunity for task switching. When using the Pomodoro method, a student can easily see whether the task needs to be continued after a break or whether it's time for a new task to begin.

Teaching children early how to inspect and adapt is crucial. Steve remembers when one of his daughters was in third grade, she came home and showed him her spelling test grade for the week. Normally, she was a perfect speller, so when he noticed that she missed four words, he was surprised. He first acknowledged that she still got a relatively good score but asked why she missed more than usual. After attempting to blame other students for distracting her, she admitted that she'd been rushing through her tests and hadn't been practicing as much as she could have each day between the pretest and the final test.

Instead of treating her as having done something wrong, he asked her how she thought she could do better on next week's test and avoid rushing through it. She remembered that at the beginning of the year, she was doing short practice tests every day of the week, not just at the beginning and the night before the test. They agreed it would be good to try that again, and she implemented her new plan the following week. She was able to learn from her own experiences and own the solution for improvement.

Graduating from high school

High school students have a specific set of needs geared toward their goals in life after high school. Until graduation, most students focus on grade-by-grade or school-level movement, but at high school level, they're taking electives and beginning to steer themselves toward their own goals. High school is an opportunity for students to take hold of the reins and guide themselves. A high school student may have many goals, from wanting to go to a four-year university to wanting to work right away (and everything in between). The best way to achieve that goal is to use each year as a stepping stone.

In this section, we focus on the popular goal of getting into college. If a student's goal is to attend college, a specific backlog geared toward college requirements needs to be set. Items on this list should include all the nonscholarly work that needs to be done. Researching schools takes longer than a student might expect, for example, and should be done as early as possible so that future sprints can include activities tailored toward meeting admission requirements. Task boards are effective tools for progressing on important product backlog items.

Prioritization for high schoolers is key. Few students can take every academic subject, play every sport, score perfectly on exams, and participate in every activity — and they definitely can't do these things at the same time. By using prioritization, a student can edit out items that don't directly support her product goal and focus on release goals that are important both personally and for getting into the right college. Using these release goals in working toward their product goal helps the student create milestones. Having release goals allows them to organize decomposed requirements into sprints.

Here's how this breakdown might look for a high school student:

>> **Product Goal:** Get into a four-year university.

>> **Release goal supporting the product goal:** Score more than 1,400 on the Scholastic Aptitude Test (SAT).

>> **Sprint goal supporting release goal:** Score more than 720 on five practice SAT math tests.

>> **Requirement level supporting sprint:** Find an SAT tutor, spend three hours studying the SAT book this week, focus on SAT math concepts, and ask the tutor about SAT-level geometry.

Expectations are high, and students are expected to become knowledgeable in a broad base of subjects. Also, competition to make it into college and receive scholarships is extremely high. Students have various mixtures of teachers and classes, so workloads vary from student to student and from term to term.

The sprint cycle of inspecting and adapting provides the framework that students need to adjust to varying loads and situations from term to term as they work through their roadmap.

THE STRUGGLING STUDENT

Parent/child relationships are tested to the fullest extent during the child's school years and many different parenting strategies exist for addressing the situation. The older the child gets, the more challenging education becomes.

One of Dean's high-school students missed so much class the only alternative left was to use "makeup" packets to obtain the lost credit. After counseling together, his son set a goal "to graduate from high school with his peers in June." (20 weeks)

Next, with the help of the high school counselor, they identified all the classes with missing credits and made a prioritized product backlog consisting of 21 packets. They also learned that packets could only be accomplished one at a time, and new packets would not be given until the test had been passed for the previous packet. Their definition of *done* became clear. The first packet was purchased and pulled, and his son went to work.

(continued)

(continued)

Each week, they plotted their progress on a burndown chart, counting down the weeks until graduation by the number of packets to complete. The burndown was kept in the family room for all to see.

At first, they noticed they were trending off and needed to make adjustments, so Dean and his son discussed the goal again and possible causes. The next week, they checked again and made another adjustment. Dean's son reduced his work hours to focus more on the packets. At the end of each week, they continued to discuss the progress and learned whether there were other adjustments that needed to be made.

And he did it! With a broad smile on his face, Dean's son walked with his schoolmates to graduation, learning that he could accomplish hard things, even in a seemingly overwhelming and insurmountable situation. Best of all, Dean's son learned his father was there to support him in reaching difficult goals.

In 2014, a guest blog post written by Alexis Wiggins went viral. The post detailed the challenges she noticed as she first shadowed a tenth-grade student and then a twelfth-grade student for one day. Of primary concern to her were the constant strain of sitting all day and the passivity expected from learning. By incorporating scrum into at-home study, a student can take charge of learning in another way. While students can't control in-class lectures, they can find alternative ways aside from sitting and memorizing when at home. This is also where a student's product backlog can heavily influence progression. If extracurricular activities are an important factor in your product goal, try choosing one that allows for physicalities, such as sports, or a tactile club, such as art, to allow different methods of learning into your goal progression. If extracurricular physical activities aren't appropriate or available, try incorporating physically active breaks when using the Pomodoro technique for studying.

Achieving in college

College is the perfect opportunity for a student to use scrum. For any college student whose goal includes employability after graduation, implementing scrum practices helps prepare for a career.

The curriculum for each class may be decided by a teacher, but the overall educational content is up to the student. Deciding what to major in is a huge task for a student, regardless of the decisions being made before or during college. Inspection and adaptation still influence students on the sprint level to improve their learning, but with college, these tasks need to be brought to release or even product goal level. A student may find at the end of a semester (release level), for example, that biology isn't a study that he wants to continue to pursue and that another subject has become a high-priority interest. As his interests evolve, he adjusts his product goal and roadmap so that they provide the boundaries and direction for each release (term) and sprint (week).

College is also a time to pursue team building within a scrum framework. College group projects are an opportunity to use scrum for planning, reviewing, coordinating, establishing team agreements, and responding to changes. Holding scrum events and using a task board give immediate visibility of who is working on each portion of the project and how the project is progressing. Students should keep group meetings as short as possible by using daily scrums. If the group needs to address an impediment or swarm on a sprint backlog item that has lagged, that visibility allows the project to progress quickly.

EVOLVING EDUCATION GOAL

A student's goals may change throughout the course of their educational career. For example, consider the following goal set by a student as a freshman and notice how it evolves as they inspect and adapt along the way. At the start of ninth grade, the student knows they want to graduate from high school with a minimum 3.8 grade-point average (GPA) to qualify to attend an Ivy League school.

The student may not have done much research on what's required of Ivy League schools or may not know that more than just a certain GPA is required to get into college. They may not even know what career they want after graduation. This goal is still a fine start, however.

By the end of the student's ninth-grade year, they know a 3.8 GPA probably won't be enough. The student learns what test scores they need for entrance, as well as the required extracurricular leadership, service, and activities. They enjoyed a couple of social-sciences classes that gave them some insights into what career they wanted. At the beginning of tenth grade, the student has an updated goal: to qualify to attend Yale, Stanford, or Harvard after high school.

The student's roadmap and backlog include things such as "earn a minimum 4.2 GPA, score at least 30 on my ACT and a 1,500 on my SAT, and save enough money to pay for half of a trip to South America (Mom and Dad will pay for the other half) for humanitarian work before the end of my junior year."

At the end of each year, this student's goal and roadmap will probably evolve because they know more than they did when they started. Regularly inspecting and adapting at logical intervals allows the student to seek guidance from trusted parents and advisers to make informed decisions.

In addition, students can tailor successful completion of projects to their own learning styles. College-level projects are frequently defined by a definition of *done* (the rubric provided by the professor), but getting to *done* is left up to the learner.

TIP

Team-building and task-pairing techniques apply in collegiate study. Students don't have to have a group project to review one another's work before completion. They can use sprint reviews to elevate their work before final submission (the release to the customer, who is the teacher).

Subsets of release and sprint goals are similar to what was done at the high school level, but in the collegiate atmosphere, goals may include building relationships with professors who can refer you for scholarships or jobs or seeking specific internships to gain job skills. Students can build a strong working relationship with professors by including their feedback and using it to improve their own work.

TIP

Credit hours, like velocity (see Chapter 4), may tell only part of the story. Just because a student took 12 credits last term doesn't mean that 12 credits is the right number next term. A three-credit class last term may not require the same amount of effort outside class as a totally different three-credit class next term. Doing an internship next term may require taking fewer credits than last term. Perhaps a student can take more online credits next term than last.

SPRINT CYCLE FOR A COLLEGE STUDENT

Scrum for students breaks sprints into one week each. Students review the roadmap and focus on the current release, selecting backlog items for the sprint, which are broken into activities that can be done in a day or less. If 30 pages need to be read for class B, the total might be broken down to 10 pages per day for three of the seven days of the sprint. At the end of the first day of reading, the student knows whether 10 pages is the right amount for the remaining days. Another requirement for the sprint might be to research a specific topic for an upcoming writing assignment.

Some of these activities may need to be timeboxed. For example, the research may need to be done in two hours or less. Because of work and class schedules, a student may have only enough time for 60 minutes of reading. Based on time available and work left to be done, each day the student has to decide how he can best use that time.

At the roadmap, release, sprint, and daily levels, students prioritize and order their work to be done and adjust as needed.

At the end of each sprint, a student reviews their completed work against the goal and adjusts the remaining product backlog accordingly. Also, the student runs a retrospective on their process and identifies impediments that keep them from attaining goals and actions to improve. For example, perhaps reading is taking too long, and the student explores options for improving speed, such as a speed-reading course. Note-taking workshops are probably offered through the school, or perhaps a tutor is needed for one subject. This review of goals and processes for attaining those goals happens every week, and tweaks and adjustments can be made against a limited amount of work — quickly, rather than the typical cramming required to make up for procrastination.

6

The Part of Tens

Chapter **19**

Ten Key Benefits of Scrum

This chapter lists ten important benefits provided by scrum to organizations, teams, products, and individuals.

REMEMBER

To take advantage of scrum benefits, you need to trust in empiricism, learn more about the scrum framework by using it, and continually inspect and adapt your scrum implementation.

Higher Customer Satisfaction

Scrum teams are committed to iteratively and incrementally delivering products that lead to higher customer satisfaction. Scrum teams have happier customers because they

» Collaborate with customers to collect product feedback throughout the process so customers get what they really need.

» Enable a product owner who is an expert on product requirements and customer needs or knows where to get that information. (Check out Chapter 2 for more information about the product owner's accountability.)

>> Keep the product backlog updated and prioritized to respond quickly to feedback. (You can find out about the product backlog in Chapter 3.)

>> Demonstrate working functionality to stakeholders in every sprint review. Customers love products that are simple to use and work. (Chapter 6 shows you how to conduct a sprint review.)

>> Deliver products to market quicker and more often with every release.

Better Product Quality

Customers demand quality products. Agile methods have excellent safeguards to ensure the quality is as high as possible. Scrum teams help ensure quality by doing the following:

>> Take a proactive approach to quality to prevent product problems by teaming up on tasks and early demonstrations of releasable product increments for feedback.

>> Embrace technological excellence, good design, and sustainable development.

>> Continuously refactor existing solutions to keep technical debt at a low level.

>> Define and elaborate requirements just in time so that knowledge of product features is as relevant as possible.

>> Build acceptance criteria into user stories so the developers understand them better and the product owner can accurately validate them.

>> Incorporate continuous integration and thorough validation into the development process, allowing the developers to address issues while they're fresh.

>> Take advantage of automated testing tools (when applicable), ensuring that new product increments do not break previous increments.

>> Conduct sprint retrospectives, allowing the scrum team to improve processes and work continuously.

>> Complete work using the definition of *done*: developed, validated, integrated, and documented.

You can find more information about agile quality in Chapter 7.

Reduced Risk

Agile product development techniques virtually eliminate the chance of absolute failure — spending large amounts of time and money with no or low return on investment. Scrum teams reduce risk by doing the following:

>> Develop in sprints, ensuring a short time between initial investment and either failing fast or knowing that a product or an approach will work. Front-load risk by ensuring the product backlog is stacked with the most valuable and riskiest items first.

>> Always have a working, integrated product, starting with the first sprint, so that some value is added as shippable functionality every sprint, ensuring the product won't fail completely.

>> Develop requirements according to the sprint's definition of *done* so that sponsors have completed usable functionality, regardless of what may happen with the product or service in the future.

>> Provide constant feedback on products and processes through the following:

- Daily scrum meetings and constant developer communication

- Regular daily clarification about requirements and review and acceptance of features by the product owner

- Sprint reviews, with stakeholder and customer input about completed product functionality

- Sprint retrospectives, where the scrum team plans process improvement

- Releases, where the end user can see and react to new features regularly

>> Generate revenue early with self-funding products, allowing organizations to pay for a product with little upfront expense.

Improved Performance Visibility

With agile product development, every team member has the opportunity to know how the product development is going at any given time. Teams can provide a high level of performance visibility by doing the following:

>> Place a high value on open, honest communication among the scrum team, stakeholders, customers, and anyone in an organization who wants to know about a product.

>> Provide daily measurements of sprint performance with sprint backlog updates. Sprint backlogs can be available for anyone in an organization to review.

>> Provide daily insight into the developers' immediate progress and roadblocks through the daily scrum meeting. Although only the scrum team may speak at the daily scrum meeting, any product team member may observe or listen.

>> Physically display progress by using task boards and posting sprint burndown charts daily in the developers' work area.

>> Demonstrate accomplishments in sprint reviews. Anyone within an organization may attend a sprint review. Stakeholders who regularly engage in sprint reviews know immediately whether a scrum team is demonstrating quality and value.

As described in the following sections, improved product development visibility can lead to greater investment control and predictability.

Increased Investment Control

Scrum teams have numerous opportunities to control investment performance and make corrections as needed because of the following:

>> Adjusting priorities throughout development allows the organization to have fixed-time and fixed-price products while accommodating the change.

>> Embracing change allows the team to react to outside factors such as market demand.

>> Daily scrum meetings allow the scrum team to quickly address issues as they arise.

>> Daily updates to sprint backlogs mean sprint burndown charts accurately reflect sprint performance, allowing the scrum team to make changes the moment it sees problems.

>> Face-to-face conversations remove roadblocks to communication and issue resolution.

>> Sprint reviews let stakeholders see working products and provide input about the products before release.

>> Sprint retrospectives enable the scrum team to make informed course adjustments at the end of every sprint to enhance product quality, increase development team performance, and refine processes.

The many opportunities to inspect and adapt throughout agile product development allow all product team members — the product owner, developers, scrum master, and stakeholders — to exercise control and ultimately create better products.

Increased Collaboration and Ownership

When developers take responsibility for products, they can produce great results. Developers collaborate and take ownership of product quality and performance by doing the following:

» Make sure that the developers, the product owner, and the scrum master work closely together daily.

» Conduct goal-driven release and sprint planning meetings, allowing the developers to commit to the sprint goal and organize their work to achieve it.

» Hold daily scrum meetings led by the developers, where developers organize around work completed, future work, roadblocks, and team morale.

» Conduct sprint reviews, where the developers can demonstrate and discuss the product directly with stakeholders. Engaged and collaborative stakeholders participate and share in the ownership of the product creating alignment rather than finger-pointing.

» Conduct sprint retrospectives, allowing developers to review past work and recommend better practices with every sprint.

» Work in a near-proximity/co-located environment, allowing for instant communication and collaboration among developers. If you're on a distributed team, stay connected to your team's video conference.

» Make decisions by consensus, using techniques such as estimation poker and the fist of five.

You can find out how developers estimate effort for requirements, decompose requirements, and gain team consensus in Chapter 4. To discover more about sprint planning, see Chapter 5. For more information about the daily scrum, sprint reviews, and retrospectives, check out Chapter 6.

More Relevant Metrics

The metrics used by scrum teams to estimate time and cost, measure performance, and make decisions are often more relevant and accurate than metrics on traditional projects. Agile metrics should encourage sustainable team progress and efficiency in a way that works best for the team to deliver value to the customer early and often. With agile product development, you provide metrics by doing the following:

>> Determine timelines and budgets based on each team's actual performance and capabilities.

>> Make sure that the team that will be doing the work, and no one else, provides effort estimates for requirements.

>> Use relative estimates, rather than absolute hours or days, to accurately tailor estimated effort to an individual team's knowledge and capabilities.

>> Regularly refine estimated effort, time, and cost as the scrum team learns more about the product.

>> Update the sprint burndown chart every day to provide accurate visibility about how the team is progressing within each sprint.

>> Compare the cost of future development with the value of that future development, which helps teams determine when to end development and redeploy capital to a new investment opportunity.

>> Monitoring the manager-to-creator ratio is another helpful metric for striking the proper balance between organizational management and the people who produce the product.

>> Measuring individual, team, and organizational skill versatility is a great way to support capability development. Gaining T-shaped skills, discussed in Chapter 4, helps team members feel more fulfilled in their careers and increases team and organizational velocity and value.

>> Satisfaction surveys can provide valuable insight into both team and customer perspectives.

WARNING

You might notice that velocity is missing from this list. *Velocity* (a measure of development speed, as detailed in Chapter 4) is a tool you can use to determine timelines and costs, but it works only when tailored to an individual team. Team A's velocity has no bearing on Team B's velocity. Also, velocity is great for measurement and trending but doesn't work as a control mechanism. Trying to make the team meet a certain velocity number only disrupts team performance and thwarts self-management.

If you're interested in finding out more about relative estimating, be sure to check out Chapter 4.

Improved Predictability

Agile product development techniques help the team accurately predict how things will go as product development progresses. Here are some practices, artifacts, and tools for improved predictability:

>> Keeping sprint lengths and team member allocation the same throughout development allows the scrum team to know the exact cost for each sprint.

>> Using development speed allows the team to predict timelines and budgets for releases, the remaining product backlog, or any group of requirements.

>> Using the information from daily scrum meetings, sprint burndown charts, and task boards allows the team to predict performance for each sprint.

You can find more information about sprint lengths in Chapter 5.

Optimized Team Structures

Self-management puts decisions normally made by a manager or the organization into scrum team members' hands. Because of the limited size of teams — which consist of less than ten people — agile product development efforts can have multiple scrum teams, if necessary. Self-management and size-limiting mean that agile product development can provide unique opportunities to customize team structures and work environments. Here are a few examples:

>> Developers may organize their team structure around people with specific work styles and personalities. Organization around work styles provides these benefits:

- Allows team members to work the way they want to work
- Encourages team members to expand their skills to fit into teams they like
- Helps increase team performance because people who do good work like to work together and naturally gravitate toward one another

>> Scrum teams can make tailored decisions to balance team members' professional and personal lives.

>> Even technical issues benefit greatly from decentralized, self-managed decision-making.

>> Because teams estimate their work, product owners can determine how many scrum teams may be required to accomplish the items on a product backlog.

>> Ultimately, scrum teams can make their own rules about whom they work with and how they work.

REMEMBER

The idea of team customization allows agile workplaces to have more diversity. Organizations with traditional management styles tend to have monolithic teams where everyone follows the same rules. Agile work environments are much like the old salad bowl analogy. Just like salads can have ingredients with wildly different tastes that make a delicious dish, agile product development can have people on teams with very diverse strengths that fit in to make great products.

Higher Team Morale

Working with happy people who enjoy their jobs can be satisfying and rewarding. Agile product development improves the morale of scrum teams in these ways:

>> Being part of a self-managing team allows people to be creative, innovative, and acknowledged for their contributions.

>> Focusing on sustainable work practices ensures that people don't burn out from stress or overwork.

>> Encouraging a servant-leader approach assists scrum teams in self-management and actively avoids command-and-control methods.

>> Having a dedicated scrum master, who serves the scrum team, removes impediments, and shields the developers from external interferences.

>> Having a dedicated product owner who serves the scrum team ensures the team is always clear on priority, value, and business risk.

>> Providing a supportive and trusting environment increases people's overall motivation and morale. People benefit from improved autonomy, mastery, purpose, and belongingness.

>> Having face-to-face conversations helps reduce the frustration of miscommunication.

>> Working cross-functionally allows developers to learn new skills and to grow by teaching others.

You can learn more about product owner and scrum master dynamics in Chapter 2 and developers in Chapter 4.

Chapter 20

Ten Key Factors for Enabling Scrum

Here are ten key factors that determine whether an agile transition to scrum will succeed. You don't need all issues resolved before you begin. You just need to be aware of them and have a plan to address them as early in your journey as possible.

TIP We have found that these ten factors are the strongest indicators of success. There may be other factors that make a difference for some organizations, but we've found that if you get these right, the likelihood of your success increases dramatically.

Dedicated Team Members

Products are considered long-term assets requiring stable, dedicated, and even permanent teams. Permanent teams retain knowledge about their product and customers. Their high performance is built over years of retrospective and hard work. Minor adjustments to the team may need to be made due to career opportunities and the like, but for the most part organizations should work to disrupt team makeup as little as possible.

REMEMBER

A team is a group of people who share a common goal, work together collaboratively towards that goal, and succeed and struggle together. A working group is simply a group of people who maintain individual accountability and focus on individual goals. Scrum teams are teams. Learn more in Chapter 4.

Further, it's critical for these dedicated team members — product owner, developers, and scrum master — to focus on a single objective at a time. If team members are jumping between contexts hourly, daily, weekly, or even monthly, their effectiveness is minimized due to the increased cost of just trying to keep up with multiple task lists. The time lost from the continual cognitive demobilization and remobilization involved with task switching is costly.

TIP

If you think you don't have enough people to dedicate to your scrum teams, you definitely don't have enough people to thrash them across multiple priorities simultaneously. The American Psychological Association reports that task switching wastes as much as 40 percent of time.

Variance in equals variance out.

Collaborative Environment

The Agile Manifesto lists individuals and interactions as the first value. You get this value right by creating environments where team members can have clear, effective, and direct communication throughout development with each other and their customers and stakeholders.

While face-to-face, co-located teams are ideal for communicating complex issues, it's not always the environment in which you'll find yourself. Video conferencing and digital whiteboards are indispensable. Small teams (see Chapter 4 about effective scrum team size) who can work synchronously throughout the day are the best and most agile (near proximity, same time zones, and so on). Beware that relying on written communications, especially those intended to resolve issues, are prone to costly delays and misunderstandings.

Done Means Releasable

Ending sprints with nonreleasable product increments is an antipattern to becoming more agile. *Done* means potentially releasable. A sprint that ends without potentially releasable functionality is, by definition, not a sprint.

Developers get to *done* by swarming on user stories — working together on one user story at a time until it is complete before starting the next. Developers hold each other accountable by ensuring that all rules for their definition of *done*, including test automation, are satisfied before starting a new user story. Product owners review completed work against the scrum team's definition of *done* (as well as the user story's acceptance criteria — see Chapter 3) before approving and moving on to a new user story.

Empowered Product Owner

The product owner's role is to optimize the value produced by the developers. The product owner's responsibility requires someone knowledgeable about the product and customer who is available to the developers throughout each day, empowered to make priority decisions, and empowered to clarify immediately, so developers don't wait or make inappropriate decisions about the product's direction.

Organizations with the following product owner characteristics will struggle significantly to deliver valuable and shippable functionality at the end of every sprint:

>> The product owner struggles to make tough business decisions.

>> The product owner is not accessible to the developers because they have too many other things to do besides support the developers and work directly with customers and stakeholders.

>> More than one product owner is named by the organization for a single product, confusing the developers as to whom to go to for clarification.

>> Stakeholders undermine decisions made by the product owner.

Although all roles on the scrum team are vital and equally important, an unempowered and ineffective product owner usually causes scrum teams to ultimately fail at delivering the value customers need from the team. See Chapter 2 for more on the product owner role.

Don't Ignore Reality

Scrum won't solve any problems for you, but it will expose them. Scrum will expose weaknesses and gaps in process, policies, organizational structures, skill sets, accountabilities, artifacts, meeting effectiveness, transparency, and myriad other topics. What you decide to do with what is exposed is up to you. Scrum provides an iterative inspection and adapts the framework for addressing items as they're exposed.

REMEMBER

Your organization is perfectly engineered to get the results you are getting today. If you want to get better results, you are going to have to change things. Scrum will show you what needs to change. Make those changes.

Scrum teams should address what is exposed on their own when they have control over the exposed issue. When they don't have control over the exposed issue, there should be a path for escalating those items to those in the organization who own the status quo and who can affect change to support scrum teams getting better and better at delivering customer value. An effective way to resolve escalated items exposed by scrum is to use the agile transition team discussed in Chapter 21.

Clear Product Goal and Roadmap

Although the product owner owns the product goal and product roadmap, many people affect the clarity of these agile artifacts. Product owners need access to and strong working relationships with stakeholders and customers throughout product development to ensure that the product goal and roadmap continually reflect what the customer and market need. The developers must also be crystal clear on the purpose of everything it works on, from the product goal to the individual user story. Purpose-driven development delivers business and customer value while mitigating risk effectively.

Without a clear purpose, people wander and lack ownership. When all team members understand the purpose, they come together. Remember the agile principle, "The best architectures, requirements, and designs emerge from self-organizing teams."

We discuss the mechanics of developing the product goal in Chapter 2 and the product roadmap in Chapter 3.

Developer Versatility

You probably won't start your first agile product development effort with developers who have the ideal level of cross-functional skills required for every item in your product backlog. However, the goal should be to achieve cross-functional skill coverage as soon as possible. Your team will also be challenged to meet its sprint goal if you have single points of failure in any one skill.

From day one, you need people on your team with the intellectual curiosity and interest to learn new things, experiment, mentor, receive mentoring, and work together to get things done as quickly as possible. This versatility was discussed more in Chapter 4.

Scrum Master Clout

Servant leadership provides the solution as you depart from command-and-control leadership to empower the people doing the work to make decisions. With formal authority, a scrum master would be viewed as a manager — someone to report to. Scrum masters should not be given formal authority but should rather be empowered by leadership to work with members of the scrum team, stakeholders, and other third parties to clear the way so that the developers can function unhindered.

If scrum masters have organizational *clout*, which is informal and a socially earned ability to influence, they can best serve their teams to optimize their working environment. In Chapter 2, we talked more about different types of clout. Provide training and mentorship to ensure that your scrum masters develop servant leadership skills and put off the tendencies of commanding and directing.

Leadership Support for Learning

When organizational leaders decide to become agile, their mindset has to change. Too often, we see leadership directives without any follow-through for supporting the learning process needed to implement the changes. Realistically, organizational transformations take one to three years from when leadership buys in. Buying in means much more than writing the check for the training or coaching services. It means leaders get involved and learn what they need to do to lead the transformation from within, buying in with their time, effort, and actions.

The bottom line: If support for learning is merely lip service, scrum teams will pick up on it early, will lose motivation to try new things, and will go back to waiting for top-down directives on how to do their job.

Leverage Industry Experts

Good coaching at leadership and team levels increase your chances of success. Professional coaching and mentoring from trusted agile experts provide support in the following forms:

>> In-the-moment course correction when discipline starts to slip or mistakes are made

>> Reinforcing training

>> One-on-one mentoring for specific role-based challenges

>> Executive leadership style and mindset adjustments

Chapter **21**

Ten Key Resources for Scrum

Many organizations, websites, blogs, and resources exist to help you get the most out of scrum and other agile techniques. We've suggested many already throughout the chapters of this book. In this chapter, we've compiled a list of additional key resources that you can use to support your journey with scrum.

Scrum For Dummies Cheat Sheet

www.dummies.com/cheatsheet/scrum

You can use my online Cheat Sheet as a companion to this book as you start implementing the scrum framework outlined in the previous chapters. You'll find helpful resources there for staying on track with scrum. Visit www.dummies.com and search for this book's title.

The Scrum Guide

http://scrumguides.org

Jeff Sutherland and Ken Schwaber, co-creators of scrum, offer *The Scrum Guide: The Definitive Guide to Scrum: The Rules of the Game* in more than 30 languages at http://scrumguides.org. *The Scrum Guide* is available in both online and PDF formats and is free to use. The guide outlines scrum theory in fewer than 13 pages and defines each scrum accountability, artifact, and event. This is the definitive source for defining scrum and is a great resource for returning to the basics.

Scrum Alliance

http://scrumalliance.org

The Scrum Alliance is a not-for-profit professional membership organization that promotes understanding and use of scrum. The alliance achieves this goal by promoting scrum training and certification classes, hosting international and regional scrum gatherings, and supporting scrum user groups globally. Find a user group near you: https://www.scrumalliance.org/resources/groups.

The Scrum Alliance site is rich in blog entries, white papers, case studies, and other tools for learning and working with scrum. Scrum Alliance certifications include tracks for

>> **Foundational**: Certified ScrumMaster (CSM), Certified Scrum Product Owner (CSPO), Certified Scrum Developer CSD)

>> **Advanced**: Advanced Certified ScrumMaster (A-CSM), Advanced Certified Scrum Product Owner (A-CSPO), Advanced Certified Scrum Developer (A-CSD)

>> **Professional**: Certified Scrum Professional ScrumMaster (CSP-SM), Certified Scrum Professional Product Owner (CSP-PO), Certified Scrum Professional Developer (CSP-D)

>> **Leadership**: Certified Agile Leadership Essentials (CAL-E), Certified Agile Leadership for Teams (CAL-T), Certified Agile Leadership for Organizations (CAL-O), Certified Agile Leadership II (CAL II)

>> **Coaching**: Certified Team Coach (CTC), Certified Enterprise Coach (CEC)

>> **Training**: Certified Scrum Trainer (CST)

Agile Alliance

http://agilealliance.org

The Agile Alliance is the original global agile community, with a mission to help advance the 12 Agile Principles and common agile practices, regardless of approach. The Agile Alliance site has an extensive resources section that includes articles, videos, presentations, and an index of independent agile community groups across the world, which can be found at https://www.agilealliance.org/communities/

Business Agility Institute

http://businessagility.institute

Business Agility Institute (BAI) is a global research and advocacy organization for business agility, which is defined as "a set of organizational capabilities, behaviors, and ways of working that affords your business the freedom, flexibility, and resilience to achieve its purpose. *No matter what the future brings.*"

BAI provides an operating model for business agility, an extensive library of hundreds of case studies, research publications, and videos. They also provide a network of meetups, chapters, and individual opportunities worldwide. The annual State of Business Agility reports can be found here, as well.

State of Agile Report

Digital.ai's State of Agile Report provides key insights from the longest continuous annual survey of agile techniques and practices (fifteen years and counting). Each year's report highlights important milestones of its origins in software development to what we're seeing currently with enterprise adoption. Access the latest report, as well as previous reports at http://digital.ai/resource-center/analyst-reports/state-of-agile-report

ScrumPLoP

http://scrumplop.org

Pattern Languages of Programs (PLoP) are methods of describing design practices within fields of expertise and often have conferences organized around them for shared learning. ScrumPLoP publishes patterns written by scrum professionals, many of which were written by Jeff Sutherland, co-creator of scrum. These practical patterns have been used successfully by organizations to get started with scrum.

Certification Resources

Several organizations provide scrum and agile-related certifications that are widely recognized:

>> **Scrum Alliance** is the most widely recognized scrum certification body, a global nonprofit with more than 1 million people certified worldwide. Read about each certification in the Scrum Alliance section at http://scrumalliance.org.

>> **Scrum.org**, founded and led by scrum co-creator Ken Schwaber, provides tools and resources for scrum practitioners to deliver value through assessments and certifications, including scrum with kanban as well as scrum and user experience at http://scrum.org.

>> **Scruminc**, founded and led by scrum co-creator Jeff Sutherland, also offers scrum training, resources, and certifications at http://scruminc.com.

>> **ICAgile (International Consurtium for Agile)** provides learning across a broader array of agile techniques and related skills including coaching, facilitation, agile engineering, agile testing, finance, marketing, product ownership, enterprise agility, lean portfolio management, and leadership. http://icagile.com.

Scaling Scrum Resources

Many frameworks and models exist for dealing with multiple scrum teams working together in collaborative ways. The following are the most common enterprise-scale models, which we address in more detail in Chapter 13.

- **Large-Scale Scrum (LeSS)** is a scrum-scaling method discussed in Chapter 13. Regardless of whether you implement LeSS, the LeSS website provides useful patterns and options for addressing the challenges of scrum when there are multiple scrum teams. It is also a good resource for understanding how to implement a systems-thinking approach to get scrum right at the team level before scaling across an organization. Learn more at http://less.works.

- **Scrum@Scale** facilitates alignment and coordination of scrum teams working together through the scrum of scrums model, coordinating communication, impediment removal, priorities, requirement refinement, and planning. Learn more at http://scrumatscale.com.

- **Nexus** is a framework that describes how multiple scrum teams — a *Nexus* — work together under a Nexus integration team on the same product backlog and under the guidance of a single product owner to deliver potentially shippable functionality every sprint. Learn more at http://scrum.org/resources/scaling-scrum.

- **Scaled Agile Framework (SAFe)** is a knowledge base for implementing agile practices and one framework for implementing scrum at scale. Use the interactive "Big Picture" graphic on the landing page to click through to see highlights of the roles, teams, activities, and artifacts. Learn more at http://scaledagileframework.com.

Platinum Edge

http://platinumedge.com

Visit our blog to get the latest insights on practices, tools, and innovative solutions emerging from our work with Global 1,000 companies and the dynamic agile community.

We also provide the following services:

- **Agile assessments:** Assessment of your current organizational structure and processes to create an agile implementation strategy that delivers bottom-line results.

- **Recruiting:** We help you find the best fit for your needs to bootstrap your scrum product development, including scrum masters, scrum product owners, and scrum developers.

>> **Training:** We offer public and private customized corporate agile and scrum training and certification, regardless of your level of knowledge:

- Certified ScrumMaster classes (CSM)

- Certified Scrum Product Owner classes (CSPO)

- Certified Scrum Developer classes (CSD)

- Path to CSP (such as Advanced Certified ScrumMaster (A-CSM) or Certified Scrum Professional ScrumMaster (CSP-SM) and similar for other scrum accountabilities)

- Agile Leadership (CAL and custom leadership training)

- Scaling techniques, including Scrum @ Scale, Large-Scale Scrum, and Scaled Agile Framework

>> **Coaching and Mentoring:** Coaches working with your teams to start off correctly and support in-the-moment course correction. Follow up on agile coaching and training with agile mentoring to ensure that the right practices occur in the real world.

Index

Numerics

Scrum at Scale model, 264–265
as a Scrum role, 12
in sprint review process, 128
why they love Scrum, 34–35
product release
about, 79
adapting as you, 154
customizing size of, 153–154
on demand, 153
frequency of, 153
inspecting as you, 154
for news media, 223
product roadmap. *See also* roadmap to value
about, 47–48, 380
creating, 50–51, 351
in estimation refinement, 79
long view of, 48–49
setting timeframes, 51–52
tools for, 49–50
production, as a stage in video-game development, 161
products
changes in, 218
for news media, 223
profit-and-loss potential, 244
project and portfolio management (PPM), 236–237
project planning
about, 47
breaking down requirements, 52–55
common practices, 62–66
in families, 337
product backlog, 56–62
product roadmap, 47–52
terminology, 55–56
project-manager, in construction, 174
projects
customizing, 167
disconnecting between business objectives and, 251
employing transparency in, 140
increased control with scrum, 372–373
principles for, 21–23
prioritizing, 248–250

setting goals in family life, 335–336
publishing
about, 215
applying scrum in, 218–219
changes in, 216–220
news media, 220–224
pull model, push model *vs.*, 113–114
purpose-driven development, 97
push model, pull model *vs.*, 113–114

Q
quality
increased, in healthcare, 192–194
increased, with scrum, 370
queuing theory, 103

R
racing in reverse, 248
readers, changes in, 216–217
"A Real-Life Example of Agile, Incremental Delivery of an Infrastructure Project in Bangalore, India," 177–178
recruiting, by Platinum Edge, 387
reducing stress, 355
refactoring
about, 159
code, 152–153
in publishing industry, 216–218
in software development, 152–154
regulations, in healthcare, 195–197
rejection, handling, 125–126
relative compensation, 276–277
relative estimating, 80
releasable, 10, 378–379
release
about, 79
adapting as you, 154
customizing size of, 153–154
on demand, 153
frequency of, 153
inspecting as you, 154
for news media, 223

About the Authors

Mark C. Layton, known globally as *Mr. Agile,* is an organizational strategist and Scrum Alliance certification instructor with more than 20 years in the project/program management field. He is the Past President and Executive V.P. of the Project Management Institute (PMI) Southern Nevada Chapter and the Los Angeles chair for the Agile Leadership Network. He is the author of the international *Agile Project Management For Dummies* and *Scrum For Dummies* book series and creator of the *Agile Foundations Complete Video Course.* He is the founder and managing member of Platinum Edge, LLC — an enterprise transformation company that uses organizational design to help businesses with their agile transformation journey.

Before founding Platinum Edge in 2001, Mark developed his expertise as a consulting firm executive, a program management coach, and an in-the-trenches project leader. He also spent 11 years as a Cryptographic Specialist for the U.S. Air Force, where he earned both Commendation and Achievement medals for his accomplishments.

Mark holds MBAs from the University of California, Los Angeles, and the National University of Singapore; a B.Sc. (*summa cum laude*) in Behavioral Science from Pitzer College/University of La Verne; and an A.S. in Electronic Systems from the Air Force's Air College. He is also a Distinguished Graduate of the Air Force's Leadership School, a Certified Scrum Trainer (CST), a certified Project Management Professional (PMP), a recipient of Stanford University's advanced project management certification (SCPM), and a certified Scaled Agile Framework Program Consultant (SAFe SPC).

In addition to his books and videos, Mark is a frequent speaker at major conferences on Lean, Scrum, DevSecOps, and other agile solutions.

Additional information can be found at platinumedge.com.

Steven J. Ostermiller is a trainer, coach, and mentor who helps organizations evolve to maximize business value and minimize risk through Lean and Agile principles and practices. He is the founder and executive director of Utah Agile (in partnership with Agile Alliance, Scrum Alliance, and Silicon Slopes), a nonprofit professional community committed to increasing agility for businesses, technology, and individuals. Steve developed and taught the agile project management curriculum for Ensign College and serves on its project management advisory board. He is co-author of *Agile Project Management For Dummies* and technical editor of Pearson Education's *Agile Foundations Complete Video Course.*

Steve's expertise comes from nearly 20 years of successes and failures as a project manager, product manager, operations executive, scrum master, agile coach, trainer, and consultant. He has worked with executive leadership and product development teams in a variety of industries on the Fortune lists. He is a Scrum Alliance Certified Scrum Trainer (CST), ICAgile Certified Professional in Coaching and Facilitation (ICP-ACC & ICP-ATF), Project Management Professional (PMP), and holds a B.S. in Business Management/Organizational Behavior from Brigham Young University Marriott School of Management.

Dean J. Kynaston is also an experienced scrum master, coach, and mentor with nearly 20 years of experience empowering leaders, teams, and individuals to become more agile. With Steve, he taught the agile project management curriculum at Ensign College in Salt Lake City, Utah. Dean was also a co-author of *Agile Project Management For Dummies* and the author of multiple Platinum Edge (http://www.platinumedge.com) blog articles.

A Platinum Edge alumni himself and former Project Management Professional (PMP), Dean has worked with multiple organizations and seen much success in applying the agile values and principles. He has worked with executive leadership and individual teams in both for-and nonprofit industries, particularly in real estate, construction, automotive, health care, pharmaceuticals, and government. He holds an MBA from Boise State University. He is a Certified Scrum Professional (CSP-SM and CSP-PO) and holds a B.S. in Business Management with an emphasis in Finance from the Marriott School of Management at Brigham Young University. As a busy father of eight children and a new grandson, Dean also finds many opportunities to use scrum with his family team.

Dedication

To Nica and Aiden — for changing my life in so many wonderful ways.

— Mark C. Layton

To Mom & Dad — my most trusted stakeholders from the beginning.

— Steven J. Ostermiller

To my wife and family, who help me welcome change even late in my development. So grateful for my tribe.

— Dean Kynaston

Authors' Acknowledgments

We'd like to thank the numerous people who again contributed to this book's first and second editions and helped make them a reality. Namely, the industry advisors whose input showed scrum's broader uses: Amber Allen (LAUSD) and Renee Jumper on education; Anna Kennedy (author of *Business Development For Dummies* [published by John Wiley & Sons, Inc.]) on business development, marketing and sales (and for modernizing that chapter in this edition); Brian Dreyer on video-game and business development; Adi Ekowibowo, Farid Kazimi, Charles Park, and Scot Kramarich on video-game development; Kelly Anderson on talent management (HR); Hiren Vashi, Lisa White, Doc Dochtermann, and Sunil Bhandari on health care; Lowell Feil, Rob Carstons, and Steffanie Ducher for enterprise resource planning (ERP); Brady Mortensen on publishing; Mogenns Gilmour, Joe Justice, and J.J. Sutherland on hardware development; Elana Glazer on manufacturing; and Dean Leffingwell, Alex Yakyma, Patrick Roach, Bas Vodde, and Craig Larman on enterprise scaling models.

Thank you to everyone who added even more value to this third edition. Zuzi Sochova for your experience and technical refinements; Caroline Patchen for bringing words to life through graphic visualizations; and John Miller for expanding on the impact of scrum in education in the services chapter.

A special thanks to Jeff Sutherland and Ken Schwaber, the co-creators of scrum, and many others who have pioneered scrum since the early days. We all work better because of you.

We'd also like to say thank you to the amazing team at Wiley & Sons: Rick Kughen, whose patience and wisdom made this happen, and the many, many others who contributed their time and expertise to make this book the guide we hoped it would be.

Publisher's Acknowledgments

Acquisitions Editor: Elizabeth Stilwell
Project Editor: Rick Kughen
Copy Editor: Rick Kughen
Technical Editor: Zuzi Sochova

Production Editor: Magesh Elangovan
Cover Image: © Michael Nivelet/Shutterstock

Leverage the power

Dummies is the global leader in the reference category and one of the most trusted and highly regarded brands in the world. No longer just focused on books, customers now have access to the dummies content they need in the format they want. Together we'll craft a solution that engages your customers, stands out from the competition, and helps you meet your goals.

Advertising & Sponsorships

Connect with an engaged audience on a powerful multimedia site, and position your message alongside expert how-to content. Dummies.com is a one-stop shop for free, online information and know-how curated by a team of experts.

- Targeted ads
- Video
- Email Marketing
- Microsites
- Sweepstakes sponsorship

20 MILLION PAGE VIEWS EVERY SINGLE MONTH

15 MILLION UNIQUE VISITORS PER MONTH

43% OF ALL VISITORS ACCESS THE SITE VIA THEIR MOBILE DEVICES

700,000 NEWSLETTER SUBSCRIPTIONS TO THE INBOXES OF **300,000** UNIQUE INDIVIDUALS EVERY WEEK

# of dummies

Custom Publishing

Reach a global audience in any language by creating a solution that will differentiate you from competitors, amplify your message, and encourage customers to make a buying decision.

- Apps
- Books
- eBooks
- Video
- Audio
- Webinars

Brand Licensing & Content

Leverage the strength of the world's most popular reference brand to reach new audiences and channels of distribution.

For more information, visit dummies.com/biz

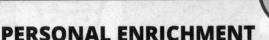

PERSONAL ENRICHMENT

Staying Sharp
9781119187790
USA $26.00
CAN $31.99
UK £19.99

Facebook
9781119179030
USA $21.99
CAN $25.99
UK £16.99

Guitar
9781119293354
USA $24.99
CAN $29.99
UK £17.99

Investing
9781119293347
USA $22.99
CAN $27.99
UK £16.99

Beekeeping
9781119310068
USA $22.99
CAN $27.99
UK £16.99

Digital Photography
9781119235606
USA $24.99
CAN $29.99
UK £17.99

Meditation
9781119251163
USA $24.99
CAN $29.99
UK £17.99

Pregnancy
9781119235491
USA $26.99
CAN $31.99
UK £19.99

Samsung Galaxy S7
9781119279952
USA $24.99
CAN $29.99
UK £17.99

iPhone
9781119283133
USA $24.99
CAN $29.99
UK £17.99

Crocheting
9781119287117
USA $24.99
CAN $29.99
UK £16.99

Nutrition
9781119130246
USA $22.99
CAN $27.99
UK £16.99

PROFESSIONAL DEVELOPMENT

Windows 10
9781119311041
USA $24.99
CAN $29.99
UK £17.99

AutoCAD
9781119255796
USA $39.99
CAN $47.99
UK £27.99

Excel 2016
9781119293439
USA $26.99
CAN $31.99
UK £19.99

QuickBooks 2017
9781119281467
USA $26.99
CAN $31.99
UK £19.99

macOS Sierra
9781119280651
USA $29.99
CAN $35.99
UK £21.99

LinkedIn
9781119251132
USA $24.99
CAN $29.99
UK £17.99

Windows 10
9781119310563
USA $34.00
CAN $41.99
UK £24.99

SharePoint 2016
9781119181705
USA $29.99
CAN $35.99
UK £21.99

Fundamental Analysis
9781119263593
USA $26.99
CAN $31.99
UK £19.99

Networking
9781119257769
USA $29.99
CAN $35.99
UK £21.99

Office 2016
9781119293477
USA $26.99
CAN $31.99
UK £19.99

Office 365
9781119265313
USA $24.99
CAN $29.99
UK £17.99

Salesforce.com
9781119239314
USA $29.99
CAN $35.99
UK £21.99

Coding
9781119293323
USA $29.99
CAN $35.99
UK £21.99

dummies.com

dummies
A Wiley Brand

Learning Made Easy

ACADEMIC

9781119293576
USA $19.99
CAN $23.99
UK £15.99

9781119293637
USA $19.99
CAN $23.99
UK £15.99

9781119293491
USA $19.99
CAN $23.99
UK £15.99

9781119293460
USA $19.99
CAN $23.99
UK £15.99

9781119293590
USA $19.99
CAN $23.99
UK £15.99

9781119215844
USA $26.99
CAN $31.99
UK £19.99

9781119293378
USA $22.99
CAN $27.99
UK £16.99

9781119293521
USA $19.99
CAN $23.99
UK £15.99

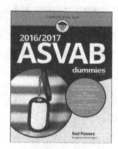

9781119239178
USA $18.99
CAN $22.99
UK £14.99

9781119263883
USA $26.99
CAN $31.99
UK £19.99

Available Everywhere Books Are Sold

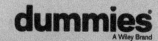

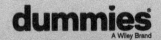